William III

PROFILES IN POWER

General Editor: Keith Robbins

LLOYD GEORGE
Martin Pugh

HITLER
Ian Kershaw

RICHELIEU
R.J. Knecht

NAPOLEON III
James McMillan

OLIVER CROMWELL
Barry Coward

NASSER
Peter Woodward

GUSTAVUS ADOLPHUS
(2nd Edn)
Michael Roberts

CHURCHILL
Keith Robbins

DE GAULLE
Andrew Shennan

FRANCO
Sheelagh Ellwood

JUÁREZ
Brian Hamnett

ALEXANDER I
Janet M. Hartley

MACMILLAN
John Turner

JOSEPH II
T.C.W. Blanning

ATATÜRK
A.L. Macfie

CAVOUR
Harry Hearder

DISRAELI
Ian Machin

CASTRO (2nd Edn)
Sebastian Balfour

PETER THE GREAT
(2nd Edn)
M.S. Anderson

FRANCIS JOSEPH
Stephen Beller

NAPOLEON
Geoffrey Ellis

KENNEDY
Hugh Brogan

ATTLEE
Robert Pearce

PÉTAIN
Nicholas Atkin

THE ELDER PITT
Marie Peters

CATHERINE DE' MEDICI
R.J. Knecht

GORBACHEV
Martin McCauley

JAMES VI AND I
Roger Lockyer

ELIZABETH I (2nd Edn)
Christopher Haigh

MAO
S.G. Breslin

BURGHLEY
Michael A.R. Graves

NEHRU
Judith M. Brown

ROBESPIERRE
John Hardman

LENIN
Beryl Williams

WILLIAM PENN
Mary K. Geiter

THE YOUNGER PITT
Michael Duffy

KAISER WILHELM II
Christopher Clark

TANAKA
David Babb

PORFIRIO DÍAZ
Paul Garner

TALLEYRAND
Philip G. Dwyer

ADENAUER
Ronald Irving

WILLIAM III
Tony Claydon

William III

Tony Claydon

An imprint of **Pearson Education**

London · New York · Toronto · Sydney · Tokyo · Singapore · Hong Kong · Cape Town
New Delhi · Madrid · Paris · Amsterdam · Munich · Milan · Stockholm

PEARSON EDUCATION LIMITED

Head Office:
Edinburgh Gate
Harlow CM20 2JE
Tel: +44 (0)1279 623623
Fax: +44 (0)1279 431059

London Office:
128 Long Acre
London WC2E 9AN
Tel: +44 (0)20 7447 2000
Fax: +44 (0)20 7240 5771
Website: www.history-minds.com

First published in Great Britain in 2002

© Pearson Education Limited 2002

The right of Tony Claydon to be identified as Author
of this Work has been asserted by him in accordance
with the Copyright, Designs and Patents Act 1988.

ISBN 0 582 40523 8

British Library Cataloguing in Publication Data
A CIP catalogue record for this book can be obtained from the British Library

Library of Congress Cataloging in Publication Data
A CIP catalog record for this book can be obtained from the
Library of Congress

10 9 8 7 6 5 4 3 2 1

Typeset by Fakenham Photosetting Limited, Fakenham, Norfolk
Printed and bound in Malaysia, LSP

The Publishers' policy is to use paper manufactured from sustainable forests.

Contents

Acknowledgements

After nearly a decade and a half studying the 1690s, I very much hope this book will be my last to concentrate on William III. This, therefore, seems an appropriate moment to thank those historians whose words – or at least whose antics – have helped me to think about the period over the years. Many could be listed: but I have been particularly grateful for the support, provocations and insights of Andrew Barclay; Hannah Barker; Jeremy Black; Jim Caudle; Jonathan Clark; Penelope Corfield; Tom Corns; Alan Cromartie; Joy Dixon; Pamela Edwards; Anne Goldgar; Mark Goldie; Jeremy Gregory; Edmund Green; Stuart Handley; David Hayton; Felicity Heal; Tony Henderson; Tim Hitchcock; Julian Hoppit; Joanna Innes; Mark Knights; Ian McBride; Roger Mettam; John Miller; John Morrill; Steven Pincus; Craig Rose; Kevin Sharpe; John Spurr; Ceri Sullivan; Stephen Taylor; Tim Wales; John Walsh; Lucy Wooding; the regulars at the Institute of Historical Research's 'Long Eighteenth Century' seminar; the participants in the University of Wales' early modern video-linked research seminar; my colleagues at the University of Wales, Bangor; and the students on my undergraduate special subject – 'Ruled by an Orange: England and Wales, 1688–1702'. How many of these people will agree with a word of what follows remains to be seen.

Maps and table

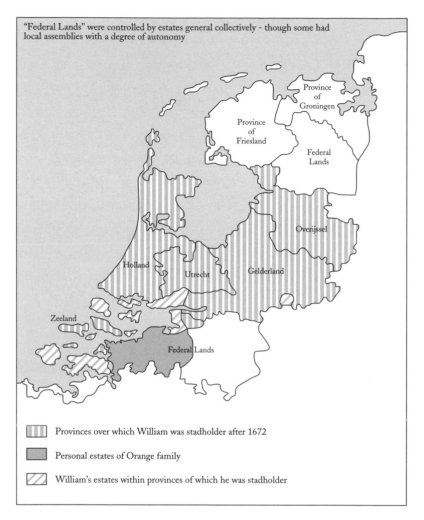

"Federal Lands" were controlled by estates general collectively - though some had local assemblies with a degree of autonomy

Province of Groningen

Province of Friesland

Province of Friesland

Federal Lands

Overijssel

Holland

Utrecht

Gelderland

Zeeland

Federal Lands

▮▮▮ Provinces over which William was stadholder after 1672

▮ Personal estates of Orange family

▨ William's estates within provinces of which he was stadholder

Map 1   William's powerbase in the Netherlands

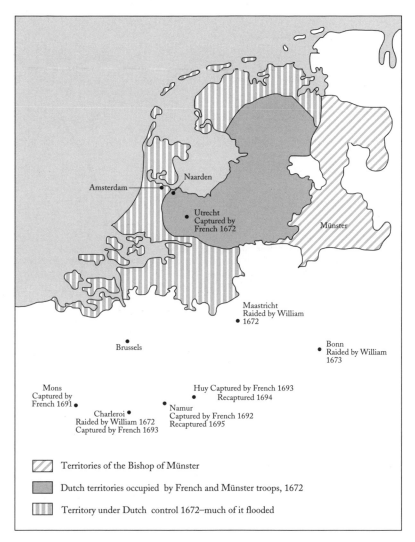

Naarden

Amsterdam

Utrecht
Captured by
French 1672

Münster

Maastricht
Raided by William
● 1672

Brussels
●

Bonn
● Raided by William
1673

Mons
Captured by
French 1691 ●

Huy Captured by French 1693
● Recaptured 1694

Charleroi ●
Raided by William 1672
Captured by French 1693

● Namur
Captured by French 1692
Recaptured 1695

	Territories of the Bishop of Münster
	Dutch territories occupied by French and Münster troops, 1672
	Territory under Dutch control 1672–much of it flooded

Map 2   William's wars in the Low Countries, 1672–78; 1689–97

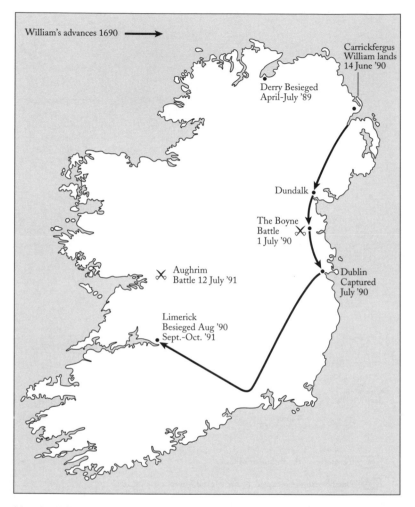

Map 3   William's war in Ireland, 1689–91

Simplified genealogical table of the Orange and Stuart families

Includes only people mentioned in text and their spouses.
Children <u>not</u> positioned by order of birth.
Reigning British monarchs in **bold**.

Notes on style and abbreviations

Guides to further reading may be found at the end of each chapter, before the notes.

In the text, dates of events which occur in Britain and Ireland are given old style (that is, according to the now-abandoned Julian calendar which was used in those islands until the mid-eighteenth century and which was running behind the later Gregorian calendar); but with the year assumed to start on 1 January (some people in the late seventeenth century did not change the year number until Lady Day, 25 March). Dates of events on the European continent are given according to the modern, Gregorian, style which was already in use in those parts. The spelling within quotations has been modernised.

In the notes, the titles of some publications have been shortened – but spellings have not been modernised as this can create problems finding them in comprehensive catalogues. The place of publication of pre-1900 works is London unless otherwise stated; post-1900 works are described by publisher. Numbers in bold are volume numbers. The following abbreviations are used:

CJ	*Commons Journals*
CSPD	*Calendar of State Papers Domestic*
CUP	Cambridge University Press
HMC	Historical Manuscripts Commission
LJ	*Lords Journals*
MUP	Manchester University Press
OUP	Oxford University Press

Timeline: the main events of William's career

1649   Execution of Charles I of England (William's grandfather).

1650   Death of William II (William's father); William born.

1651   William christened; Mary Stuart (William's mother) unsuccessfully demands his appointment as stadholder of Holland.

1654   Act of exclusion bars William from Holland's stadholdership.

1660   Death of Mary Stuart; restoration of Charles II (William's uncle) to Stuart thrones.

1662   William barred from all offices in Holland and Zeeland.

1666   De Witt dismisses William's household servants and takes charge of his education.

1667   Perpetual edict abolishes Holland's stadholdership.

1668   William installed as 'first noble of Zeeland'; pro-Orange party begins to make political progress in Holland by allying with 'middle party'.

1670   William appointed to Dutch Council of State.

1672   William appointed captain-general and admiral of the Netherlands; France and Münster invade the Netherlands in alliance with England; riots against de Witt in Holland and Zeeland; William appointed stadholder of Holland and Zeeland; William refuses Charles II's offer of sovereignty over a reduced United Provinces; William leads Dutch military resistance and launches expedition to Maastrict and Charleroi; William appointed stadholder of Utrecht, Gelderland and Overijssel – to be operational when provinces liberated; de Witt murdered by mob in The Hague.

1673   William evicts French forces from Naarden; raids Bonn, forcing French troops to withdraw from Dutch soil; liberates Utrecht; masterminds propaganda campaign in England to undermine support for the war.

1674   England and Münster forced out of war – provinces of Gelderland and Overijssel liberated; William's stadholdership of Holland, Zeeland and Utrecht made hereditary in his male line

1675   Federal captain-generalship and admiralship made hereditary in William's male line; William offered sovereignty of Gelderland –

but refuses it after opposition in other provinces; criticism of Orange ambition begins to grow in Netherlands.

1677 William travels to England to marry Princess Mary (Charles II's eldest niece and second in line to English throne after her father James); marriage causes unease in Netherlands about Orange ties to royalty; French advances in Spanish Netherlands lead to considerable war-weariness in Holland.

1678 Treaty of Nijmegen makes peace between Netherlands and France against William's wishes.

1679 William persuades estates general to reject French offer of prolonged truce; initially supports Charles II in resisting English parliament's demands that his brother (the future James II) be excluded from the throne.

1680 William begins to reconsider exclusion of James – comes to believe it would preserve harmony between king and parliament in London and secure England for the anti-French cause.

1681 William persuades estates general to lift French siege of Luxembourg.

1683 William persuades estates general to supply troops to resist French in Spanish Netherlands and presses for increase in troop numbers; William's pressure culminates in an armed occupation of Amsterdam (city had led resistance to military demands).

1684 William denounces Amsterdam in states of Holland; Amsterdam's representatives walk out and make clear they will not pay for William's aggressive foreign policy; Amsterdam secures control of estates general; estates general refuse to counter French occupation of Luxembourg; William converted to more conciliatory policy.

1685 Accession of James II to Stuart thrones; Duke of Monmouth (illegitimate, but Protestant son of Charles II) fails to replace James when invading England; William supports James against Monmouth; Louis XIV revokes edict of Nantes, removing legal protection for French Protestants and alienating Dutch opinion.

1686 James extends prerogative-stretching campaign to emancipate Catholics; Mary explains to William he will exercise her royal power when she becomes queen of England.

1687 William uses agents to make contact with opponents of James in England; makes his opposition to James's policies known publicly; Mary of Modena (James's Catholic wife) announces pregnancy; William and Protestant English fear a son would displace his wife in English succession.

1688

April?   William decides to invade England.

June   Birth of James II's son, James Edward Stuart; leaders among William's contacts in England issue invitation for him to intervene.

October   Manifesto published, justifying William's intervention and calling for English support.

November   William lands at Torbay; advances through Exeter to Salisbury; risings in favour of William in the North of England; James retreats from Salisbury.

December   James sends negotiators to meet prince at Hungerford; attempts to flee England; is captured and returns to London; William invited to capital; is given authority to organise convention; moves James to Rochester; James's second and successful flight.

1689

January   English convention meets, begins to debate succession and declaration of rights.

February   William offered throne of England and Ireland jointly with Mary, along with declaration of rights and changes to oaths of loyalty; English convention made a parliament; William's first speech to English parliament urges war on Louis and promises co-operation between king and legislature; toleration and comprehension bills introduced to English House of Lords; Dutch declare war on France after Louis invades Rhineland.

March   James lands in Ireland where majority Catholics under Tyrconnell have risen for him; Scots convention meets to discuss succession; Scots Jacobites withdraw from convention after letters from James and William read; William calls for abolition of the test in speech to English parliament; English tories resist further concessions to dissent; English parliament delays a revenue settlement

April   William offered Scots throne by the convention but is also sent unpalatable 'claim of right' and 'articles of grievance' which would limit powers of Scots monarch; Williamite forces besieged in Londonderry; English toleration act passed; William abandons repeal of the English tests and sidelines comprehension by sending it for consideration by convocation.

May	English declaration of war; William concludes First Grand Alliance, committing Britain, Netherlands, Austria, Brandenburg and Spain to reverse France's recent territorial gains.
June	William offers English Commons audit of royal accounts.
July	Siege of Londonderry broken; Scots Jacobites victorious at Killiecrankie; Halifax notes William becoming more sympathetic to tories in England.
August	Schomberg lands in Ulster to reclaim Ireland for William; defeat of Scots Jacobites at Dunkeld.
September	Schomberg's advance stalls at Dundalk.
December	Declaration of rights enacted as bill of rights; whigs alienate William by attacks on tories and objections to his travelling to Ireland; William dissolves English parliament to strengthen tory representation.

1690

March	William's second English parliament meets for the first time; king appoints predominantly tory ministry under Nottingham; revenue settlement reached – William to receive excise for life, customs for four years.
April	William accepts claim of right and articles of grievance in Scotland.
June	William lands in Ireland, leaving Mary exercising authority in London; French victory over English fleet at Beachy Head – but French unable to follow up victory.
July	William's victory over James at the Boyne.
August	William returns to London after failure to evict Jacobites from strongholds in western Ireland.

1691

January	Committee of public accounts established; William travels to Netherlands.
April	French capture Mons.
July	Ginkel leads Williamite forces to victory over Irish Jacobites at Aughrim.
October	Treaty of Limerick gives generous terms to Irish Jacobites to surrender the city (their last stronghold); William returns to England.

1692

February	Glencoe massacre ends Jacobite resistance in Scots Highlands.
March	William travels to Netherlands.
May	French fleet defeated at La Hogue.
June	French capture Namur.
August	Stalemate at battle of Steenkirk.
September	William returns to England.
October	Irish parliament meets, but proves unmanageable because of anger over Limerick treaty.
November	William asks for advice in speech to English parliament. Attacks on Nottingham's conduct of the war.

1693

March	William travels to Netherlands.
July	William defeated by French at Landan; French capture Huy; English Smyrna-bound merchant fleet captured by French.
October	French capture Charleroi; William returns to England.
November	William heeds Sunderland's advice to move towards whig ministry; Nottingham resigns as secretary of state.

1694

January	William vetoes English place bill; Commons protest, king sends conciliatory reply.
March	William begins programme of whig appointments to ministry.
April	Bank of England founded.
May	William travels to Netherlands.
September	Recapture of Huy from French.
October	William returns to England.
November	William surrenders to Commons pressure and accepts Triennial Act.
December	Death of Mary from smallpox.

1695

May	William travels to Netherlands.
June	Company of Scotland founded.
August	William re-captures Namur; Irish parliament meets — begins framing penal legislation against Catholics, contradicting the spirit of the Limerick treaty.
October	William returns to England.
November	William's third English parliament meets for the first time (election to shore up whig ministry).

December	English merchant community complains about Company of Scotland to English parliament, William begins moves to foil Darien scheme.

1696

February	Assassination plot against William; many tories refuse to join association to protect monarch – objecting to swearing William a 'rightful' king.
May	William travels to Netherlands; begins to explore peace proposals.
October	William returns to England.

1697

April	William travels to Netherlands.
September	Treaty of Ryswick ends war.
November	William returns to England.
December	Campaign begins in English Commons to disband army; William instructs ministers to ask for a standing force of 35,000; Commons vote for only 10,000 men; displaced tories returning to local offices.

1698

July	Company of Scotland sends first expedition to Darien – William instructs English governors in Caribbean not to aid it.
October	William concludes first partition treaty with France to avoid war on death of king of Spain – most of empire to go to electoral prince of Bavaria
December	William's fourth English parliament meets for the first time (election under the terms of the Triennial Act) and votes to reduce army to 7,000 men; William talks openly of abdication.

1699

February	William surrenders to Commons, accepting cuts in army numbers; William begins easing whigs out of office in disappointment at their performance in defending his armed forces.
May	William accommodates English Commons with Irish woollens act, causing uproar in Ireland.
November	William begins to consider union of England and Scotland.

1700

March   Second partition treaty – division of Spanish empire rene-
         gotiated between Louis and William on death of electoral
         prince of Bavaria; final abandonment of Darien colony by
         Company of Scotland.

April   William accepts English parliament's act of resumptions
         which confiscates Irish land granted to his supporters and
         causes further uproar in Ireland; Somers (last of the leading
         whigs) dismissed from office.

November Death of king of Spain – Louis accepts the late monarch's
         will leaving whole Spanish empire to his second grandson,
         effectively reneging on partition treaties.

December William begins programme of tory appointments to
         ministry.

1701

February William allows meeting of convocation (bending to tory
         ministers' demands); William's fourth English parliament
         meets for the first time; William pressures English parlia-
         ment to re-arm the kingdom against Louis's ambition.

September Death of James II; Louis XIV recognises James Edward
         Stuart as king of England; William concludes Second Grand
         Alliance, committing Britain, Netherlands, Brandenburg and
         Austria to deny Spanish throne to the French.

December William (disappointed with tory ministry's response to
         French threat) begins to consider swing back to whigs.

1702

February William suffers horse-riding accident in Hyde Park.

March   William's dies at Kensington Palace.

Introduction:
William III in British and Irish History

※

For anyone attending to the news, the situation in Britain on 20 November 1688 was grim. Two great armies – those of King James II, and of his invading son-in-law, William, Prince of Orange – faced each other on Salisbury plain. Between them these commanders had amassed over 40,000 soldiers. James's men belonged to the professional armed forces he had built up in the three years since he had come to the throne. Most of William's were crack Dutch troops brought over from his power base in the Netherlands. With such a concentration of military numbers and expertise, it was clear there would be heavy casualties if blows were struck. Sixty miles to the east, London was tense. Within days the capital would be swept by rumours that hordes of wild Irishmen were coming to massacre its inhabitants. These rumours would spark riots which would leave parts of the city in flames. Meanwhile, port towns along the south coast were slipping out of royal control, and in the north of England, risings were taking place against the court. In all these places, horrified loyalists protested, and sometimes brought their support for their sovereign to clash of arms. Further afield in Ireland, forces still backing James began to organise to help their beleaguered monarch. Many believed this might lead to an invasion of England which could give substance to Londoners' paranoid fears. As these events unfolded, Scotland awaited news, nervously gathering into camps which would fall upon one another in the new year. To many, therefore, the prospect of all-encompassing war was real. The king's injunction to his subjects to pray that God might avert the coming 'effusions of Christian blood' was no over-reaction.[1]

What made the threat of civil conflict still more plausible, was that the tensions of 1688 came at the end of a lifetime of crisis. For nearly three generations, the Stuart realms had been unable to attain a political stability which could guarantee internal peace. Most famously, the three kingdoms of Scotland, Ireland and England/Wales had been plunged into prolonged domestic conflict in the mid-seventeenth century. From 1637 to 1646 a horrifying cycle of rebellion and warfare had shattered the peace of every county, and had caused the death of many as a fifth of the islands' inhabitants. Nor had violence ceased with the end of this 'First Civil War'. After 1646 the spectre of military force had returned in a series of clashes, risings and martial interventions. Full-scale battles had occurred somewhere in Britain or Ireland in 1648, 1649, 1650, 1651 and 1685. Violent risings had had to be suppressed in 1649, 1655, 1659, 1661, 1663, 1666, 1679 and 1685. Military coups against governments had occurred in 1648, 1653, 1659 and 1660. Rumoured plots to assassinate the sovereign had dominated 1678 and 1683. Judicial murder of subjects had seemed the only way to keep order in 1660, 1661, 1663, 1683 and 1685; and had been threatened against leading subjects in 1667 and 1678. In 1649, the execution of the king himself had proved that nobody stood above the bloodshed. Given such a history, the mood in December 1688 was understandable. The standoff near Salisbury looked like the latest stage in an unending theatre of horror, which might easily plunge the nations back into their nightmare of disorder.

Despite its inauspicious autumn, however, 1688 is not remembered in British history as a bad year. Since the time itself, it has been celebrated as the date of a 'glorious' Revolution'.[2] There has been much debate about the appropriateness of this tag for William III's usurpation of his father-in-law, but in at least three respects its gloriousness is not in doubt. First, in England, tension ebbed after 20 November. King James retreated from Salisbury and abandoned the realm without striking a blow. William was then brought to the throne after a peaceful occupation of London and the meeting of a constitutional convention which offered him, and his wife Mary, the crown. Second, 1688 marked the point when Britain and Ireland began to escape their cycle of violence. No further battles would ever be fought on English or Welsh soil and, although William's coronation caused rebellion and warfare in Ireland, this was over by 1691, and Irish history was then largely peaceful for a century. War was also sparked in Scotland in 1689. However, while this rumbled on until 1692, and although there were further armed risings in 1708, 1715 and 1745, conflict was to be far less feverish in the eighteenth century than it had been in the seventeenth. By the mid-Georgian period, Scotland had gained a European reputation as the most enlightened of nations.

A third reason to call the revolution of 1688 'glorious' was that it marked a more general turning point in British and Irish history. Not only did violence rapidly die away after the event, many of the underlying causes of that violence seemed to be suddenly eased. For example, many of the earlier conflicts had centred around a basic constitutional deadlock. A series of disputes about the boundaries of royal and parliamentary power had fed the various crises of the century, and had ensured that for much of the Stuart era sovereigns were terrified to call their legislatures. After 1688, however, this deadlock was dramatically broken. Parliaments in all three realms met frequently and regularly, and worked with the crown without falling into intractable constitutional disputes. Similarly, difficulties surrounding the size and growth of the state were solved. Up to William's arrival, crown attempts to secure sufficient military force, tax revenue and administrative manpower, had been met by a hysterical opposition which had imagined absolutist ambition behind the court's actions. By the mid-1690s, however, parliaments had voted the king the means to raise an army and navy of over 100,000 men, and had accepted unprecedented burdens of taxation, bureaucracy and public debt. This progress allowed Britain to emerge as Europe's greatest power. Again, in the sphere of religion, 1688 seemed to bring a breakthrough. Before William's arrival, diversity of faith within and between the Stuart realms had been the prime cause of armed conflict. There had proved no way to contain religious plurality in societies that demanded that all subjects be included in monopolistic state churches, and this failure had led both to the mid-century civil wars, and to subsequent tensions and crises. From William's time forward, by contrast, disagreements of faith seemed far less dangerous. Disputes about religion continued, but de facto and de jure toleration took heat out of the situation, and theological positions found expression chiefly within peaceful – if robust – contests in parliaments. Finally, tensions between the three kingdoms of England, Scotland and Ireland, were eased. Jurisdictional clashes between the different realms, the difficulty of governing all three from a single point, and the ability of conflicts in one kingdom to destabilise its near neighbours, have long been recognised as important causes of the mid-century conflicts. After 1688, however, the 'British problem' ceased to be more than an occasional irritant. By 1710 methods ranging from parliamentary union to parliamentary management had been found to co-ordinate policy in the three realms, and it was not until the late eighteenth century that the kingdoms would again cause serious difficulties for one another.

This astonishing escape from the disaster which had threatened in November 1688 demands an explanation. For some years after the Glorious Revolution itself, accounts of the change in Britain and Ireland's fortunes were primarily providential, European and centred on William III. A Protestant God, it was argued, had taken pity on nations which had tried – however falteringly – to lead the continent towards his true faith, and had sent them a foreign, but miraculous, ruler to cure their ills. Acting as heaven's lieutenant, William had healed rifts in the realms, he had brought their peoples back to a godliness which the Catholic-tinged luxury

of the Stuart courts had endangered and, most importantly, he had reminded them of their duty to protect Protestants everywhere from the
forces of European popery. By doing all this, he had regained divine
favour for his new subjects, and had earned them the blessings of peace
and security. This message was broadcast through a mass of media – from
panegyric poems and heroically decorated pottery, to streams of pulpit
polemic issued on special days established to thank God for the mercy of
1688.[3]

More recent historians have been sceptical of such claims. Their explanations have moved away from providence, from the European context
and from William, towards structural shifts within British politics and
society. Thus, for example, much has been made of the rise of political
parties in the 1680s and subsequent decades. Parties are seen as having
restructured the way internal disputes were managed, redirecting energies
from plot and rebellion to propaganda and electioneering, and ritualising
conflict into peaceful contest in Commons and constituencies.[4] Similarly,
much store has been put on the rise of a 'public sphere' in late Stuart
England. It has been suggested that the emergence of a series of arenas for
public debate – especially the free press and urban meeting places such as
coffee houses – provided safe forums for the expression of disagreement,
and taught the nations rules of civilised debate.[5] Again, there have been a
number of socio-economic explanations for the return to stability. The
ending of inflation and the pressure of population growth in the second
half of the seventeenth century may have removed underlying social difficulties, and the growth of trade and of the professions may have eased
tensions by providing livelihoods for important sections of the political
nation.[6] A victory for the capitalist gentry in the mid-century civil wars
may have ended a destabilising stage in British class struggle.[7] Again, ideological and cultural shifts have been invoked to explain the end of conflict.
A process of 'secularisation' may have made people more sceptical of religious views of the world, and therefore less likely to go to war to fulfil
some vision of a godly state.[8] Programmes of radical reform may have
discredited themselves in the debacles of the mid-century, so that their
capacity to disrupt the ordered running of a conservative society may
have been reduced.[9]

Obviously, all such explanations might have a role in accounting for
Britain and Ireland's return to stability after 1688. They point to important changes, which may well have allowed the Stuart realm to regain an
equilibrium. Yet for all the force of recent theories, it is possible that something was lost in the abandonment of the earliest versions of the nations'
escape from their seventeenth-century horror. While it would be difficult

for a modern writer to reassert divine intervention as a causal factor in history, there may still be important insights to be gained from taking seriously both William III's personal role, and the European context of late Stuart politics. Gaining such insights is the central point of this study. By examining William's main objectives (objectives which will be shown to have been overwhelmingly continental rather than British in focus), and by studying his political skills (how he used and presented his power), this book will argue that it was the actions of a monarch whose motivation lay beyond his own realms which did most to return the Stuart realms to stability. Possibly, it will be suggested, British and Irish politics had reached a internal deadlock by the late Stuart era which required an external – if not providentially miraculous – intervention to break. Only when a man of foreign political training and foreign political concerns was called to head the British and Irish political system could solutions to the problems of that system be found.

Notes

There are many fine accounts of the seventeenth century – but still the clearest and best is Barry Coward, *The Stuart Age* (Longman, 2nd edn, 1994). The most stimulating recent analysis of instability is Jonathan Scott, *England's Troubles* (CUP, 2000).

1   [Edmund Bohun], *The History of the Desertion* (1689), p.18.
2   For an early use of the word glorious, see *An Order of the Lords ... for a Publick Thanksgiving* (1688).
3   Tony Claydon, *William III and the Godly Revolution* (CUP, 1996).
4   E.g. Brian Hill, *The Growth of Parliamentary Parties, 1689–1742* (Allen & Unwin, 1976), ch. 1.
5   E.g. John Brewer, *The Pleasures of the Imagination* (Harvard UP, 1998).
6   E.g. Geoffrey Holmes,'The achievement of stability', in John Cannon (ed.), *The Whig Ascendancy* (Arnold, 1981).
7   E.g. Christopher Hill, 'A bourgeois revolution?', in J.G.A. Pocock (ed.), *Three British Revolutions* (Princeton UP, 1980).
8   E.g. C.J. Sommerville, *The Secularization of Early Modern England* (OUP, 1992).
9   E.g. William Lamont, *Godly Rule: Politics and Religion, 1603–1659* (Macmillan, 1969).

Part One:

William's Life

Chapter One

An Orange: William's career, 1650–88

The shape of William's Dutch career

William's life began inauspiciously on 4 November 1650. Although born in the grand surroundings of the Binnenhof Palace in The Hague, and born into two of Europe's premier dynasties, events immediately preceding his arrival cast a deep shadow over his prospects. Most dramatically, his father, William II, Prince of Orange, had died eight days earlier from smallpox and had left his wife, Mary Stuart, alone with her child. As importantly, the elder William had damaged his son's prospects by acts of political folly. To start, he had lent heavily to Charles I of England during Britain's civil wars. This had landed the family in financial trouble once Charles had been defeated and executed in 1649; and had also fostered opposition to the dynasty in their native lands. In that republican state – the United Provinces of the Netherlands – popular sentiment had baulked at Orange support for a royal cause. Worse still, the old prince had attempted a coup in Holland the autumn of 1650. When this failed (the Dutch resisted William's armed demands that they pay for a larger military), the clan's reputation sunk further. An anti-Orange 'states' party mobilised and managed to deny the family the offices it had traditionally held in the republic. Thus, although the baby's christening in The Hague's Great Church on 5 January 1651 was a glittering affair, the service was pure bluster. At two months old, the new Prince of Orange was the head of a greatly weakened house. The essential key to analysing William's subsequent career is to appreciate exactly what had been squandered towards the end of his father's life. Had it not been for the disasters of 1649–50, the infant prince could have expected a high status within Europe's ruling elites. Much of his energy would therefore be devoted to recovering positions he should simply have inherited, and all his actions must be understood in this context.

The first position William had forfeited was as a member of the British ruling family. His mother had been a daughter of King Charles I, so if that king had not been deposed, the infant prince would have gained considerable influence as the grandchild of the reigning British monarch. Charles's execution greatly weakened the baby William, both by undermining his associations with royalty, and ensuring he would have no support from powerful relatives in London. This lost Stuart heritage remained important to William throughout his life. He was to spend much energy trying to restore the family's fortunes, both in his early career and, more obviously, once he wore the Stuart crown. Thus although he was too young to help his relatives back onto the throne in 1660 (beyond making a public appearance as they travelled back to England); in the decades after the restoration he gave political advice to his uncles – the kings Charles II and James II; and he married back into the clan in 1677. In 1688, William's concern for his mother's family was part of his reason for invading England, and he tried to uphold the powers and dignities of the royal house once he reigned in London.

However, while the prince's Stuart inheritance was near the heart of his identity, it was not the central focus of his ambition. Given that he was brought up in Holland, rather than England; and given that his uncles at first overshadowed him in the British realms, it was always the loss of his *father*'s status that he felt most keenly. Before 1650, the Orange family had dominated the Netherlands, and had cut considerable figures on the world stage. For example, they were the hereditary and sovereign princes of Orange, the city-state in Provence. They were also major landowners and nobles elsewhere, holding a string of estates and titles across France, the Low Countries, Burgundy and Germany. Moreover, Orange leadership of the struggle for Dutch independence from Spain had made the family appear the founders of the new nation. Although they had never been crowned kings, their charisma had allowed them to bask in popular adulation and to attain a quasi-monarchical status in the Netherlands. As we shall see below, the United Provinces remained a republic, governed by a network of committees and assemblies dominated by representatives of urban merchants. However, such was the status of the Orange dynasty, that it enjoyed considerable sway in these bodies, and had an almost automatic claim on some of the crucial offices of the state. For instance, William's ancestors had usually been made the captain-general and the admiral of the republic, and had thus gained command of the state's armed forces. Similarly they had been appointed stadholders of most of the individual provinces. These stadholderships – remnants from the days of the Habsburg viceroys – bestowed huge powers of patronage and the right to maintain internal order. In addition, the Orange family's battle with Spain had given them a providential claim to be the godly champions of European Protestantism. It had also constructed a heroic image as resisters of continental hegemony, the last great hope of battling and oppressed nations. Taken together, this Orange identity offered the most glittering prizes to the infant William. Being part of the British ruling family might bring some prestige, but if he could recover his father's family from the disasters which had robbed it of its wealth, reputation and offices, he would cut a far more impressive figure than a minor Stuart.

If restoring Orange power in Europe would be the new prince's central objective, the circumstances in which this recovery would be attempted provide further keys to understanding the man. The first of these was William's need to oppose Louis XIV. From the 1660s, this French monarch engaged in a vigorous territorial expansion on his eastern border. This not only threatened the small states and principalities in its path, but also promised to allow France to dominate Europe, as it involved military and diplomatic offensives which cowed most of the powers of the continent. This French aggression was central to William's career. While it posed a threat to the recovery of his position, it also provided an opportunity for his own advance. Louis endangered virtually all the foundations of Orange influence – but at the same time opposing him would allow William to perform all the roles which had traditionally brought his house such prestige.

At the most personal level, the French threatened William's own patrimony. Eastward expansion would absorb many of his family's lordships in Burgundy, Flanders and along the Rhine; and Louis added insult to injury when he first occupied and then annexed the city of Orange. As worryingly, France endangered the basis of William's political power in the Netherlands. Given that the United Provinces stood in the way of Louis's encroachments, the French were determined to neutralise the republic, and especially to emasculate the Orange family who had stiffened its resistance in the past. For much of the time the court at Versailles did this by encouraging the anti-Orange 'states' party in Dutch politics. This grouping, centred on the commercial city of Amsterdam, and therefore reluctant to see trade-disrupting warfare, promoted a policy of appeasing Louis and worked to exclude the more bellicose supporters of the prince from power. Between 1650 and 1672, the alliance between France and the states party was triumphant, keeping the Orange faction away from any real influence in the Provinces. In the early 1680s, the pact was almost as successful, effectively blocking William's attempts to mobilise against Versailles. In other periods, however, Louis's hostility to Orangeism was less subtle. For two periods during William's lifetime (from 1672 to 1678, and again from

1689 to 1697), Versailles tried to control the Netherlands simply by wiping them off the map. The French waged war on the republic, sometimes coming close to total conquest, or exhausting the Dutch to the point of collapse. Thus if Louis was not attempting to prevent William leading the Netherlands, he was trying to ensure there would be no Netherlands to lead. Opposing the French king was therefore essential to Orange survival.

Yet while Louis posed a threat, he also provided an opportunity. Countering the French would allow William to claim the charismatic mantle of his ancestors. For example, he could appeal, as they had done, to Dutch patriotism. Leading the struggle for national survival, William could ape the earlier princes of Orange who had inspired the republic to free itself from Spain. Furthermore, the new leader of the house could claim, like his forefathers, to be the godly champion of protestantism. Since Louis's territorial expansion coincided with persecutions of the reformed faith – both in France and in the newly conquered lands – William could present himself as the providential protector of the Protestant religion. He could reprise the role of his ancestors who had vanquished the Habsburg inquisition in the Low Countries, and had weighed in on the Protestant side of the Thirty Years War (1618–48). Finally, the new prince could lead resistance to single-power hegemony in Europe, just as his house had traditionally done. In the sixteenth and early seventeenth century, the Orange family had built alliances against the potential 'universal monarchy' of Spain. Now, the Spanish threat may have subsided, but William could point to the danger of French domination, and again present his dynasty as the champion of freedom-loving nations. Taken together, these roles would burnish the image of the house of Orange. Magnified, as they would be, by propaganda, they could re-ignite the Dutch popular enthusiasm, and regain the heroic status, on which the clan had thrived.

After Louis's expansionism, the second important context in which William would try to restore the fortunes of his house was the peculiar constitution of the Netherlands. As has already been suggested, the United Provinces was a structurally complex republic, in which the Orange family only exercised power through appointment to public office, and popular support. No individual could monopolise authority within this structure, since the location of this ultimate authority was impenetrably obscure. Technically, sovereignty in the Netherlands rested with the seven individual provinces. It was therefore supposed to lie in the provincial assemblies, or 'states', which governed each of these: but many factors disordered this basic arrangement. First, the provincial states were dominated by delegates from the Dutch towns, meaning that individual municipal councils were very influential. Second, each province could appoint a 'stadholder', whose authority could parallel and challenge that of the states, especially since this person had the right to appoint town magistrates. Third, an 'estates general' took decisions for the United Provinces at the federal level: though whether its power overrode the sovereignty of its constituent provinces was endlessly debated. Fourth, certain offices, such as the captain-generalship, parallelled the estates general in the federal sphere, and so confused authority there, just as the stadholderships did in each province. Fifth, traditions of unanimity – both within provincial states and the estates general – meant that individual towns or provinces could claim a veto on policy. Sixth, the fact that most state revenue came from the province of Holland – and within Holland from the city of Amsterdam – gave these two entities a disproportionate power. They had to be squared before anything was done. Overall, there-fore, gaining the traditional Orange influence in the Netherlands would be nightmarishly complicated. It would be troubled further by Dutch pride in their republicanism, which meant that any attempt to clarify the system by establishing a monarchy, or other regal office, would result in deep unpopularity. William would need to develop a dazzling array of political skills in order to dominate his native land.

Most obviously, the young prince would have to learn to work with representative assemblies. Since the United Provinces had such a diffuse power structure, William could not expect to command obedience, but rather had to become a sort of persuader-in-chief. Certainly, the traditional Orange offices would bestow authority, but the prince would need to get himself appointed to these by the states or estates general and, even if he were put in post, many of his powers could only be used effectively with the co-operation of the assemblies. For example, the captain-general's com-mand of the army was supervised by a committee of the estates general, and his authority would anyway be meaningless if Amsterdam refused to provide finance for the military. Thus William would have to learn the arts of collaboration with representative bodies. Above all he would have to learn the two essential skills of compromise and public relations. The first was needed because he would never gain all that he wanted from such a complex network of committees and particular interests. He would therefore need know what his core aims were – and be willing to sacrifice subsidiary desires – as the price for securing his fundamental objectives. William would need an ability in public relations because propaganda played a vital role in Dutch politics. It is true that, while republican, the United Provinces were hardly democratic. The sovereign assemblies were drawn from the landed nobility and wealthy merchant oligarchies, not ordinary people. Nevertheless, popularising political positions would still be crucial. With power dispersed among a relatively large number of people, persuasion would be a key tool of power, and there were moments when popular opinion could sway the political elites. As we shall see, street demonstrations could make Dutch towns ungovernable. At these points, even urban oligarchs would be forced to bend, and fall in behind the men or policies who had swayed the mob.

Considered together, there is one striking feature about these circumstances which would shape the infant prince of Orange's career. That was the overwhelmingly *Dutch* and *European* focus of the future monarch of Britain and Ireland. William was a Stuart, and would be interested in the Stuart realms – but his ambitions would always be continental, and his formative political experiences would be in the Netherlands. Recovering his father's position meant gaining authority in the United Provinces; it meant leading a house with interests which stretched from Provence to Germany; and it meant posing as the hero of international Protestantism. Restoring his family's fortunes also meant opposing the continent-embracing ambitions of the 'universal monarch' Louis XIV and learning to master a fiendishly confused Dutch political system. Thus while William would ultimately gain his greatest formal power from his coronation in Westminster Abbey, the British islands would rarely be at the centre of his thoughts. His destiny and identity as an Orange dictated different and far wider horizons.

The course of William's Dutch career

Of course, lying in his cradle in The Hague in 1650, William was unaware of these considerations, and was unable to do much to advance his cause. Indeed, for the first eighteen years of his life, his fate was in the hands of squabbling pretenders to leadership of the Orange house, whose political incompetence weakened the clan even further than it had been damaged under William II. Until the new prince began to take his own initiatives in the later 1660s his recovery was plotted by his mother; by his paternal grandmother Amalia; by his uncle Frederick William of Friesland; and by members of William's own household. However, these conspirators were so determined to do one another down, and were so incapable of building political alliances, that the states party outmanoeuvred them easily. Led by the strategically brilliant John de Witt, the republicans ensured that the federal and provincial offices which had traditionally been held by the princes of Orange remained vacant. In 1654, for example, they secured an 'act of exclusion' by which Holland agreed never to appoint William stadholder. In 1662 they persuaded Holland and Zeeland to reject appointment of the young prince to any office for at least six years, and got this extended by an extra half decade when this period was up. In 1667 they voted a 'perpetual edict' through the governing assembly in Holland which abolished the province's stadholdership, and committed the states to reject William's appointment as federal captain-general if he had become a stadholder anywhere else. Perhaps the greatest personal humiliation came in 1666. Then de Witt proved strong enough to storm the young prince's own household. Removing William's governor and personal servants, he insisted on supervising the raising of the child himself, and attempted to indoctrinate him in republican principles.[1]

The only advantages gained from this period of William's life were determination and experience. Repeated disasters can only have focused the prince on the need to reverse his fortunes, and this sense of dynastic destiny would have been reinforced by his upbringing. Until 1666 William was raised by a coterie of loyal family servants. These people, led by Frederick van Zuylestein, an illegitimate son of William's grandfather, instilled a keen sense of his paternal clan's proper, but squandered, dignities. They reminded William of the glories of his Orange heritage, and trained him in theory and practicalities of warfare – the mastery of which would befit the great military aristocrat they hoped he would become. They also taught the prince a love of hunting, and probably weakened any Stuart identity bestowed by William's mother Mary. She anyway spent much of her time away with her exiled brother, the future Charles II, and died before William was ten. Yet while William was being raised as a proud (and personally somewhat haughty) prince of Orange, the manner of his guardians' political defeats was teaching valuable lessons about dealing with an open political system. Mary, Amalia and the rest had failed because they had stood on their dignity as they campaigned for their heir. They had insisted uncompromisingly on the rights of his family in public, and had conspired incompetently in private, rather than trying to build wide or popular alliances. For instance, in 1650, William's mother had written to the states of Holland demanding that her newborn son be appointed stadholder immediately. This was in spite of the surge of republican sentiment which dictated tact, and the absurdity of asking a baby to exercise this difficult office. Similarly, members of William's household had been exposed plotting against the states party regime in the mid-1660s. This had destroyed the servants' credit just as de Witt was preparing to remove them, and made it easy for him to control the young prince. Orange shenanigans had thus alienated the Dutch public, and allowed the states party to accuse its opponents of arrogance and treason. Reviewing such debacles, William must have concluded he must behave with greater finesse. Ironically aided by de Witt's education (which stressed the political skills of managing a republic, and set daily exercises requiring the prince to solve problems of political negotiation and persuasion), the young man was trained to temper his princely pride, and to realise the importance of building broad support.

These lessons proved their worth in the vital years 1668–1672. In this period, de Witt's hold on the United Provinces finally began to weaken. Partly this was because his long dominance irritated rivals among republicans, who felt they were being excluded from influence and patronage. These men began to form a 'middle party', willing to team up with Orangeists to check their enemy. More importantly, the Dutch began to lose faith in de Witt's handling of foreign affairs. From the late 1660s, Louis XIV began to emerge as a serious threat to the Provinces, and the states' policy of appeasement began to look suicidal. As the French king expanded towards Dutch borders, and as it became likely that he planned to remove a vital buffer by absorbing the Spanish Netherlands, de Witt's record of allying with France, and of saving money on the army, began to tell heavily against him. Obviously, these circumstances provided an opportunity for William. As he came of age, he abandoned the profitless plot and postures of the older Orange leaders, and instead began to succeed through political co-operation and appeals to the public. Under William, his supporters began to work with the 'middle party', giving the Orangeists influence even in de Witt's strongholds of Amsterdam and Holland. At the same time, they began to make more successful appeals to popular opinion, preaching up the new prince as the patriotic heir of his ancestors. Stressing that France was the new Spain in its universal ambition, the Williamite party insisted that only the latest leader of the Orange house could fulfil its traditional role and lead the Dutch fight for independence.

As a result, the prince began to make progress. In 1668 he travelled to Middelburg to accept the position as 'First Noble of Zeeland'. This was an old family honour, which brought him great influence with that province, and enabled him to launch a claim for wider power through the impressive ceremonial of his installation.[2] In 1670, he managed to secure a position on the Council of State, with his ancestors' traditional concluding vote. The Council was a federal advisory body, which brought the prince close to the centres of the republic's power. Early in 1672, pressure from Zeeland and the inland provinces overcame Holland's resistance to further Orange advance, and William regained the federal military offices of admiral and captain-general. This brought command of the Netherlands' armed forces – albeit in collaboration with a balancing committee of the estates general to salve republican sentiments. By the time he was twenty-one, therefore, the main strands of William's career were already becoming clear. His central objectives were the recovery of his family's position, and resistance to the king of France: but both of these would be conditioned by the political skills essential to the Dutch republic.

This pattern was set in stone as William swept to dominance in 1672. At first glance, this triumph seems extraordinary. As captain-general, the prince was in charge of the Dutch army, and should, therefore, have suffered in the military disaster of the year. Early in the spring, Louis XIV (in alliance with England, and the bishop of Münster) launched a devastating attack on the United Provinces. As the English navy harried the Dutch fleet in the North Sea, French and German troops poured into the Netherlands from Münster's territories in the east, and swept the Dutch forces before them. Within weeks they had occupied most of the inland provinces and had captured Utrecht. The only areas left to the estates general were Friesland in the far north-west, and the maritime provinces of Holland and Zeeland, which were only kept out of Louis's hands by breaching the dykes and flooding the land in front of his advancing armies. As commander during this catastrophe, William should have been destroyed. That he instead came to dominate the Netherlands was the defining moment of his life. In 1672 he discovered a series of political techniques and positions which he found could promote him in the most unpromising circumstances.

Most importantly, of course, William benefited from Louis's invasion because it vindicated Orange warnings about France. Since the late 1660s, William's party had insisted that the Netherlands arm themselves against French expansion, and had criticised de Witt's attachment to negotiation. In 1672, the prince's hostility to Louis was shown to be justified in the most emphatic manner possible, and the Dutch population rallied behind the Orange stance. Furthermore, William's own behaviour during the crisis allowed him to pose as the pre-eminent Dutch patriot. Though the army he commanded was routed, his own campaign looked heroic. As soon as it became clear that Louis would invade, the prince worked night and day to bolster Dutch fortifications, and made the inspiring – if strategically ridiculous – pledge to defend the line of the Ijsell river with his own life.[3] Against this selfless patriotism, the states party appeared shabby. Although de Witt laboured tirelessly to organise the war effort, it was his earlier skimping on the army which seemed to have led to the crisis, and meetings with French agents to explore peace proposals looked like the preamble to surrender. As a result, popular anger grew against a man who did not seem to share William's determination to 'die in the last ditch' of his homeland.[4] The anger was fanned by a huge outpouring of Orange propaganda. As France advanced, pamphlets, prints and pulpit fulminations spread the message that the Dutch were betrayed and that only William could save them. Vitally, this propaganda added the image of Protestant saviour to Dutch patriot in Williamite iconography. Sermons and broadsides depicted the French invasion as an apocalyptic moment. God's true people faced annihilation by satanic popish forces, and only heaven's providential champion, the Prince of Orange, could prevent this. Meanwhile, prints depicted French Catholic atrocities against Dutch Protestants in occupied territories. In doing this they copied the style of earlier illustrations of Spanish cruelties during the wars of independence, and so reminded the audience that it had traditionally been the Orange family who had opposed ungodly persecution of the reformed faith.[5] Added to popular anger at de Witt, this apocalyptism produced a popular, Williamite hysteria. By the last days of June there were riotous demands in many Dutch cities to restore the prince to all his family's old dignities.

At this stage, it might well have been easy for William to seize power. Political authority was collapsing in the face of military crisis; 'states' party magistrates were losing control of the streets of their own cities; and William could have used his forces and urban mobs to take advantage. However, although the prince saw how much stronger his patriotic and Protestant francophobia was making him, he was also cautious. He had a genuine repugnance for illegal action, but he was probably also aware that over-ambition could damage him. He knew that in 1650 his father had overplayed his hand, and awakened republican horror of monarchical ambition. The son appeared to have learned this lesson. In 1672 he was careful to remain within the bounds of the Netherlands' constitution and to ensure he retained the support of the Dutch political classes. So even as he swept to power, William waited for the provincial states and the estates general to promote him, and refused any new royal status. Thus in late June when pro-Orange rioting in Dordrecht forced the town's magistrates to beg the prince to come to the city and accept their acclamations, he was extremely reluctant. He took much persuading to go, and refused to pro-claim himself Holland's stadholder, even when the mob trapped him and the municipal leaders in an inn until they had offered him the post. When, days later, the states of Holland and Zeeland tried to calm popular hysteria by voting for the prince to take up the two provincial stadholder-ships, he still hesitated. Even though the offer was now formal and con-stitutional, William had sworn not to accept these offices under the 1667 perpetual edict, and had to be reassured this oath was no longer valid before he took on the jobs. At the public ceremony installing him as Holland's stadholder in The Hague on 9 June, he showed no great public enthusiasm for the promotion. He remained silent and stoney-faced through the inauguration, so maintaining the impression that he was accepting only out of duty and overwhelming popular demand.

Crucially, William refused any suggestion that he be elevated to a sovereign position. One of the Netherlands' assailants, his uncle Charles II, had assumed the prince was keen to become king of Holland. Part of his motivation for attacking the Provinces had been to humiliate their republican leaders, and persuade them to raise his nephew to a royal title.[6] In the summer of 1672 the Dutch political classes were so desperate that they might have accepted this solution if it would halt the French advance. Charles, however, had misread his young relation. William, though ambitious, was determined to work within the Dutch constitution, and with the underlying Dutch preference for republican forms. He therefore rejected English offers of sovereignty over a territorially reduced Netherlands in return for a truce, instead telling his uncle – probably correctly – that his countrymen were far more attached to their liberties than they would be to any royal ruler.[7] The result of this restraint on ambition was impressive. There was no backlash against his promotion – indeed, his popularity and control only increased once he had regained the stadholderships. On 20 August, de Witt was lynched and murdered by a mob in The Hague. William was appalled by this, but nevertheless used the hostility to his dead rival and his supporters which it demonstrated.[8] In the second half of the year, William began a systematic purge of states party magistrates. In town councils, provincial states and the federal bureaucracy, de Witt's supporters were replaced by cabals of the prince's men.

By the autumn of 1672, then, William had refused coronation, but had gained all his family's old offices, and political dominance in the Netherlands. The circumstances in which this happened, and the lessons he had learnt from them, were to shape the rest of his career. First, William had discovered the power of francophobia, patriotism and Protestantism to promote his cause. By standing against French aggression, for Dutch liberties, and in opposition to persecuting Catholicism, he had become the most powerful figure in the republic. Second, he had confirmed the importance of propaganda in open political systems. He had been swept to power on a wave of popular support, whipped up by the gale of anti-states publicity. Third, and somewhat by contrast, William had found that the danger of over-ambition which had destroyed his father could be avoided by close co-operation with the popular and the political classes of the Netherlands. The prince avoided a backlash against his elevation by remaining within constitutional norms. He had let the populace rather than his coterie demand his promotion, and he had waited for the formal bestowal of power by the provincial states. Finally, 1672 bound William inextricably to the cause of defeating Louis XIV. If he had earlier opposed the French in anger at their encroachments on family lands, or because it gave him a way to criticise de Witt, his entire survival now depended on beating the French king. He had accepted leadership of a country battling for its existence against France; he had set himself up as the prime obstacle to Louis's ambitions; and had cemented himself in power on this platform.

The clearest consequence of these events was William's obsessive dedication to military action against France. From the moment of his promotion, the defeat of Louis was the prince's chief objective. In fact, containing the French became a kind of monomania which endangered the rest of his personality. Naturally focused and serious, William became a driven, and somewhat isolated, man. For the rest of his life the prince always strove to get to the battlefield, showing a preference for the front over the ease of his palaces. He was visibly impatient with the trivial socialising of the Dutch – and later the English – court, and his very few close friends (men such as Hans Bentinck) tended to be soldiers who had shared his military experiences. Later, as we shall see, these traits were to cause him political problems. In immediate aftermath of 1672, however, they helped him apply himself to the Dutch cause, and to gain even further popularity as he led his nation in war.

After his elevation, William's immediate concern was to eject French troops from the occupied Netherlands. Given the scale of the initial defeat, he achieved this remarkably quickly, relying on the Dutch spirit of resistance, and rapid alliance building with powers who had become concerned with Louis's aggrandisement. Over the late summer, William built up the Dutch army behind its flood defences, and used often brutal discipline to give it a new effectiveness. He also benefited from naval success against the English, and the mobilisation of Spain and Austria against Versailles' ambition. By autumn he made his first foray from the redoubt, leading his troops in an expedition to Maastricht and Charleroi. This did not recapture significant territory, but it did force the French to withdraw troops from the siege of Holland and Zeeland, and gave allied soldiers more time to organise. In 1673, successes were greater with William winkling the French from Naarden, and then joining the Spanish and Austrians in a daring raid outside the Provinces to Bonn. This forced the French to withdraw almost all their troops from the Netherlands, while in 1674 Dutch resistance forced England and Münster out of the war, and liberated the provinces of Gelderland and Overijssel. From then on, the war was fought outside the republic's borders. French troops faced Dutch, Spanish and Austrian armies in the lands of the Habsburg Netherlands around Brussels. The conflict conformed to the seventeenth-century pattern of tedious sieges of fortress cities, which inexorably drained the resources of the protagonists. This second stage of the war did not go as well as the initial eviction of Louis's army, but it had reasserted Dutch independence by 1678, when exhaustion brought a peace at the treaty of Nijmegen.

Obviously, the bulk of William's energy from 1672 to 1678 was spent containing Louis. He was still captain-general and admiral of the republic and so was commander-in-chief of the armed forces. He led most of the land expeditions personally, and when in The Hague he spent most of his time organising the war effort. As might be expected from the prince's personal convictions and political circumstances, this commitment to defeating the French continued even after the peace of Nijmegen. Even though there were no longer active armies to lead, William maintained his bellicose stance, constantly urging the Dutch to preserve their armed forces in a state of readiness, and to intervene against the new encroachments which the French began to make on their eastern borders. In 1679 he persuaded the estates general to reject Louis's offer of a truce, arguing that it would prevent the Dutch resisting further French expansion. In 1681, William negotiated an anti-Bourbon alliance with Sweden; and in a speech of 7 March 1682, he convinced the republic to send 8,000 troops to frighten Louis into lifting a siege of Luxembourg. In 1683, William again persuaded the estates to send soldiers to resist France outside their borders, this time in the Spanish Netherlands, and throughout this period he urged expansion of the armed forces.

Thus the whole decade after 1672 confirmed that William was dedicated to resisting Louis. It also confirmed the pattern of this resistance bringing the prince domestic political benefit. All through the war, Orange supporters magnified William's heroic actions and mobilised considerable popular support. In fact, the Orange party built an impressive publicity machine. Centring on Gaspar Fagel, a close political ally of the prince, this employed writers, preachers and engravers to polish William's halo, and then used the highly developed Dutch printing industry to spread their products widely and cheaply.[9] In the propaganda produced, William was held up as the patriotic and Protestant saviour. He was the providential redeemer of the fatherland, the heir to the ancestors who had first freed and established the Dutch republic. All this puffing had its effect. At least in early years of his dominance, William enjoyed such a level of popular approval that he advanced his personal status beyond the old inheritance of his family, and was able to sweep almost all opposition aside. As the inland provinces of Utrecht, Gelderland and Overijssel were liberated from the French, the estates general granted the prince powers to reconstitute their governments. He awarded himself expanded rights to remodel and purge town administrations, and put his own supporters in charge. At a federal level, he found he was able to bypass the old bureaucrats who had controlled the republic under the states party, and operated through ad hoc commissions given to his close political allies and personal friends.[10] Titles also followed the prince's dominance. He easily gained the stadholderships of the liberated provinces, and in 1674 secured an extraordinary privilege when the states of Holland voted to make its stadholder hereditary in his male line. Zeeland and Utrecht soon followed Holland's example and, the following year, the federal military offices were made hereditary as well. As early as 1675, therefore, the wisdom of William's refusal of Charles II's offer of sovereignty was becoming clear. By rejecting royal status in 1672, and instead continuing to fight Louis and his allies, the prince had come pretty close to royal power three years later. Even better, he exercised this power over the whole Netherlands, not the territorial rump which Charles had envisaged.

Yet while the first decade of William's dominance demonstrated how much power resisting the French could bring, it also reasserted the other lesson of 1672. It reminded the prince that he must work with the Dutch, respecting their republican sentiments and structures. In truth, William's triumph was never as complete as the summary above would suggest. Much of his power came from the willing co-operation of the Dutch political classes: when this was withdrawn, the prince suffered serious reverses. On three occasions in particular, a lack of compromise and negotiation with other forces in the republic nearly led to disaster. The prince learned from each of these setbacks and modified his political strategy. Together they were almost as formative as his first miraculous year in power.

The first reverse came as early as 1675. In this year, the states of the newly liberated province of Gelderland voted to make William – not their stadholder – but their sovereign duke. This would have given the prince an entirely new regal status within the Netherlands, and was a sign of quite how far his hold over the political classes had gone. Yet, although William had bowled over the Gelderland elites, elsewhere the offer of sovereignty set off the sort of backlash which William had avoided in 1672. In Holland and Zeeland, public opinion began to fear that any acceptance of a dukedom in Gelderland might unravel the whole Dutch constitution. The United Provinces would no longer be a federation of republican states, and princes of Orange might use the precedent of Gelderland to demand sovereign powers elsewhere. As such fears found expression in the press, and in governing assemblies, William suddenly found his control weakening. Half of the states of Zeeland objected to William's promotion; and in Holland, the Orangeists lost their majority in the provincial assembly as delegates from traditionally Williamite towns such as Leiden and Haarlem joined the always sceptical Amsterdam in vigorous protest. In the face of these pressures William backed down. On meeting the states of Gelderland on 20 February, he rejected the dukedom, and satisfied himself with the standard stadholdership. This incident re-enforced the importance of respecting existing constitutional arrangements. In the Netherlands, it seemed, power came from popularity and political alliance. Attempts to institutionalise this power in new monarchical offices meant it dissolved away.

William's second major reverse came in 1678. The prince himself had not wanted to make peace with Louis in this year. He objected to the treaty of Nijmegen because he believed the French would still be dangerous until definitively defeated on the battlefield, and because he did not trust Versailles to abide by any terms. He therefore argued against negotiations in the months leading up to the treaty, and went on fighting for a while even after it had been signed. The treaty itself was concluded on 10 August, but William used delays in its formal ratification as an excuse to attack the French lines at Mons on the 14th. Despite these actions, William lost the political battle. When Louis first approached the estates general with a suggestion that peace be concluded on the basis of pre-war borders and a trade deal, the majority of representatives were very interested. They opened negotiations, and came to a settlement in the face of the prince's protests. There were several reasons for this defeat. The Dutch were exhausted by the long military effort, and had not been doing well on the battlefield in the last years of the war, so Louis's peace terms came as a relief. Commercial interests centred in Amsterdam were also influential. The city would support and pay for a war of liberation, but was less interested in a war to humiliate Louis if it meant heavy taxes and disruption of trade. Most importantly, however, William's popularity had declined in the second half of the war. He had stopped delivering heroic military victories and many came to see him as the overbearing head of a corrupt and monopolistic faction. Two factors in particular underlay the prince's sudden lack of support. First, in 1677, he had married his cousin, Princess Mary Stuart. The prince had hoped this would secure friendly relations between England and the United Provinces, but the Dutch were more suspicious. They saw the match as tying William more closely into the Stuart royal house; and they knew it could soon make him consort of a reigning British queen (only Mary's father James stood before her in the succession once Charles II had died). The Dutch therefore worried that the prince's marriage was a prelude to his seeking royal status at home. Second, William lost popularity because of the poor quality of the people he had appointed over the preceding years. Whereas the old states party had been drawn from the respected and public-spirited elites of Dutch towns, the men William had drafted in to replace them were often outsiders or upstarts, who abused their new influence for personal gain.[11] As a result of all this, public opinion soured in the later years of the war. Pamphlets and pulpits criticised William's rule, complaining about the cost of the conflict, the trade slump it had produced, and the prince's military adventures outside the Provinces. Above all they attacked the arrogance of the Orange party. They accused the prince of using prerogative and purge to destroy opposing forces. In these circumstances, the prince found he had little political capital to deploy against calls for peace. The republic came to a treaty in defiance of their captain-general, who was left charging the French army without his country's sanction.

The treaty of Nijmegen was a disaster for William. However, it did continue his political education. It reminded him once again to mind public opinion, this time teaching what damage accusations of ambition and corruption could do. From 1678, the prince was noticeably more conciliatory in his handling of the Dutch. In particular, he was careful to show he shared others' concerns about administrative dishonesty. He permitted the rehabilitation of many of the magistrates excluded in the early 1670s, and admitted to the poor quality of some of their replacements. This lesson was emphatically reasserted in the prince's last major reverse in 1683–84. In this winter, William came dangerously close to repeating the mistakes of his father. Although he had been working well with the representative assemblies since Nijmegen, his frustration at having to bargain and compromise burst out in one last act of political folly. Through 1683, William had been working hard to convince the estates general that the republic needed to raise 16,000 extra soldiers to counter Louis's expansion. When Amsterdam led successful opposition to this demand, the stadholder's patience snapped. In November, he led a delegation from towns which agreed with his policy, and made a full ceremonial – and armed – entry into the leading Dutch city. In January the next year his supporters argued that decisions to raise troops did not have to be unanimous in the states of Holland (effectively removing Amsterdam's traditional veto), and in February he personally presented evidence to this body that the city's magistrates had been in treasonous correspondence with Louis.

All this, of course, followed the pattern of 1650. Three decades earlier, William's father had tried to bully Amsterdam into increasing the size of the army with a show of armed force. Unfortunately, the results of the initiative were also very similar. Just as in the earlier incident, Orange high-handedness backfired. Neither the magistrates of Amsterdam, nor the populace, were impressed by William's visit, and mob hostility soon persuaded the prince to withdraw. In the states, Amsterdam protested against the Orange interpretations of the constitution which removed their veto, and simply walked out when accused of treason. This effectively scuppered any further business. Neither Holland nor the Netherlands could function without the tax revenue Amsterdam supplied, and it was certain no extra troops would be forthcoming until the great city had been mollified. Consequently, the Provinces were forced in behind Amsterdam's peace policy. In May the states of Holland passed a resolution forbidding its troops to fight outside its boundaries. The republic did nothing when Louis occupied Luxembourg; and then accepted a twenty-year truce from the French in return for accepting all of their recent gains. For William, this was a personal as well as political catastrophe. He had imperilled his careful restoration of his family's position since 1668, and could only watch as the republic accepted France's absorption of the clan's ancient estates. 1683–84 was also, however, a final, and at last a conclusive, demonstration that William had to act with compromise and respect for constitutional forms. From the ruins of his position, the stadholder began again to build up trust with the political classes by tact and negotiation. Never again did he try strong-arm tactics. From this point forth, he never attempted any major political initiative without ensuring he had squared the Dutch political classes, and especially the magistrates of Amsterdam, first.[12] Slowly he won the Dutch back round. He appointed men of talent from across the political spectrum to offices in his control, he treated representative bodies with deference, and reassured them constantly that he was the servant, not the usurping master, of the state.

In 1688–89, William's mature political style paid its most handsome dividends. In that year he persuaded the Dutch republic to launch one of the most daring and impressive amphibious operations in history, as the Provinces' fleet and army backed the prince's invasion of England. 1688–89, was of course, to be a turning point in William's career, raising him to still greater dignities and powers. This chapter, however, has suggested that the truly defining moments of his life may have come earlier, and had a far more European and Dutch focus than the English and British events of the Glorious Revolution. For this prince of Orange, the important years had been 1650, 1672, 1675, 1678 and 1683. In the first, he had inherited a situation in which restoration of his paternal family's position in the United Provinces, and in the whole continent of Europe, became the most urgent priority. In the second, the recovery of this position had become inextricably linked with the containment of France and the defence of the Netherlands, and with the Protestant and patriotic propaganda this policy could generate. In the last three years, William had learned that skills of compromise and humility were essential in dealing with representative assemblies, and that popular opinion could only be won by respect for constitutional forms and the people's attachment to their liberties. By 1689 these earlier years had bred a new kind of king in Britain, who would have different priorities and attributes to his predecessors. In Part Two of this book, we will see how this new kind of king could solve the structural problems of his new kingdoms. Before that, however, we must examine whether becoming ruler of the British realms changed William. Might the long dormant Stuart side of his inheritance re-awaken once he sat on the Stuart thrones?

Notes

The best general accounts of William's early career in English are contained in Stephen Baxter, *William III* (Longmans, 1966); Jonathan Israel, *The Dutch Republic* (OUP, 1995); and Herbert H. Rowen, *The Princes of Orange* (CUP, 1988). Relations with de Witt can be traced in Herbert H. Rowen, *John de Witt* (Princeton UP, 1978). J.L. Price, *Holland and the Dutch Republic in the Seventeenth Century* (Clarendon Press, 1994) is a good guide to the Dutch constitution.

1 De Witt's influence rubbed off – William was later to call him 'one of the greatest men of the age', Gilbert Burnet, *The History of My Own Times* (1723–34), **1**, 321.

2 BL Sloane Ms 1908, f.19 – travel diary of Edward Browne.

3 Rowen, *de Witt*, p. 830.

4 Burnet, *History*, **1**, 327.

5 Simon Schama, *The Embarrassment of Riches* (Collins, 1987), pp. 275–7.

6 See his letter to the prince, Arthur Bryant (ed.), *The Letters, Speeches and Declarations of King Charles II* (1935), p. 257.

7 Burnet, *History*, **1**, 598.

8 For William's reaction, see N. Japikse (ed.), *Correspondentie van Willem III en van Hans Willem Bentinck* (Rijks Geschiedkundige Publicatie, 1927), **2**, 744–5.

9 John Carswell, *The Descent on England* (Cresset, 1969), pp. 24–35.

10 D.J. Roorda, 'The peace of Nijmegen', in J.A.H. Bots (ed.), *The Peace of Nijmegen, 1676–9* (APA, 1980), p. 20.

11 Israel, *Dutch Republic,* pp. 810–11.

12 Ibid, p. 836.

🏵️

Chapter Two

A Stuart? William's British Career, 1688–1702

William and the invasion of England

On 5 November 1688, William landed at Torbay in Devon. He thus began an invasion of the Stuart realms which had been months in preparation, and which would rapidly lead to his seizure of the throne in London. Although William's army was not as large as that of James, he benefited from political circumstances which redressed the balance between his 21,000 men and the 40,000 of his opponent. Most importantly, William had been plotting with the group of high-placed English politicians for weeks before the expedition. As a result, pre-planned defections from James's court and army undermined morale in the king's military, and brought their leader to the brink of a nervous breakdown. Armed risings by William's allies in the north of England also sapped James's confidence, and led him first to withdraw without ever really engaging the prince, and then to slip out of the country. He first fled on the night of 11 December, but was detained in Kent and brought back to the capital. William then ordered that he be transferred to Rochester – supposedly for his own safety, but actually because it would allow him to remove himself easily to France. The king finally left two days before Christmas.

After this dissolution of the established regime, William's path to the throne was fairly clear. He first occupied London after the terrified inhabitants asked him to come to guarantee order, and then made rapid political advance. Meeting a 'provisional government' of peers assembled in the Guildhall, he secured agreement that a national convention should meet, to be constituted in the same way as a parliament. This body would decide the future of the English constitution, with the clear possibility that it might offer William the crown. Not all welcomed the prince's progress. Indeed many had supported him because they thought he had promised to rescue James from evil counsellors, not take power himself. However, in the confused days of the winter, it rapidly become clear that there was little alternative to William's elevation. When the convention met in

Westminster in late January, it initially debated a range of constitutional solutions to the disappearance of James, but soon concluded that election of the Prince of Orange as king was its only real choice. The prince privately threatened to return to the Netherlands if he was not offered the throne, and everyone gathered in London knew that this would spell anarchy. William was the only guarantor of order in a country whose central authority had broken down. He was also the only defender of the realm against the expelled ruler. By February James had teamed up with Louis XIV; he was preparing to lead a rebellion which had broken out against William's authority in Ireland; and was threatening terrible vengeance on those who had acquiesced in his fall. Consequently, the convention agreed in mid-February to offer William the crown: albeit in a novel 'joint monarchy' with his wife. The crown of Ireland followed that of England automatically under constitutional law, though re-establishing London's actual control would be difficult given the rebellion. In Scotland, which had mirrored England's pattern of events (a collapse of central authority followed by a convention), William and Mary were made monarchs on 11 May.

The obvious question about this elevation is why William decided to pursue it. In particular, it is important to decide whether the Glorious Revolution marked a change in the prince's priorities. Until 1688, William had been an Orange, determined to maintain that family's position on the continent by containing France. In 1688, however, it was conceivable that William became more of a Stuart. He turned his attention to the British realms; he left the United Provinces at a moment when it was facing renewed war with Louis XIV; and took with him a large armed force which could perhaps have been more prudently used shoring up the defences of the United Provinces. Once in England, he worked to gain the crown there, and for months he concentrated on British politics while leaving the running of the Netherlands in the hands of loyal deputies. On one interpretation of events, this could simply be seen as Stuart ambition displacing William's Orange identity. A man frustrated by the limitations placed on his power in Holland may have plotted to seize the full glory of his mother's family's throne. Certainly, there are difficulties with this view. At the start of James's reign, William seemed keen to establish a close working relationship with his uncle, and lent him considerable support when Charles's illegitimate son, the duke of Monmouth, invaded England to claim its crown for the Protestant religion. It therefore seems unlikely that William had had any long-standing intention of ousting the legitimate monarch. Yet even if a simple theory of growing Stuart ambition is rejected, there is still an argument that the 1688 invasion was driven by a new concentration on the prince's British heritage. William may not have worked consistently to gain the throne in England – but he could still have acted in order to safeguard a Stuart crown in which he had considerable interest, and which he had come to believe was in great danger.

The key here is to analyse exactly when William decided to invade. Direct evidence of this decision is scant, but what there is suggests it was taken in the spring of 1688. This was when Gilbert Burnet (the exiled Scots clergyman who had arrived in Holland in 1686 and rapidly wormed his way to the heart of Orange councils) was later to claim that the expedition had been conceived, and it was only after the spring that concrete military, diplomatic and conspiratorial preparations began. The important thing about this date is that it marked the stage when James's rule emerged as a serious threat to William's interest in the Stuart throne. Up to this point, the prince could believe his British heritage was secure, and that at some point it would come down to him. During the spring, however, William's advantages as a Stuart seemed in real danger, and intervention appeared essential to secure them.

It is true that things had begun to go wrong in Britain and Ireland from the moment James came to the throne. In the years 1685 to 1687, William's younger uncle steadily squandered his early popularity. His efforts to promote his own Catholic religion fanned the flames of English anti-popery, and his use of his prerogative to promote his religious policies sparked fears of monarchical absolutism. However, until the spring of 1688, William did not see these trends as threats to his own position, and expressed only mild concern about them. First, the prince knew that he would soon exercise considerable influence in England. James was ageing, he had no male children, and his heir was therefore William's wife Mary. She had promised the prince that he would exercise actual executive power when she came to the English throne.[1] Second, although James was unpopular, this did not pose an immediate threat to the Stuart crown. At the end of 1687, the English were nowhere near rebellion. They were fearful of resistance after the experience of the civil war; they were reassured that parliament could ultimately frustrate the king's policies (since Catholicism could only be legalised by statute); and they comforted themselves that the heir and her husband were staunch Protestants. Thus while William may have disapproved of his uncle's policies in his first few years, there were no grounds to worry that James was endangering the prince's Stuart inheritance.

By the spring of 1688, by contrast, things begun to change. William's interest in the Stuart throne looked much more precarious, and it might have started to look sensible to take action to save it. To start, it became doubtful that the prince would come to control the Stuart realms. In the winter of 1687–88, James's wife, Mary of Modena, announced she was pregnant. As the new year wore on, it looked increasingly probable that she would carry a child to full term which could be a son to displace Mary's claims. As dangerously, the English king's policies stoked political tensions to the point where it was possible the Stuart monarchy would not survive at all. William, in close contact with many leading figures in London, began to hear more talk of rebellion as James made it clear he was prepared to remodel the franchise for parliament to secure a pro-Catholic legislature; and when he eventually celebrated the birth of a boy who would perpetuate his Catholic regime. Rumours that the new heir was actually suppositious (many said he had been smuggled into the birthing chamber in a warming pan) crystallised the threats to William's position. They fed further English anger at the court, and suggested the lengths to which some might go to keep the Prince of Orange from power. In the light of all this, William's decision to invade in the spring looks like an attempt to salvage his Stuart interests. Whether he intended to seize the throne from the first (as James's supporters alleged), or whether he merely hoped to get his uncle to reverse his policies and to investigate the legitimacy of his son (as his own manifesto claimed), his position in his maternal family seemed uppermost.[2] He was ensuring he gained the eminence in the dynasty which he had long anticipated, and was saving the clan from political suicide.

Yet, although William's Stuart identity was clearly important to him in 1688, it is not possible to interpret his expedition solely in terms of this. In fact, William's decision to invade England makes more sense as a continuation of his earlier career, with its Dutch and European focus, than as a startling new direction. Throughout the revolution, this Stuart remained an Orange at heart, and the continental traditions and position of his father's family remained the keys to understanding the man.

To see this, one should first remember that the invasion was not William's first intervention in British politics. On several occasions in the 1670s and earlier 1680s he had focused his attention on the Stuart realms: but as might be expected during these years when the prince was trying to save his inheritance from France, it was European, rather than British concerns which led to his interest. This was most obviously true of his propaganda campaign in London during the second Anglo-Dutch war. Between 1672 and 1674, William had sponsored anti-French feeling in England, and contacted anti-French politicians there, in order to turn public opinion against Charles II's attack on the Netherlands.[3] This was successful (parliamentary opposition forced Charles to make peace) and it represented a dramatic sabotage of Stuart policy by the Prince of Orange. In 1677, William had married back into the Stuart family. Again, however, this had more to do with continental concerns than any loyalty to his mother's clan. In the late 1670s domestic politics had forced Charles II to adopt an anti-French stance. William pursued his match with Mary in hopes of securing the new mood sufficiently to have England come in on the Dutch side of the war. Similarly, William's intervention in the English 'exclusion crisis' (1679–81) was dictated by Orange interests. When parliament first demanded that James be excluded from the succession because he was a Catholic, the prince was hostile to the idea. Initially he was Stuart enough to resent legislative encroachment on the English monarchy, and backed Charles's policy of resistance. However, as time went by, and as it became clear that the debate over exclusion was rupturing relations between the English crown and parliament, the prince changed his mind. He advised Charles to surrender, because he realised this would be the only way to restore that harmony between monarchy and legislature which would be essential if the British realms were ever to be an effective bulwark to France.[4] Again, William's Orange priorities cut across any Stuart view of the world. Finally, William had intervened in England in the early years of James's reign. Although helping to rescue the new monarch from the Monmouth rebellion in 1685, the prince continued to put Orange interests first. To James's annoyance, he counselled against the king's religious policies – and even contacted the ruler's opponents – as he tried to heal the internal breach which stopped England acting as a balance to France. Earlier engagement, therefore, suggested William was interested in the British realms as part of his continental strategy. It makes sense to interpret the 1688 expedition as part of the same pattern.

Another reason for stressing Orange considerations in William's invasion, is that James had come to endanger the prince's European objectives as much as his Stuart heritage by the time he chose to invade. While William *was* horrified at the damage James was doing to the ruling dynasty's position in London, and may well have been angered by his wife's displacement from the succession, he was still more horrified by the prospect of his uncle driving his kingdom into dependence on France. By the spring of 1688, the prince was faced by three very frightening scenarios in London. Each of these threatened to destroy his European strategy by placing England in the scale against him, and each would demand urgent action. First, James might alienate his subjects so far that he would have rely on pensions from Louis to survive. This had happened to his brother Charles II, and that experience had taught that the price for such support was diplomatic, or military, co-operation with Versailles. For William such an alliance re-awakened the terrors of 1672. Second, James might spark a civil war in England. This would certainly destroy the Stuart realms as an effective counterweight to Versailles; and would provide many opportunities for Louis to make political hay in the domestic chaos. Third, any civil war might result in a republican government. As the history of the 1650s had showed, such a regime would be no friend to the Orange family. Republicans traditionally viewed the Orange house as ambitious for monarchical status; and the record suggested they would be as likely to ally with France as with a United Provinces led by a relative of the displaced king.[5] Thus, as William explained to Dutch politicians over the summer of 1688, the main justification for intervening in England was to prevent French advance. The estates general agreed to finance the expedition, and to risk the aggrandisement of their old rival, only because they knew they could not afford to allow the Stuart realms to slip into Louis's camp.

A final reason to think William had his eyes on Europe in 1688, was that his behaviour was puzzling and inconsistent if considered from a solely Stuart perspective. During the revolution, the prince's aims seemed to shift constantly, and it is difficult to explain this with any simple desire for the British crowns. The confusion centred on the changing scale of Orange ambition. In the initial stages of his expedition, William seemed only to want a free parliament which would rescue James from evil counsellors. This was all his manifesto, published in October, asked for; and this limited demand informed the prince's early, cautious, attitude in England.[6] Until James's first flight from London in mid-December, William refused to blame his uncle personally for bad policies; he continued to address him as the sovereign of the kingdom; and he held back from directly usurping his legal authority.[7] By contrast, after the flight, the prince's ambitions seemed to grow swiftly. Once his uncle was broken, William accepted virtually the full powers of monarchy to maintain order while the convention assembled, and he began to act in a regally high-handed manner. He effectively man-handled James back out of the kingdom when his first flight was interrupted; and he bullied the convention, once it had met, into accepting that he should have the throne. In early February, by another contrast, William again reduced his demands. Once he was certain of the crown, he seemed willing to accept new and far-reaching limitations on his power. He tolerated a public declaration of parliament's rights (see below), and the dilution of his majesty which was involved when the convention insisted he share his throne with his wife.[8]

It is difficult to see how simple concern for Stuart interests could explain these shifts, or even account for any of the individual stages of William's policy. For example, the prince's initial demand for a free parliament threatened the rights of the dynasty and the dignity of the office he was soon to hold. As this free legislature was supposed to reverse recent royal policies, and investigate the birth of James's son, the demand suggested an enhanced role for parliament in checking the monarchy. Admittedly, the next stage of the prince's policy fitted defence of his Stuart interests better. In mid-December it became clear that William was aiming to displace his uncle, and his handling of the convention in January and February suggested a man comfortable with the plenitude of royal power. Yet while the prince appeared more authoritative in the deepest months of winter, he did not seem entirely committed to his dynasty's dignity. After all, he bullied the head of the clan into abjuring his realm, and then supported the argument that the throne was vacant and that the convention had the right to fill it. This implied that the English nation could take constitutional decisions perfectly effectively without any Stuart monarch, and suggested a rather weak link between the hereditary claims of the dynasty and the crown. The final stage in William's revolution also make little sense as a defence of his dynastic interests. The new king accepted a wholesale reduction and ad hoc remodelling of the Stuart monarchy. These included limits on its prerogative in the declaration of parliamentary rights; limits on its future hereditary claims in the form of an outright ban on a Catholic ruler; and the joint monarchy, whose establishment suggested the nation could simply redesign sovereignty at will.

By contrast, William's Orange and European outlook *can* account for the prince's variable stance over the winter of 1688–89. If it is assumed that the prime purpose of the invasion was to bring England into play against France, William's behaviour begins to make sense. Stated simply, the prince was engaged in a sustained attempt to seize control of English foreign policy, the strategy for which had to alter as circumstances changed. At first, William was not sure that he had brought enough force to displace his uncle from the throne. He therefore limited his demands to a free parliament – not wishing to alienate those Englishmen who were fed up with James, but would be outraged at his removal by a foreign force. Yet even though a free parliament would be unlikely to grant William the crown in the autumn of 1688, it would be good enough for the prince, since it would certainly secure the English foreign policy which he desired. This was because the mood in England was viciously Francophobic. The chorus of complaint against the court which had been growing since 1685 had accused James of being in the grip of French agents, and of being encouraged by Louis to impose a French style of government in England.[9] With such public opinion, the prince knew a free legislature would insist England join William's anti-French alliance, and since the presence of the Dutch army in England would guarantee the parliament got its way, he also knew he could saddle James with this Orange foreign policy. In the early stages of the expedition, therefore, a call for a free parliament would be enough to secure his basic goal. Of course, William never had to rely on such a body because the old king fled the country. After mid-December, William felt confident enough to try to seize the throne, and his assertiveness grew accordingly. The motive for this new ambition, however, remained Orange rather than Stuart. William probably did believe he would be a better custodian of his mother's heritage than his uncle, but his real desire was to gain control of the Stuart military and turn it against the French. This was why he was prepared to accept the convention filling a vacant throne. The implied attack on Stuart majesty was outweighed by the practical control of foreign policy which the move brought. This attitude carried over into the last stage of the revolution. William could swallow the declaration of rights, the joint monarchy, and the limitations on the future hereditary entitlements of his family, because none of these changes directly challenged the king's control of the armed forces or foreign policy. Certainly, parliament's new role meant William would have to work closely with it to organise and finance the struggle against Louis. However, the basic direction of foreign affairs and command of the military remained with the monarch, who could ensure the Stuart realms stayed in the anti-French camp.

Overall, therefore, an Orange explanation for the 1688 invasion looks most convincing. Of course William was concentrating upon the Stuart realms when he organised his expedition, and he came to desire the Stuart throne if he had not wanted it from the very start. Yet while these considerations were important, they did not seem to have played more than occasional roles in determining William's action. The only consistent principle behind what he did was the old Orange one of resisting Louis. The marquis of Halifax, who became a close confidant of the new king in 1689, once noted that William was so obsessed with defeating France 'that it would incline one to think, he took England only in his way'.[10] This was not a bad summary of the prince's whole policy.

William's career as king in Britain and Ireland

If England had been just a stepping stone to France over the winter of 1688–89, it was conceivable it would not remain so. Once William began to spend time in England, it was possible he would come to have a new affection for his mother's homeland, and that British concerns would loom larger in his mind. In fact there is evidence that the prince developed a deeper attachment to the Stuart realms once he sat on their thrones. For example, after 1689, he barely visited the United Provinces. He did not return to the continent until 1691, and then only spent campaigning summers in Flanders with brief trips to The Hague on his way to and from London. In 1697, even these regular journeys stopped once war in the Low Countries ceased. The bulk of William's time in his last eleven years was therefore spent in London – and much of it was employed dealing with the British political nations, attempting to make them stronger, and trying to preserve the Stuart family's role within them. As we shall see, the new king devoted considerable political skill to working effectively with parliament and gave attention to the fiscal and military resources of his new realms. He also fought hard for the dignity of the royal family. He persisted with stubborn political campaigns to prevent the weakening of the prerogative, and worked hard to preserve the magnificence of court. He staged sumptuous ceremonies such as his coronation, and the funeral of Mary in 1695; and built an impressive new palace at Hampton Court.[11] All in all, William looked like a pretty good Stuart after 1688. The interests of his maternal family and of his maternal homelands seem to have come suddenly to the fore.

Yet examined more closely, the last stage of William's career fits smoothly with the rest. Although the prince clearly had a Stuart identity, an Orange and European strategy remained at the heart of his vision, and his time as king of England, Scotland and Ireland was dedicated to the battle with Louis. Indeed, the direction in which the monarch would take his new realms was evident even before he had mounted the throne. During the invasion, William had ordered Admiral Herbert, who was one of his conspiratorial contacts, to use the English ships under his command to attack the French fleet, even though England was not yet at war with France.[12] Once William had secured the crown, he forged on with this war policy. His very first speech to the Westminster parliament – on 18 February – stressed the hazard faced by 'our Allies abroad, and particularly that of Holland'.[13] He therefore urged his audience to help the Dutch, who by this stage were back at war with Louis, opposing his massive incursion into the Rhineland. In Scotland similarly, the elevation of the Prince of Orange was understood to involve hostility to France, and the nation began to mobilise immediately. By early summer, the new king's enthusiasm had locked the British and Irish realms into a vast anti-French confederacy. The 'First Grand Alliance' – concluded in The Hague in the late spring – married the Stuart islands with Spain, Austria, a league of German princes and the United Provinces in a determination to reverse all of France's territorial gains since 1659. These powers resolved to fight until this humiliation of Versailles had been achieved.

Once he had secured his new countries for the Orange cause, William continued to promote his *paternal* family's interests as his priority. The obsession was most evident in his determination to lead the war against Louis personally. It is true that the king spent over half his time in London after 1689, and that much of his energy was spent dealing with English politicians – but this was only because the consent of the Commons at Westminster was essential to keep funds flowing for the war effort; and anyway, William's time in England was concentrated in the winter when it was too cold and wet for effective military operations. Whenever active conflict was occurring, the king made every effort to be in the thick of the fighting. In fact his determination to get to the front line overrode con-siderations for the personal safety of the reigning Stuart monarch, and for the internal political stability of the Stuart realms. For example, he expressed his wish to go to Ireland in the summer of 1689 to help defeat the French troops whom Louis had sent to aid James with his Dublin-based rebellion. This was despite the danger to his person, and the fact that the new regime in London was nowhere near settled enough to sur-vive the absence, let alone the death, of its new monarch. Ministers had to work hard to persuade the king that he must remain in England estab-lishing a stable government and new procedures of business in a post-rev-olutionary age. By 1690, William's urge to cross the Irish Sea had become irresistible. He went in June, even though this meant sacking the minis-ters who opposed the trip; ignoring the pleas of Scots politicians who begged him to go to Edinburgh to settle the regime there; and overruling those who (rightly) worried that his plans to leave executive power in England in the hands of a regency council would result in chaotic fac-tionalism. Fortunately, the king survived his campaign in Ireland, and even scored a major victory at the battle of the Boyne. Unfortunately for his new subjects, however, he was not persuaded to greater caution by the narrow escape he had had on the battlefield (he had been wounded by a bullet in the arm), or by the equally narrow escape Britain had had while he was away (the French had proved unable to capitalise on a major naval victory in the Channel). Ireland may have been secure from Louis after the final defeat of the Jacobite forces in 1691– but Flanders was not, and William determined to lead his armies there too. Every summer from 1691 to 1697 he crossed to the Low Countries, and after brief visits to The Hague, spent months at a time at the front. Still ignoring the personal danger to the leader of the Stuart house, and the political difficulties his trips caused back in the Stuart realms, he witnessed at first hand the French advances of 1691–93; and then himself led the reversal of fortunes which culminated in his capture of Namur in 1695.

Nor was it only on the battlefield that William's continuing commitment to the defeat of France was displayed. Even when in Britain, it was the continental interests of his paternal family which dominated William's actions. Throughout the war, his overriding objective was to persuade the Westminster parliament to keep voting for money, for supplies and for men to send to the battlefields. This was the burden of speech after speech to the English Commons. For example, on 19 October 1689 he asked his legislators to give 'what you think fit ... to the Charges of the War'.[14] On 27 January 1690 he thanked the houses for the 'readiness you had showed me to supply me with Money for carrying on the war'; and on 2 October the same year he warned them of the consequences if the conflict were not 'prosecuted with vigour'.[15] Overall, William's speeches down to 1697 ran on a fairly fixed formula. Almost every time he reminded MPs of the situation on the continent. Almost every time he apologised for having to ask for supplies – but asked for them anyway. Almost every time he urged that they put aside all matters which might delay or distract them from voting funds for the military, and thanked them for their concern in his cause.

William's political concentration on the war did not stop with parliamentary rhetoric. It was most impressively revealed in his willingness to sacrifice almost any other objective to the struggle in Ireland and Flanders. The history of the 1690s show that the king did have some aims in Britain beside military finance, but it also demonstrates he would never pursue these if they obstructed his continental strategy. For instance, William wished to preserve the power of the crown. In the early part of his reign he defended his prerogatives against Commons' encroachment, opposing attempts to control his influence over the sitting and composition of the legislature. Yet, as we shall see, this resistance lasted only until MPs threatened to cut royal revenue if the king did not retreat. Once supply for the war had been endangered in this way, William surrendered, and important court powers were lost (see Chapter Three). Similarly, the incoming monarch hoped to grant a generous religious toleration in Britain. Once, however, he had realised that such liberality would alienate key political factions, and reduce their enthusiasm for his military leadership, the king's generosity disappeared. As a result, monopolistic state churches were retained in all three realms, and were allowed to act against those who did not belong (see Chapters Four and Six). Again, the new king

had hoped to reconcile the whig and tory parties who had divided English politics in the years before he arrived. Soon after taking the throne, William urged people to forgive past injuries, and tried to force them to work together by establishing mixed ministries. But, as we shall again see later, this desire for political harmony would also be sacrificed for military expediency. When it became clear that mixed ministries led to tension in government, and particularly to doubts about the direction of the war, the king abandoned his commitment to balance and ruled through single factions who might be more effective in wartime leadership (see Chapter Four). Taken together, these sacrifices to William's European strategy represented a triumph of Orange over Stuart interests. The war to defend Flanders kept going – but the Stuart crown lost ancient powers, abandoned its control of ecclesiastical policy, and was usurped by party leaders as the focus of domestic politics.

Whatever the effect on the old British dynasty, William's dedication to conflict reaped rewards. The 1695 capture of Namur proved a turning point in the war – securing the safety of Holland, and William's position on the English throne. Although the allies had few great successes in the following campaigning seasons, it was clear that their efforts were exhausting France, and Louis became much more interested in sporadic peace feelers which both sides had put out since 1692. In the summer of 1697, a deal between the war-weary nations was agreed and signed at the town of Ryswick. In return for an end to the Grand Alliance's attacks on him, Louis would give up his recent territorial gains, he would accept Dutch control of 'barrier fortresses' in the Spanish Netherlands, he would recognise William's British titles, and he would cease to support James's efforts to regain his thrones.

After this treaty, one might suppose William's obsession with France would at last wane. In fact, it remained dominant even in the years of peace at the end of his life – and even though a more relaxed attitude to continental threats would have benefited his British and Irish subjects. From a purely domestic point of view, the interests of the island realms would have best been served by a rapid return to peacetime conditions. The war had been a considerable strain – enough of a strain indeed, to have forced the treaty negotiations – and there were a number of problems which could best be solved by rapid demobilisation. Most pressingly, the war had resulted in huge public debt. Even though levels of taxation had been raised massively in the years since 1689, this had never covered the enormous expenditure on the military, with the result that the crown owed £19 million by 1697. Reducing the cost of the military was therefore an urgent priority. The war had also placed a considerable strain on the economy. Heavy taxation had depressed demand; trade had been disrupted by naval warfare and a commercial boycott of France; and the nation's stock of gold and silver had been depleted as it had flowed out to buy supplies for the English army in Flanders. In the mid-decade, these factors had led to a crisis which had led to real dearth at home, and delays in payments to the military abroad. For economic as well as fiscal reasons, therefore, a full and lasting end to the struggle with France seemed essential. William, however, was as reluctant as ever to see this happen.

It is true that in the years immediately after Ryswick, William was prepared to try new methods to secure long-term Orange goals. Facing the risk that the French ruling house might inherit the entire Spanish empire on the death of its heirless ruler, King Carlos II, William did not react with his usual martial aggression. Recognising that his realms and allies needed time to recover after 1697 (and realising that France, too, was exhausted), he decided to negotiate with Louis about the future of Spain. Persuading Versailles that Europe would not stand by while the Bourbons took all of the Habsburg's possessions, William sealed deals by which the French royal house would take only part of the empire on Carlos's death. In the 'First Partition Treaty', signed on 1 October 1698, Louis would take only Naples and Tuscany, with the bulk of Spain's territories (Iberia, Milan, Flanders and America) going to the electoral prince of Bavaria. When that prince died months later, William negotiated again, this time securing the 'Second Partition Treaty' (15 March 1700). This granted Milan to France along with other Italian dominions, and left everything else to a cadet branch of the Austrian Habsburgs. Twice in two years, therefore, William had concluded agreements with his old enemy to avoid the risk of war.

Yet while the partition treaties might seem to reveal a new William, less obsessed with the Orange cause and more in tune with the needs of his British nations, they did not really represent a change in policy. Most obviously, they represented a change in methodology, not objective. The aim was still to contain France, albeit with fences of diplomacy rather than gunpowder. Moreover, peaceful negotiation was only one half of William's strategy in the years after 1697. If he was willing to talk, he still prepared for open conflict. From the treaty of Ryswick to his death in early 1702, he continued to keep his British realms on a war footing – whatever domestic opposition and economic strain this might entail.

The continuing determination to uphold the military option was most evident in the king's attitude to the army once peace was declared. Given the expense of keeping a large military force, the majority of the English political nation wanted to demobilise rapidly after 1697. The king, however, disagreed. He wanted a powerful army ready to counter any move which France might make, and to give him a realistic military threat to back him in his negotiations with Versailles. Consequently, in his speech opening parliament on 3 December 1697, William stated that England could not be 'safe' without a substantial army, and he asked his ministers to secure agreement to a force of 35,000.[16] The result of this royal position was the king's most serious rupture with parliament. General determination to demobilise meant William's servants lost control of the Commons, and that parliament voted to reduce the military to only 10,000 soldiers by the end of the session in spring 1698. In normal circumstances, William might well have bowed to his legislators, as he had in the disputes of the early 1690s. Now, however, the king saw parliament undermining his ability to control France, and dug in. He continued to demand large forces in speeches to parliament even when it was clear which way the wind was blowing. He refused to allow his ministers to suggest 15,000 men as a compromise figure over the winter of 1697–98, and over the following summer he attempted to defy parliament by hiding extra troops in the Irish establishment and among the officer corps. As a result, the Commons re-assembled in the autumn in even more belligerent mood. Furious that William had retained over 14,000 men instead of the 10,000 they had voted for, they resolved to cut the army down further to only 7,000 soldiers. This was very nearly the end for William. By late December 1698, the king was talking openly at court about abdication – or at least retiring to Holland and leaving the English to their own devices.[17] Only Herculean efforts by the king's chief minister, John Somers, got him to calm down and stay at his post. William's Orange commitment to containing France had nearly led to his abandoning his Stuart throne altogether.

The old continental cause dominated even the very last months of William's life. In October 1700 Carlos II of Spain finally died. This should have meant that the second partition treaty came into operation, and that the Spanish empire would be divided between France and the Austrian Habsburgs. Unfortunately for European peace, however, Louis had two problems accepting this course of events. First, Carlos's will ignored all international agreements and left his *entire* territory to the king of France's second grandson. Although this should not lead to a union of France and Spain (since the kingdoms would remain in different branches of the French royal house), it would probably give Versailles considerable influence in Madrid, and was therefore too tempting a prize to resist. Second, Louis came to realise that partition was deeply unpopular outside his own and William's courts. The treaties had been negotiated between the two sides without consulting other powers: when they were revealed they were opposed by the Spanish elites (who did not want to see the division of their imperium), and by the Austrians, who had hoped to gain the whole empire. Louis therefore realised he would probably have to go to war to impose the partition treaty, even if he stood by it. He consequently decided to accept Carlos's will, reasoning that if conflict were inevitable, he might as well fight for the bigger reward.

Surprisingly, English reaction to Louis's betrayal was calm. The partition treaties had been as unpopular in London as they had been in Madrid and Vienna. They had been concluded without informing parliament; and they granted France huge advantages in Italy, which might allow her to dominate the Mediterranean and threaten England's trade. Carlos's will, by contrast, promised to keep the Italian possessions outside the direct control of Versailles. If objecting to it meant a return to war, then many Englishmen were happier to acquiesce in the French breach of faith. This was the reaction even of William's ministers in 1700–1. The tory administration of the day opposed rapid remobilisation, while its supporters in the Commons attempted to impeach the group of whig ministers whom they held responsible for the partition treaties. William's response, however, was furious. After a brief attempt to re-open negotiations with Louis and rescue the principle of partition, he reverted to his familiar bellicose stance. Struggling against the British reluctance to return to conflict, he pushed for massive remobilisation and worked to rebuild the alliances of 1689–97. By the autumn of 1701 he was appealing to parliament for a vigorous response to Louis (who had begun to play into his hands by occupying territory in the Spanish Netherlands, and recognising James II's son as king of England on his father's death). He was also supporting a propaganda campaign to persuade the English public to back war; and was beginning to think about sacking his tory ministers to replace them by the more aggressively anti-French whigs. The formal success of his campaign was demonstrated on 7 September 1701. Then, only six months before William's death, the British realms joined the Second Grand Alliance. This tied them to a continuing 'Orange' policy, uniting them with the United Provinces and Austria in opposition to Louis's claims on Spain.

Conclusion

William died on 8 March 1702 . Two weeks earlier his horse had tripped over a molehill in Hyde Park. Although the king had survived the fall, and even began to make a recovery, the accident probably weakened his resistance to the pulmonary fever which set in on 5 March and claimed his life three days later. As he expired, the Stuart realms were preparing to return to war with France. He had pushed them to do this even though they had not regained their full strength from their earlier bruising conflict. He had urged war, even though the policy filled public opinion with dread and led to tensions between monarch, ministry and parliament. William had thus remained an Orange right to the end. He certainly cared about the prestige of the Stuart crown, and had clear regard for the interests of the Stuart realms, but all this would be sacrificed if they hampered the great aim of controlling Louis XIV.

William's priorities were obvious to his contemporaries. Indeed they were to cause his deepest political difficulties in governing the Stuart realms. Throughout his reign, there were constant complaints that the monarch cared little about Britain; that he took advice only from a small coterie of Dutchmen; and that he wished to bleed his new kingdoms dry to defend his old country. These complaints rapidly became the burden of Jacobite attacks on the king. Those who still supported James's rights to the throne used their underground presses to ask why the new regime was taxing its subjects so heavily, disrupting their trade in war and sending their sons to die in Flanders – especially when Louis's prime threat was to the Netherlands, not the British. More worryingly, such questions began to circulate among those who had initially supported the revolution. Even in parliament there were doubts about the wisdom of sacrificing the nation to foreign goals. MPs at Westminster wanted to know why England was engaged as a principal in the war, when it was the Dutch who were most obviously in danger of conquest. They objected when English soldiers were commanded by Dutch generals (fearing that such leaders would hold English lives cheap); and they were suspicious of the king's close reliance on foreign counsellors (such as his old friend Bentinck, whom he made earl of Portland, and installed as his closest court servant, the groom of the stole).[18] The most dramatic expression of such fears came immediately after William's death. When addressing her first legislature, his successor Queen Anne stated that she knew her heart was entirely English. Many took this to be a dark reflection on her brother-in-law's record, and a promise to consider her realm more fully than he had ever done.

William's continental priorities, then, risked unpopularity. Unfortunately, this danger was compounded by what his obsession had done to his personality as well as his policies. As we noted earlier, concentration on the military containment of France had made William a driven and isolated man. In Holland this had meant he was not as sociable as some of his countrymen might have wished: in London it was very nearly disastrous. Here was a new, unfamiliar and questionably legitimate ruler, who urgently needed to introduce himself to his new subjects and get himself liked. Yet here was a man who hated large gatherings; who trusted only a small circle of people (most of whom were Dutch and had fought alongside him in Flanders); and thought that only active battle was a truly valuable use of his time. Consequently, William withdrew from his new subjects, just as he should have been getting to know them.

The breakdown in contact was very nearly total. William, for instance, showed great reluctance to participate in the social round which had traditionally cemented English monarchs to the political elite. He cut back on royal balls, dances and public dinners – and looked pretty miserable when he deigned to attend them. He did not enjoy horse racing, and was anyway rarely around in the summers when high society decamped to Newmarket to follow this (now-kingless) sport of kings. He went little to the theatre, or other entertainments, and a respiratory complaint forced him to withdraw from smokey palaces in central London to live in the impressive – but more distant – apartments he had built at Kensington and Hampton Court. Most damagingly, William disliked talking to people. It was almost impossible to get an audience with him and, when one did, he was short to the point of insult. Indeed, it was said that people were less angered by their exclusion from the king, than by his rudeness on the occasions when they managed to break through it. It was not that William had difficulties with language. Although most comfortable in French, and obviously fluent in Dutch, his very early years with Mary Stuart had ensured that English was actually his mother tongue. Rather, the king's reluctance to communicate sprang from his sense of mission and of his status as saviour of Europe. They meant he was impatient with small talk, and had too high a notion of his special position to waste time with people he thought inconsequential. With this attitude the king became the despair of some of his closest allies. Gilbert Burnet – who came over with William in the invasion as his chaplain, and became one of his chief advisors on public relations – constantly urged him to be more welcoming and outgoing, but his later writings are full of frustration that he never made much progress with his patron. Some even worried that William's exclusion of all but a few very close male friends fuelled rumours of unnatural vice.[20] There were stories (then, as now, impossible to substantiate) that the king engaged in homosexual affairs: first with Bentinck, and then with Arnald van Keppel, the handsome young courtier who replaced Bentinck in the royal favour in the 1690s, and who was created earl of Albemarle.

In fact, William's obsession with France risked such dangerous unpopularity that he can be counted extremely lucky to have been rescued by four countervailing advantages. First, and most basically, his subjects were grateful to him. He had saved them from popery in 1688, and this made them willing to forgive many subsequent slights. Second, although personally haughty, William's experiences in the Netherlands had taught him to be politically open. As we shall see, his refusal to have subjects as friends was moderated by his willingness to work with a wide spectrum of them in government and to trust important public roles to many more. Third, for all his social reticence, the king *was* prepared to mount spectacles to satisfy the popular appetite for pomp. William may not have been physically impressive (he was almost diminutively short, his hooked nose made him instantly recognisable on coins and cartoons but did not render him handsome, and a bout of smallpox in the mid-1670s had ensured he was thin and pale), but he was willing to participate in glittering ceremonies. He was highly visible during his invasion (for instance, entering Exeter in a grand procession mounted on a white horse), and went on to have an impressive coronation. Afterwards, he displayed himself regularly to his people at Lord Mayor's Shows in London, in progresses through the rest of the country and at a series of thanksgivings for military victories.

Finally, and most vitally, William was fortunate in the support of his joint-monarch, his wife. Mary and the prince had not got on well for their first decade after their marriage in 1677, but once a misunderstanding about her political ambition had been sorted out (she made it clear she had none), and once her husband began to be more discreet about his interest in other women at the Dutch court, they made an effective partnership. In particular, Mary did much to soothe fears that the crown had fallen into the hands of a foreigner. As an English-born Stuart, she looked more like an appropriate ruler for the new realms than her husband, and she tried to compensate for her spouse's seeming lack of interest in his subjects. Unlike William, she did not leave the country for months every summer. Unlike him, she was gracious and charming, and attracted people to her. Unlike her husband, she enjoyed dancing, theatre and gossip – even if she later felt guilty for her less-than-godly behaviour. Thus even though she exercised little independent power (when left in charge during William's summer campaigns, she consulted with him constantly by letter), Mary's death at the end of 1694 was a major blow. The king's shattering grief was genuine and personal: but it must also have been political. The queen had stood as his protection. She had deflected charges that the monarchy now cared nothing for its realm, and that the nation was being run as an outpost of Dutch foreign policy. It is noticeable that

William's greatest domestic defeats, for example over the standing army, came after her funeral.[21]

Taken overall, therefore, there is no doubt that William remained an Orange to his dying day, and that his subjects outside the Netherlands resented this. They were put off by his personal fixations, and they feared that he placed the interests of Europe above their own. Yet while the people of the time complained about royal Orangeness, three hundred years later it is less clear that William's foreign focus damaged them. Certainly, the anti-French cause took the king away from his kingdoms – both physically and mentally – for much of his reign. But in the circumstances of the late seventeenth century, this may have been no bad thing. For over fifty years, the Stuart realms had been governed by men who had concentrated on their position in London. The result had been civil war and constitutional crisis. As we are about to see, it may have taken someone with no great experience of British politics, and no overwhelming interest in the British kingdoms, to find solutions. The determination to defeat Louis may have given William the wider vision needed to see past log-jams in British politics: the training in people management he had received in the United Provinces may have equipped him with the skills required to implement his remedies. William was a pretty marginal Stuart. Given that family's record in government, however, it would be hard to argue that this was a misfortune.

Notes

The best narratives of the 1688/9 revolution are probably J.R. Jones, *The Revolution of 1688 in England* (Weidenfeld & Nicolson, 1984); and W.A. Speck, *Reluctant Revolutionaries* (Clarendon Press, 1988). Robert Beddard, *Kingdom without a King* (Phaidon, 1988) provides a close account of the invasion itself, while Dutch participation and the military history is well handled in Jonathan Israel, 'The Dutch role in the Glorious Revolution', in Jonathan Israel (ed.), *The Anglo-Dutch Moment* (CUP, 1991). Baxter, *William III* continues its excellent biography through to the king's death, and chapter 17 gives a full analysis of when and why he decided to invade England. An admirably clear account of the progress of the war, politics and diplomacy is provided by Craig Rose, *England in the 1690s* (Blackwell, 1999). The economic strains of war in Britain can be followed in D.W. Jones, *War and Economy in the Age of William and Marlborough* (OUP, 1988); while the disputes over army demobilisation are covered in John Childs, *The British Army of William III, 1689–1702* (MUP, 1987).

1 Burnet, *History*, **1**, 692–3.

2 For the alternative interpretations see James's declaration in *London Gazette*, **2397** (1688); and William's manifesto – *The Declaration of His Highness, William Henry, Prince of*

Orange, of the Reasons Inducing Him to Appear in Arms in the Kingdom of England (The Hague, 1688).

3 K.H.D. Haley, *William of Orange and the English Opposition, 1672–1674* (Clarendon Press, 1953).

4 R.W. Blencowe (ed.), *Diary of the Times of Charles the Second by the Honourable Henry Sidney* (1843), **2**, 46, 78, 84, 139, 149.

5 See Steven Pincus, *Protestantism and Patriotism: Ideologies and the Making of English Foreign Policy, 1650–1668* (CUP, 1996), parts 1–2.

6 *Declaration of His Highness.*

7 Jones, *Revolution of 1688*, ch. 10.

8 See below, pp. 66–7.

9 Steven Pincus, 'The English nationalist revolution of 1688', in Tony Claydon and Ian McBride (eds), *Protestantism and National Identity, 1650–1850* (CUP, 1998), pp. 75–104.

10 'The "Spencer House" journals', quoted in H.C. Foxcroft, *The Life and Letters of Sir George Savile* (1898), **2**, 203–47.

11 Lois G. Schwoerer, 'The coronation of William and Mary'; and W.A. Speck, 'William – and Mary?', both in Lois G. Schwoerer (ed.), *The Revolutions of 1688/9* (CUP, 1991); *The King's Apartments: Hampton Court Palace*, special edition of *Apollo* Magazine **390** new series (1994).

12 Japikse, *Correspondentie*, ii, **3**, 78–9, 81.

13 *LJ*, **14**, 128.

14 *LJ*, **14**, 320.

15 *LJ*, **14**, 428, 513.

16 *LJ*, **16**, 174.

17 William Coxe (ed.), *Private and Original Correspondence of Charles Talbot, Duke of Shrewsbury* (1821), pp. 572–3.

18 For details of this criticism, see Claydon, *William III*, pp.122–6.

19 *LJ*, **17**, 68.

20 Japikse, *Correspondentie*, i, **1**, 198–9.

21 The best short and up-to-date account of Mary's role in the joint monarchy is W.A. Speck, 'William – and Mary?', in Lois G. Schwoerer (ed.), *The Revolution of 1688/9* (CUP, 1991).

William and the Stuart Realms

Chapter Three

❖

William and the English Constitution

The problem: constitutional instability in England and Wales

On 2 March 1629, William's grandfather, King Charles I, issued a proclamation explaining why he had resolved to rule without parliament for the foreseeable future. Blaming the 'malevolent dispositions of some ill affected persons of the House of Commons' for recent ruptures between the crown and the legislature, he stated that MPs and peers should depart Westminster in order that those intent on 'disturbance to the peace, and good order of our kingdom', should not have their victory.[1] Fifty-two years, two civil wars, and a series of constitutional crises later, King Charles II issued a remarkably similar declaration. Explaining why he had dissolved parliament before it had had a chance to conduct any business, he blamed 'the restless malice of ill men who are labouring to poison our people' and appealed for a little time without parliaments to 'open the eyes of all our good subjects'.[2] These two proclamations illustrate the central constitutional instability of seventeenth-century England. From the moment the Stuarts had come to the throne, they had proved incapable of living peaceably with their legislative assembly.

Tensions between monarchs and parliament had begun under James I, but they had worsened to rupture under his son Charles I. In the later 1620s, the younger king had repeatedly dissolved his legislature when it made what he thought were illegal demands to extend its influence. In 1629 he had resolved to rule without parliament until he could secure a more compliant body. The proclamation at the head of this chapter ushered in an eleven-year 'personal rule' during which resentment grew that the king was not consulting his subjects through their representatives. Commons and Lords eventually reassembled in 1640. However, since this occurred only because the king was facing rebellion in Scotland, and desperately needed revenue, it was not surprising that the mutual distrust between the crown and the legislature continued. The period 1640–42 was marked by an increasingly bitter power struggle, in which

51

the leaders of the parliamentary cause made greater and greater demands to control the king. When they finally insisted that the legislature must supervise command of his majesty's armed forces, Charles lost patience. Raising his standard to crush what he thought was rebellion, he initiated the English civil war. In 1649, struggles were temporarily stilled when the victorious parliamentary forces executed the king. These forces proved unable to build a stable new regime, however, so the monarchy was restored in 1660. Unfortunately, the old regime's problems were re-established along with that old regime. By the late 1670s battlelines were drawn in remarkably familiar places. Majorities in parliament attempted to control royal powers, while the crown stoutly defended the court's position. In 1681, as we have seen, Charles II had decided he must rule without parliaments to avoid political crisis. In 1686, his brother James II, only a year into his reign, came to much the same conclusion.

To understand the difficulties William faced with the English system of government, it is important to get to the root of the disasters just described. Fundamentally, their cause was an inherent constitutional contradiction. Given that definitive rules for the conduct of English government were not laid down, the system had to operate on a general consensus about the responsibilities, powers and limitations of public institutions. Sadly, this consensus was endangered by confusion in constitutional thinking. Over the centuries, the English had adopted their political philosophy piecemeal, so that they had ended up with a self-contradictory assortment of principles which has been labelled 'monarchical republicanism'.[3] On one hand, the English believed that their nation was a monarchy, led by a single ruler who must have unchallenged power to implement policy. People thought that monarchy had served England well under the Tudors; they knew that the country had suffered when the court had been weak – as during the Wars of the Roses; and they had been subjected to generations of royal and ecclesiatical propaganda stressing the semi-divinity of the crown. Yet, while they were monarchists, the English were also at least a species of republicans. Although convinced they should be ruled by a king, they believed their realm should be run on principles most clearly espoused in republics – particularly that government should be for the good of the whole community, that it should usually be by consent and that power should be dispersed among a large number of citizens. These ideals came partly from study of classical republics. More generally, however, they stemmed from a commitment to the English common law as the subject's defence against rulers' encroachments; and from the fact that most people experienced the state, not as royal command, but in the network of participatory committees (such as parish vestries, town corporations or county commissions) which constituted local government. Above all, the 'republican' ideals were rooted in a traditional attachment to parliament as the representative of the nation. Reassured by legal textbooks which spoke of the legislature's importance, and informed of its activities through news, law courts and election campaigns, the English took pride in the fact that they were not governed arbitrarily, but that the ruler had to consult the whole community (embodied in Commons and Lords) before taxing his subjects or changing the law. Taken together, these opposed principles meant the English lived a contradiction. They were passionate monarchists, but they were passionate 'republicans' as well.

This ambiguous political philosophy was the fundamental cause of English instability in the seventeenth century. Curiously, however, monarchical republicanism did not cause problems directly, or on its own. In fact, with a little compromise and accommodation, it had proved perfectly possible for people to live with both royal and anti-royal ideals. Under Elizabeth I, for example, the system of government had worked reasonably well because the English had shared a broad understanding about when monarchical and republican principles should operate. They had switched ideals according to circumstance, and so avoided incompatible beliefs clashing in practical situations. To take just one instance: there had been pretty wide agreement that some parts of the crown's revenue (feudal dues, and taxes on foreign trade) were 'monarchical' and could be raised without parliamentary consent. By contrast, other parts of the revenue (taxes on internal wealth and income) were governed by 'republican' principles and must be approved by the legislature. Consequently, conflict was avoided because parliament did not question some forms of royal money raising, while the crown was always careful to consult parliament before taxing people in particular other ways. The problem which William faced, therefore, was not the basic constitutional contradiction. Rather, it was that the practical accommodation which had made it work had collapsed. Over the seventeenth century the English had lost their ability to negotiate their opposed axioms of politics. Their flair for holding monarchism and republicanism in balance had disappeared in parallel paranoias. While many Englishmen had become gripped by anxiety that there was a plot at court to crush their liberties, they had been equally gripped by fears that rebels and demagogues were stirring up the mob to overthrow royal authority.

Fear of the court was one of the most persistent features of Stuart England. Throughout the century, 'country' concern that the monarchy was encroaching on the rights of individuals and other institutions of government dominated public discussion. This country ideology so sensitised people to the crown's supposed ambition that the old sense that the king had rightful powers broke down. For example, in the 1620s, certain members of the House of Commons became so convinced that monarchs were exceeding their rights that they campaigned for parliamentary control over areas previously thought the preserve of the court. These included foreign policy, choice of ministers and collection of customs duties. In the 1640s, these claims were joined by innovative requests to control the army and the calling and dissolving of parliaments; and in Charles II's reign by demands to scrutinise the crown's spending of its money. By the end of the 1670s, parliament was making quite breathtaking claims for its authority. In the 'exclusion crisis' (1679–83), leading members of the Commons and Lords used rumours of a plot at court as an excuse to try to alter the succession to the crown.

What lay behind these disruptive country concerns was a new and disturbing development in the post-Elizabethan era. Once the old queen had died, it became easy to believe that there was a popish conspiracy at court. Elizabeth's solid Protestantism was replaced by a series of royal regimes whose commitment to the reformed faith was at best ambiguous. Between 1603 and 1688, all the four reigning monarchs were married to Catholics. James II openly espoused this religion; Charles II had been a secret convert; and the artistic, ecclesiastical and political patronage of the other rulers suggested deep Catholic sympathies. In these circumstances, the ingrained tradition of English anti-popery fashioned a horrifying vision of a satanic plot at the heart of government. Papists, it was thought, were planning to use court power to rob the nation of godly Protestantism, and were determined to destroy the parliamentary constitution which supported the true religion. This belief in a Catholic plot was the most constant feature of Stuart politics, underpinned by a tradition of Protestant polemic asserting that popery was the evil behind all misfortunes.[4] Consequently, anti-popish rhetoric was central to all parliamentary attacks on the crown. It burst out in suspicion that Catholics were urging Charles I to ignore the legislature in the 1620s; it fuelled the excessive demands of the Commons in the early 1640s; and it dictated legislative attempts to exclude the Catholic James from the throne in the 1680s.

This country paranoia would have been disturbing enough. Unfortunately, however, these fears from the 'republican' side of the English psyche were parallelled by 'monarchical' nightmares. Throughout the century politicians at court came to dread a radical conspiracy to destroy the crown and replace it by democratic anarchy. These fears are clearly expressed in the 1629 and 1681 declarations which opened this chapter. In such documents, the monarchs and their supporters advanced the theory that 'ill' men were deliberately stirring up the Commons. Plotting to take advantage of constitutional stalemate, these conspirators had pushed the legislature beyond the traditional role of warning and advising the king, and had persuaded it to bring government to a halt. As with country fears, the court claimed solid evidence for its accusations. Certain groups in parliament had behaved obstructively; they had made unprecedented and disruptive claims about legislative powers; and they had been prepared to plunge the country into chaos during the civil war. As with country fears again, the court's perception of a plot drove it to shatter the old consensus about when different principles should operate. Claiming that extraordinary action was needed in the face of anti-monarchist conspirators, the Stuarts stretched their prerogatives into areas where 'republican' ideals had previously held sway. Thus Charles I and James II collected tax without parliamentary approval. Charles II and James II built an army with the same lack of consent. James II claimed to be able to nullify statute without due parliamentary repeal.

The constitutional tragedy of Stuart England was that rival conspiracy theories reinforced one another. Horror of supposed plotters drove republican and monarchical principles into new areas, where they began to encroach on one another's territory. As parliamentary leaders took controversial actions to control a crown they thought was plotting against them, the crown took this as evidence of a conspiracy against it and defended itself by expanding claims in the opposite direction. More tragically still, the fact that most English people were good monarchical republicans meant that they would respond to both these sets of fears and defences, and would rally round the competing causes. Parliamentary leaders could appeal to English 'republican' ideals and gain support for their attacks on the crown. This is why they enjoyed public backing in the 1620s; why so many were prepared to take up arms for parliament in the 1640s; and why parliamentary attempts to stop a popish conspiracy at court in 1678–81 were encouraged by mass petitions and street demonstrations. On the other hand, the crown could plug into 'monarchical' ideals, and find its own popular enthusiasm – even from people who at other times had expressed country sentiments. This is why Charles I was able to recover from nearly universal unpopularity to persuade half the country to fight for him in 1642. It is why the 1660 Restoration was greeted with bonfires and bells, and why Charles II was able to dissolve the 1681 parliament with considerable 'tory' or pro-court support. The rival conspiracy theories thus did more than push an abstract political contradiction into real political conflict. They polarised masses of people into opposed camps, and kept alive the nightmare of civil war.

This constitutional analysis has been important, because it is essential to understand the exact challenge facing William in 1689. The contradiction of 'monarchical republicanism' was the key to the instability of the seventeenth century. However, rebuilding a functional system of government did not mean that the contradiction had to be removed. The Elizabethan age had shown that the English could live with the paradox given pragmatic accommodation. Moreover, the history of the seventeenth century suggested that attempts to solve crises by debilitating monarchy, or by eliminating 'republican' sentiment, simply made things worse. Such attempts merely convinced people that there were indeed conspiracies to destroy one of their highest ideals. William's real problem, therefore, was not to abolish monarchical republicanism, but to make it work again. He had to find ways of reconciling a system of government and of political belief centred on a crowned ruler, with institutions and axioms which stressed the representation, involvement and consent of a wide political nation. Above all, he had to break the spell of the rival conspiracy theories. Only this would stop monarchism and republicanism encroaching upon one another. Only this would stop the political nation being divided between their causes.

William's constitutional advantages

The rest of this chapter will argue that William succeeded in taking the tension out of English constitutional conflict. It will argue that it was his European experience and focus which allowed him to do this. It will suggest that it took someone who was an Orange rather than a Stuart to get monarchical republicanism to function, and someone fixated on the continent rather than England to solve the country's troubles. Partly, this argument will be based on the distance which William's upbringing gave him from English paranoias. Having grown up in Holland, he was far less likely to get caught up in the conspiracy theories which so destabilised the Stuart realm. More crucially, however, it will be suggested that William's Orange inheritance gave him three specific advantages which had not been enjoyed by his purely Stuart predecessors. First, his obsession with defeating Louis XIV meant he was relatively unconcerned about preserving the royal prerogative. He was, therefore, less prone to stoke fears of absolutism. Second, his experience of parliamentary bodies was not simply that they were an obstruction to rulers. The constitution of the Netherlands had forced him to co-operate with assemblies, and as a result he was less suspicious of them and had new ideas about how they might work with monarchs. Third, William's continental career had allowed him to present himself as an unequivocally Protestant king. This meant he could dispel the fears of popery which had done so much to breed fear of the court.

William's first and most important advantage as a constitutional arbiter was that his political priority was the defeat of France rather than the preservation of the royal prerogative. This was in stark contrast to his Stuart predecessors who had put the rights of their dynasty at the heart of their vision. Raised within the Stuart households, the earlier monarchs had been brought up on a belief in the justice of crown power, and had identified no real objectives beyond the preservation, glorification and extension of this power. After the civil war, such priorities had been reinforced. Charles II and James II had suffered painful exile after the execution of their father. Their own experience therefore highlighted the threats to monarchy in England, and the absolute necessity of cementing its position. The result of these Stuart concerns was stiff resistance to parliamentary claims. Before 1688, monarchs had seen preserving the prerogative as their highest duty and had dug in at moments of tension – even if this meant precipitating constitutional crises. In huge contrast, William was relatively uninterested in the preservation of royal power. As we shall see, he wished to keep what prerogatives he could, complaining bitterly about parliament's ambitions and defending his rights with vigorous action. Yet, in the end, the Orange obsession with containing Louis took precedence. William proved unwilling to precipitate constitutional crises. Rows with the House of Commons risked that body blocking tax revenue to win its points, and this would be disastrous for the war. Consequently the new king always backed down before political tension rose too high. The king's European focus – his determination to rescue the continent from French domination – helped restore a functioning political system in England. He put the army in Flanders above his personal power, and so avoided the pitched confrontations which had marked earlier reigns.

William's second qualification as a physician of the English constitution was that he was far less suspicious of representative assemblies than his predecessors. Given that seventeenth-century parliaments had launched a series of obstreperous campaigns to roll back the power of the Stuart kings, it was understandable that earlier monarchs came to view legislatures with hostility. Kings believed their Lords and Commons were too easily infected by factious men who must be stopped if the crown were to be saved. Superficially, William's position in the Netherlands was similar. As we have seen, he too faced opposition from representative assemblies, and frequently struggled with the men sitting in the provincial states and estates general. He too could have concluded that he was facing traitors in the assemblies, and tried to rule alone. Yet there was one vital difference. In the British realms, the individual ruler was sovereign, and could legally govern without parliament. In the Provinces, however, the assemblies were sovereign. They could – as they had shown before 1672 – govern without any stadholder. William therefore did not have the option of dissolving his enemies' power base, and this taught very different political lessons.

First, the new king's Dutch experience meant he did not see strong-arm tactics as a way of dealing with difficult assemblies. The one time he had really tried these – in 1683 with Amsterdam – the result had been disastrous, and he had come to realise that opposition was better worked with and worked around than faced off. Second, William's time in Holland meant he did not automatically see opponents in assemblies as traitors. Unlike his Stuart predecessors, he had been forced to work alongside political enemies, and through this had discovered that they were not inherently evil. For example, the very representatives who had opposed him in the 1670s and early 1680s were persuaded to back him in his invasion of England once he had flattered and compromised with them, and persuaded them of the continuing danger of France. Once William was in England, he was therefore less likely to view parliamentary opposition as rebellion, and more likely to try to comprehend it. Third, William's Dutch years had taught him how to co-operate with assemblies on a daily and practical basis. Since he could get no policy approved, administered or financed without the states and estates general, he had had to find ways of involving assemblies, and had learnt parliamentary skills which had eluded his English predecessors. Finally, the Orange family's position, unlike the Stuarts', taught that representative bodies were sources of strength, not weakness. William's own career had shown that rulers who fell out with representative assemblies were badly handicapped. On the other hand, when these assemblies could be brought to rally round the prince, great things could be achieved. The glories of the early years of the 1672–78 war, and the breathtakingly successful expedition to England, proved this. Brought together, these foreign political lessons produced a very different kind of English king. Here was a man used and ready to work with parliamentary bodies – the very sort to make monarchical republicanism function again.

William's third continental advantage – his ability to present himself as a truly Protestant ruler – might seem surprising. Although he had fought the leading Catholic power in Europe for many years, he did not have an unimpeachable anti-Catholic record abroad. He had allied with Catholic powers, and had employed many Catholics in his administration and armies in the Netherlands. There was therefore evidence of a toleration of popery which – in England – might have sustained the destabilising theory of a popish plot in government. It was true that William seemed, unlike his uncles, to have remained a solid Protestant himself. Also, this time in contrast to all four of his Stuart predecessors, he had not married a popish wife. Yet given the loose attachment of his maternal family to the reformed faith, and the fact that royal marriages across Europe were usually a matter of dynastic convenience rather than denominational solidarity, these facts might have seemed somewhat accidental to an English audience.

However, probed more deeply, it is clear William's Protestantism, and his vigour in presenting it, were more central to his European experience than at first appears. On the continent, the Orange family had always benefited from its championing of the anti-Catholic cause. Within the Low Countries it had gained public support by guaranteeing Protestant freedoms in the face of popish aggression, and from the first days of the Dutch revolt against Spain (when Orange propaganda centred on images of popish inquisitors torturing the godly) it had associated itself with resistance to the counter-reformation. William's personal Protestantism, and his Protestant marriage, therefore, were no accidents. Even if he had been drawn towards Catholic doctrines or Catholic partners (and there is no evidence he ever was), his family inheritance meant he had too much to lose to give in to these temptations. Moreover, William had found vigorous Protestantism very useful in his own career. Protestant propaganda swept him to power in 1672, and united the Dutch behind his war policy. William's European experience had thus bound him into the reformation cause, and given him practice in broadcasting a Protestant image. Whereas his Stuart predecessors had centred their public presentation on traditional images of royal magnificence and majesty, William's relied far more heavily on religious messages. His propagated image in the Netherlands had stressed, not the dignity of rule, so much as his providential role as protector of the reformed faith.

Transferred to England, this Dutch image of William would have impressive results. The new king lost very little time broadcasting his religious message in his new realm. As we shall soon see, Williamite publicists began promoting their man as the saviour of the reformation even before he had disembarked at Torbay, and they continued a barrage of such propaganda throughout the reign. The effect was dramatic. In the face of overwhelming insistence on William's Protestantism, the notion of a popish conspiracy at the centre of government became hard to sustain. William's royal court could be accused of corruption or exceeding his proper powers, but it was hard to accuse it of sympathy with popery because the evidence of the king's commitment to reformed religion was just too great. As a result, parliamentary suspicion of the court began to fade, or at least to run along saner lines.

Taken with William's other legacies from his Dutch career, William's Protestantism dispelled the mutually re-enforcing fears which had disrupted political stability in Stuart England. While his religious image – and his willingness to back down at moments of constitutional crisis – eased country fears of a popish cabal at court, his willingness to work with parliaments blocked court accusations that the Commons was filled with dangerous demagogues. As we shall see in the next sections, these advantages allowed England to make a new start in her Dutch king's reign. They first secured a revolutionary settlement in 1689 which addressed the fundamental fears of the English political classes, and then provided a new model for successful relations between court and parliament in the 1690s.

William's solution: the revolutionary settlement

Whatever William's qualifications as an arbiter of British constitutional disputes, it was not instantly apparent how his action in the autumn of 1688 might help stabilise the political system. The prince of Orange had brought an armed force into the country and demanded investigation into recent court policy. He was therefore rehearsing arguments which had led to civil war in the recent past, and was helping to furnish the country with the soldiers and artillery which would make such a conflict possible. Consequently it was something of a miracle that 1688 marked a turn towards stability, rather than a further descent into chaos. The prince's dangerous actions, far from leading to bloodshed, soon produced a stabilising constitutional settlement. To understand how this extraordinary thing happened, it is important to bear in mind the advantages which William's Dutch heritage gave him. In addition, it is useful to point to parallels with 1672 which remarkably few historians have noted. In 1688 William was no novice in the art of seizing power. Sixteen years before he had come to control the Netherlands without provoking a constitutional crisis, so by the time of his invasion of England he had already had experience which would be invaluable in the Glorious Revolution. Fortunately, William found that repeating political strategies paid dividends. Following the pattern of 1672, he was able to apply lessons he had learned that year, and found that they provided effective salves for England's sores.

The first instructive parallel between 1672 and 1688 was William's extreme caution in demanding promotion. In both years, the prince had secured considerable real power. In 1672, William commanded the Dutch army, while mobs called for the prince's elevation, and his opponents lost their old control over the cities. By the end of 1688, William was occupying London with an army of loyal Dutch troops, and the 'Irish night' breakdown of order had demonstrated he was the only barrier against civil chaos. Yet on both occasions, the prince refused to use his de facto control to demand that he be raised to formal offices. Rather, he avoided any suggestion of a *coup d'état* by making it clear that he would only accept promotion from bodies which were as nearly legal as crisis circumstances would allow, and which could claim to be representative of the political classes of the nation.

In the early stages of France's invasion of the Netherlands in 1672, William showed no overt ambition at all. When the crisis struck, he had just been made captain-general of the republic's army, and he concentrated on the duties of that post rather than manoeuvring for promotion. This attention to duty included staunch loyalty to properly constituted powers of the state. He worked closely with the estates general, and even with de Witt, who remained, for the moment, in charge. Later, when French successes led to popular calls for William's elevation as stadholder, William still did not campaign for further powers, and resisted putting his name forward for any new office. Suggestions from his allies that he might now move to regain his family's old positions were met by stern reminders that he had his hands full commanding the army. Rejecting any premature or irregular acclamation, he refused to acknowledge his popular proclamation as stadholder in Dordrecht, and waited until the duly constituted authorities, the states of Holland and of Zeeland, offered him his family's traditional status.

William's pattern of behaviour in 1688–89 was more similar to 1672 than might at first appear. Of course, the Glorious Revolution opened with a spectacular breach of England's constitution. William invaded the realm in direct opposition to its sovereign's will, and James's propagandists were quick to point out the massive illegality and disloyalty of what he had done.[5] Yet, nestling within this outrageous impropriety, was a paradoxical show of deference for English institutions and an attempt to prove the prince was not an ambitious usurper. Take, as the most important example, the manifesto which William produced for his expedition. Published from The Hague in October 1688, and entitled *The Declaration of Reasons for Appearing in Arms in England*, this was widely distributed as the prince advanced, and tried to justify his actions to domestic and foreign audiences.[6] Its central appeal was for people to recognise William as the defender of the English constitution. It was the royal court, it claimed, which was breaking English law with its promotion of Catholicism and its unprecedented extensions of the prerogative: the only way to save the constitution now was to help the prince. Moreover, the manifesto proclaimed loyalty to England's sovereign institutions even as its author seemed to attack them. The document put the blame for recent miscarriages firmly on evil counsellors at court, not King James himself. Nowhere did it question the reigning monarch's title to the throne, or call for him to be deposed. The central demand of the document was – not any promotion of William – but the endlessly repeated requirement that a free parliament be allowed to meet, and exercise its established function as a physician of the nation's ills.

This lack of stated ambition on the part of the prince, and the deference to England's representative assembly, continued to echo the stance of 1672 even when James's power collapsed. After the old king had retreated from Salisbury Plain to London, William rejected the pleas of members of his camp that he himself should assume royal powers. When the prince had got as far as Hungerford in early December, many of his English supporters urged him to usurp James's authority. They argued he should countermand royal writs which James was still sending out from his London palaces, and so effectively take over royal duties. William, however, brushed this aside. He continued to advance very cautiously, and continued to address his uncle as king when James sent commissioners to negotiate with him.[7] Even after James had fled, William still refused self-promotion. Repeating his strategy of 1672, he insisted on waiting for an offer from proper authority.

Of course, in 1688–89, getting any such offer posed a problem. The only body with the constitutional power to alter the succession to the throne was a full parliament – and this could not be convened because one of its vital elements, the monarch, was missing. Technically, also, it could only be called through writs sent out under the king's great seal. James had deliberately sabotaged this process as he stole away by throwing the seal in the Thames (it was later recovered by some rather surprised fishermen). In the face of these difficulties, William might have used the impossibility of convening parliament as an excuse simply to declare himself monarch. Instead, however, he tried to keep as close to a legal accession as he could. In December he consulted with two groups of people – namely everyone resident in London who had served in the Commons under Charles II, and all peers in the capital – which came as close to a parliament as could be gathered in the chaotic circumstances. They gave William the authority to summon an even more parliament-like body, the convention, which met in January. This was constituted in every way like a normal legislature (it consisted of the House of Lords, and a 'house of commons' elected on the usual franchises from all constituencies), save that it lacked a monarch to confirm its deliberations, and had been called by letters from the prince rather than royal writ. Throughout this whole process, William advanced no open claim to the crown. When talking to the groups in London in December, when summoning the convention, and when writing to it as it first met, he stressed that the point of the meeting was to discuss the future without outside pressure, and that this convention must be the 'free parliament' for which he had called in his manifesto.[8] Even when discussions in the convention deadlocked between various possible ways of filling the throne, William kept up his front of waiting for an uncoerced offer. He did threaten to withdraw from England if not made king – but he did this privately, using his contacts to brief members about his attitude rather than publicly announcing his ambition. In fact, even in these private communications, he never actually demanded the crown. He merely warned that he would leave if he did not get it, and left the convention to decide if it was prepared to take that risk. He therefore followed what he had done in 1672 remarkably closely. Although circumstances in the real world of armies and street politics meant there was little alternative to advancing the prince, he had not simply seized power.

The advantages of this course of action also parallelled 1672. First, respect for due authority avoided adverse reaction to William's elevation, or at least delayed reaction so long that it became unimportant. Some people, such as Sir Edward Seymour, had rallied to the prince when they thought he would abide by the English constitution, but fell away horrified when they realised he was prepared to replace a reigning king. However, while this opposition was embarrassing, it was ultimately insignificant because by the time Seymour and his ilk realised their mistake, William was occupying London. Second, the prince's determination to wait for an offer from a representative assembly allowed him to demonstrate a deference to parliament. As in the Dutch takeover, this helped to calm suspicions of the new executive, and so allowed William to stabilise the political system at a deeper level.

The Prince of Orange's respect for parliament ran through his whole expedition to England. As we have seen, the great thrust of his manifesto was that only a free parliament could sort out the mess left by James's policies. In fact, the *Declaration of Reasons* was a quite remarkable milestone in relations between crown and legislature. Even though it came from a man who would soon be king, it was one of the most comprehensive statements of *country* ideology which the seventeenth century ever produced. All the classic elements of anti-court paranoia were there. The declaration asserted that there was a cabal of evil men operating at court. It claimed they were encouraging the crown to extend its prerogatives illegally, and only the legislature could prevent disaster. In the crisis, parliament must be given extraordinary powers to investigate the king, and Englishmen must support their assembly, even to the point of taking up arms. Thus, as the prince avoided making claims for himself, he flattered parliament, and set himself up as a country champion. Nor did this stop with the manifesto. William's determination to follow the example of 1672 meant he encouraged extraordinary claims for the representative assembly. When he sought the agreement of parliamentarians before summoning the convention, and when he charged that very parliament-like body with deliberating the constitutional settlement, he was acknowledging that the Lords and Commons ultimately embodied the nation's will. When he took the crown from the convention as a gift, he was acknowledging that the two houses had authority over all other institutions – including the monarchy. When accepting the idea that the throne was vacant, and that the convention had the right to fill it, he was recognising that the Lords and Commons could operate without the third element of parliament. This last implication was truly extraordinary. William's manifesto had made the already controversial point that the king could not act legally without the rest of the legislature. Over the winter he made the far more radical claim that a king-less parliament could make valid and binding decisions, even though a parliament-less king could not. Remarkably, therefore, William's adherence to his Dutch tactics helped to turn England into a sort of Netherlands. He showed so much deference to parliament that he recast the English system in a Dutch mould. The assembly at Westminster, he implied, was the sort of sovereign body which the provincial states had always been.

In the longer run, William's determination to co-operate with parliament in the constitutional settlement played an important part in providing stability. It helped to defuse country suspicion of the court. Indeed, reading the prince's manifesto, and watching his actions over the winter, the English and Welsh were reassured they were getting a king who actually shared country sentiments. Here was a man, it seemed, who trusted parliaments; who thought they embodied the nation's true interest and will; and believed that – at least in crisis situations – they held ultimate authority. The later consequences were not always comfortable for William. He soon began to fear he had preached up the power of parliament too much, and played down the 'country' elements of his propaganda. He never explicitly mentioned his original manifesto after the end of 1688. Yet, as we shall see, the impression of a trustworthy king stuck in country minds.

The second similarity between 1672 and 1688 lay in the threat posed by Louis XIV and in William's determination to counter this. In the earlier year, the French king had been at the gates of Holland with his hostile army. In the later year, Louis may not have been quite so physically close to the prince, but he was almost as menacing. He had resolved to reverse James II's fall from power, to patrol the Channel with his navy, and to send troops to Ireland. In both years, of course, William's priority was to push the French back and save the states over which he was coming to rule. In 1672 he dedicated his time to organising Dutch defences. Over the winter of 1688–89 he made preliminary military arrangements to protect England from France, and urged the English to settle the political situation quickly so they could turn their attention to French manoeuvres.[9] In both cases this dedication to defeating France brought considerable support. The Dutch viewed William as a patriotic hero, reprising his ancestors' role as national saviours. The English turned to the invading prince in desperation, since he seemed the only one who could organise defence against French invasion. Many members of the English constitutional convention swallowed doubts about dismissing a reigning monarch because they saw no other escape from the national emergency.

Clearly, William's commitment to defeating Louis helped to stabilise the political situation in England early in 1689. It ensured there was only a limited backlash against the elevation of a man who could easily be seen as an invading usurper. However, the prince's sustained opposition to France produced another similarity between 1672 and the Glorious Revolution, which tackled English difficulties at a deeper level. The similarity was that both 1672 and 1688 offered William a choice between personal power in the state, and prioritising the defeat of France. In both cases he chose his war, and reassured his people about his ambitions as he did so.

In 1672 William could either have led resistance to Louis XIV, or accepted Charles II's offer of sovereignty over a reduced rump of the Provinces. When he refused his uncle's bribe, and instead satisfied himself with the non-regal position of stadholder, William indicated he was more dedicated to defeating France than securing an increase in his immediate status and constitutional power. He calculated that his interests would be better served by uniting with his people in national defence, than by provoking their opposition by bolstering his legal power over them. In 1688–89, William found himself in a remarkably similar situation, and made the same choice. This time the need for a decision arose as the convention met. Almost as soon as this body began its deliberations, one of its members, Lord Falkland, suggested that before they discuss who should be king, the assembled company should 'consider what powers we ought to give the Crown'.[10] He argued that the current crisis provided an opportunity to protect England from 'arbitrary government' since the royal prerogative could be defined and limited before it was offered to any particular person. This suggestion struck such a chord with traditional 'country' suspicions of the crown that it found instant support across the political spectrum. Members lamented the excesses of crown action over the past two reigns; and resolved to 'proceed to secure our Religion, Laws, and Liberties' *before* moving to fill the throne.[11] Once the convention had decided to act in this way, William was faced with his choice. On one hand, he was vehemently opposed to any major reductions in the crown's prerogatives. As a Stuart, he was concerned for the traditional rights of his house, and now that he had a chance of capturing the crown he would want it to bestow as much power as possible. He therefore watched closely as a committee of the convention drew up a list of limitations on the prerogative, and worked hard behind the scenes to ensure they were not too radical.[12] On the other hand, William knew that too much effort to defend royal influence might actually damage him. He faced the danger that he might get locked into a constitutional dispute with the convention over the prerogative, and that this might delay his attempts to bring England into the war against France. The prince, therefore, reached the dilemma he had faced years before. Should he prioritise the struggle with Louis, even at some cost to his personal status and power?

As in 1672, William's obsession with Louis won through. He decided to accept a lesser prize to avoid alienating new subjects, and to organise them against the French. Thus, although William's private pressure helped defeat some far-reaching proposals to control crown power, he acquiesced when some pretty severe limitations on the crown were suggested. He convinced the convention to drop demands that kings call parliaments every year, and that he lose the right to sack judges, but the 'declaration of rights' (the popular name given to the final proposals) nonetheless abolished a series of traditional monarchical powers. These included the ability to suspend parliamentary statutes, to raise taxes and standing armies without legislative approval, to rule for long periods without meeting the Lords and Commons, to punish people without due process of law, to alter the franchise for parliamentary elections, and to imprison people for petitioning the king about their grievances. Despite these sweeping controls on the crown, William raised no protest when they were read out to him before the formal offer of the throne on 13 February 1689.[13] In this way he avoided a long drawn out constitutional tussle, and was able to persuade the convention to start talking about military mobilisation soon after the throne had been filled. At the same time, William continued to tackle the underlying problems with the English system of government. Throughout the seventeenth century, relations between crown and legislature had repeatedly foundered on exactly the issues handled by the declaration of rights. Caught up in their mutually reinforcing conspiracy theories, Englishmen had accused each other of exceeding their just powers over taxes, armies, statutes and control over parliamentary sittings. Now, William had defused tensions. Parliament believed it had secured the guarantees for which country rhetoric had long called, while the court indicated it was too concerned with the foreign threat to try to deny them.

The final similarity between 1672 and 1688 was the use made of Protestant propaganda. In the United Provinces this had helped sweep the prince to power. In England too, William advertised his godly credentials. Although some recent scholarship has called this into question and suggested the prince's publicity drive in 1688 was actually based on a defence of English law rather than religion, the overall flavour of Orange propaganda during the expedition was undeniably Protestant.[14] It is true that William's manifesto itself was not strongly anti-popish. In producing it, the prince's party had recognised they would need Catholic allies in Europe against Louis XIV, and they were careful not to offend these powers in a document which they sent to continental courts as an international justification of the invasion. The *Declaration of Reasons*, therefore, took its main stand on abuse of royal prerogative, and limited its anti-popery to observations that Catholics had benefited from the court's absolutist tendencies. However, in parts of the Williamite message aimed primarily at the English, the confessional elements were far more explicit. For example, the expedition sailed and marched under banners proclaiming 'god and the Protestant religion'.[15] As William crossed the Channel he released letters to the English navy stressing that he was coming to save their faith.[16] Prayers used among the prince's forces, and in the parts of the West Country that he came to control, emphasised defence of the reformation.[17] Most impressively, much of the propaganda machine which had polished the prince's halo in The Hague was shipped over to England in the expedition's baggage and continued its work. A shower of pamphlets, sermons and pictorial prints presented the stadholder as a providential figure – informing the English that William, like a biblical champion, was riding forth for God's true faith. Thus news reports of the expedition's progress had the prince riding on a white horse like the righteous knight of the Apocalypse, and put the words of King David into his mouth.[18] Sermons also used Davidic imagery, and hastily composed squibs and ballads gloated over the defeat of popery.[19] The prince himself played the religious hero. He told the people of Salisbury that he had come 'to secure the Protestant religion' as he marched into their city, and in January he wrote to the constitutional convention, asking that they behave as 'Protestants' as well as 'Englishmen' in their deliberations.[20]

In the Provinces, such Protestant propaganda had created the popular hysteria which had led to demands that William take power. In England, this same godly image seems to have played a similar role. From reports of William's early reception in the West Country, it appears that crowd enthusiasm was based largely on his perceived defence of the Protestant faith.[21] In December, William was invited to take charge in London because rumours of an approaching Irish Catholic army had plunged the capital into a night of panicked rioting. Relief that the Dutchman had saved the reformation filled early addresses of gratitude from the English political nation to the prince.[22] Most importantly, William's Protestant image helped the convention accept his claim to the throne. Contributors to debates in this body were keenly aware that they faced a crisis of faith as well as of the constitution, and that the prince offered the only available defence for God's true religion. In the opening sessions, one member declared that the English had been 'striving against Anti-Christ' before William arrived.[23] Subsequent debates were full of the classic anti-Roman rhetoric of 'Popery', 'Idolatry' and 'Jesuit' plotters. As the convention moved towards offering the crown to William, it frequently considered the dangers the international 'Protestant Interest' faced in this time of counter-reformation, and worried about the fate of Irish Protestants in the current Catholic revolt.[24] William's providential posture thus brought him the same support in 1688 which it had in 1672. It did more besides, however. By presenting 1688 as a religious as well as political crisis, the prince's propaganda seems to have persuaded the English to tackle one of their most deep-seated causes of tension. It finally concentrated minds on the dangers of Catholic rule in a country where anti-popery was rife, and where the government system depended on trust between executive and legislature.

Of course, great numbers of English people had been worried about 'the prospect of a popish successor' even before William launched his publicity campaign.[25] In the exclusion crisis, many had pushed to ban the Catholic James from the throne, and there were complaints about his religion throughout his reign. Yet although there was widespread alarm about popish rule before the prince of Orange arrived, the fundamental cause of instability had remained because much of the nation had not been convinced that Catholics should be barred from the throne. Many people had tried to retain their monarchical ideals even in the face of Catholic succession. They had, therefore, comforted themselves that it was covert popish plotters at court who were dangerous rather than the open spiritual preferences of a king. As a result the crisis of 1679–83 had ended in defeat for the exclusionists. James had ascended in 1685 with considerable support, and as late as the autumn of 1688 a group around the earl of Rochester had hoped to persuade James to rid himself of popish courtiers and reign in harmony with the nation.[26] In these circumstances, popish royalty remained a central cause of instability. The English had become bitterly divided over the succession, and Catholics were left at court to stoke the deepest fears of anti-Catholic subjects.

It seems to have taken William's Protestant polemic to convince the English finally to remove the danger of popish rule. Naturally the last errors of James, especially his abandoning the country, would have brought some to the conclusion that Catholics should never again be allowed power. Yet, William's propaganda must also have played a role. After all, the shift in opinion coincided exactly with the prince's publicity campaign, and was remarkably rapid and complete. Over a few weeks in the winter of 1688–89, the entire political spectrum united round the principle that papists must be excluded from executive authority in England. The convention's first substantive act was to pass a unanimous resolution that 'it hath been found by long experience that it is inconsistent with the safety and welfare of this Protestant Kingdom to be governed by a Popish Prince'.[27] This brought old exclusionists together with men who had been trying to work with James only weeks before; and it united those who supported William's claims on the throne with those who hoped to find other ways out of the political crisis. For instance, Bishop Turner of Ely wanted James to remain king. Nevertheless he argued that popery was 'a false religion, contrary to the Doctrine of Christianity', and that since Catholicism in a ruler was equivalent to madness, James's prerogatives must be exercised by a regent.[28] Previously, such consensus had eluded the English. Now, however, after William's Protestant campaign, all were persuaded. When the convention assembled there were still deep political divisions about how to proceed in the constitutional crisis, but the expedition's 1672–style polemic had helped everyone agree that papists must be kept away from actual power.

The broad principle agreed in the January resolution formed part of the final revolution settlement. A bar on Catholics inheriting the throne was incorporated into the bill of rights. The statute prevented papists from coming to the throne, and declared that if a monarch converted to Catholicism their subjects would be 'absolved of their allegiance' and the crown would pass on as if the convert were 'naturally dead'.[29] As a part of the settlement, the resolution against Catholic rule has been over-shadowed. Historians have tended to concentrate on the declaration of rights, because its list of parliamentary liberties looked more like a com-prehensive constitutional statement. Yet arguably, the resolution was both more radical, and of greater long-term significance, than the declaration. To start, while the declaration claimed only to express *existing* ideals, the 'inconsistency' declared *for the first time* that there were conditions on who could govern England. This was an idea which had been decisively rejected as recently as 1685, and which fundamentally redefined the monarchy. No longer a mystical status bestowed by divine power, king-ship now looked like an ordinary public trust with clear duties and quali-fications for exercising the office. The January resolution also did rather more to calm deep-seated tensions than the declaration of rights. Although the declaration settled disputes between crown and parliament, it did not really cut to the heart of instability in the way the 'inconsistency' did. Parliaments, after all, had been suspicious of courts because they thought they were popishly affected. The declaration of rights might have dealt with some of the excesses of crown power which were thought to stem from this popish infection, but only the 'inconsistency' dealt with the underlying problem itself. When incorporated into the bill of rights, it weakened suspicions of the court by guaranteeing that the king would never be a Catholic. When the bill decreed that monarchs could not even marry Catholics, fears were still further eased. In the convention, mem-bers lamented that it was not only Catholic plotters and Catholic mon-archs that had caused problems – the Catholic wives of the preceding four Stuart kings had been a chief point of entry for popery.[30] Now this worrying portal of evil was blocked, and Protestant Englishmen could breathe still more easily.

William's repeat of his 1672 strategies thus did more than secure his personal advancement. Because his tactics demonstrated his commitment to Protestantism, his willingness to co-operate with parliament and his prioritisation of the war with France over royal power, the prince's Dutch-style takeover moulded a stabilising settlement. It eased fears that there was a popish, anti-parliamentary conspiracy operating at court, or that the king would ride roughshod over English liberties. This pattern was to be repeated after the revolution. Throughout the rest of his reign, William deployed lessons from his foreign experience to repair the English political system.

William's solution: the policies of the 1690s

The importance of one element of William's European obsession has long been recognised. For some time, historians have argued that the new king's determination to defeat Louis XIV had a profound impact on relations between court and parliament. Desperate for war finance, William is reputed to have sold the royal prerogative by the pound. The king, it is argued, sacrificed royal power in order to keep money flowing for his army and navy, and effectively surrendered control of the English state to his legislature. This change has been seen as so important that it represented the real English revolution. The civil war and the Glorious Revolution may have looked like spectacular victories for the men gathered at Westminster, but only the changes of the 1690s fully established a parliamentary system.[31]

The evidence for this point of view is impressive and convincing. In the war years of his reign – from 1689 to 1697 – the king's commitment to containing France led him to withdraw in the face of parliamentary attacks on his position. Unlike his predecessors, who were prepared to resist the legislature even if this meant constitutional crisis and stalemate, William calculated that only grants of taxation from parliament could provide enough money to run his war effort. He therefore had to keep his legislature sitting, and he had to keep it sweet, at all times. Of course this grated. In the realm of abstract political ideals, the king believed in royal power, and frequently expressed anger at what he saw as his humiliation by the House of Commons. In the real world of politics, however, William swallowed his pride. He accommodated his legislators' demands, and steadily reduced their dread of the executive as he did so.

The process began even as William came to the throne. By the time the Prince of Orange was offered the crown, he had already surrendered some royal glory to concentrate minds on the threat of France. As we have seen, he had accepted the convention's declaration of rights to avoid a damaging dispute over the constitution which might delay England's entry into the continental alliance. While doing this, however, William had been determined to prevent any further erosion of his power. He used his occupation of London to persuade the convention to drop more radical clauses in the first draft of their statement of English liberties; and, while he gave every impression of agreeing with the broad principles of the declaration, he did not explicitly accept it as a binding condition of his taking the throne. He listened politely as the list of limitations on the crown was read out to him in the Guildhall on 13 February, but he was careful not to make any commitment to obey the terms beyond a vague promise to 'preserve your religion, laws and liberties'.[32] Yet even though William did not want any further diminution of his powers, his need for money soon forced his hand. The king's realisation that he could not afford a rupture with parliament soon meant that he abandoned the defences he had built as he came to the throne.

First to go was his equivocation over the declaration of rights. William's problems with this document began when the convention voted to declare itself a parliament. The vote, taken as soon as the succession was settled, regularised the assembly's constitutional position and gave it full power to pass laws. Although in many ways convenient, this change of status posed difficulties for William because the new parliament redrafted the declaration of rights as a statute, subsequently known as 'the bill of rights'. This would give the troublesome document a binding authority it had lacked as a simple resolution of the convention, and it would force William into a more open admission of his attitude to it. Once the bill had passed all its stages in the Lords and Commons, it would be presented to the king for royal consent. At this point, vague mouthings of harmony would not do. William would either have to bind himself to the bill by passing it into law – or would have to risk the anger of its authors by using the royal veto over the proposed legislation.

In the face of this threat, William talked like an embattled Stuart. In private conversations with his confidant, the marquis of Halifax, he detected endless conspiracies in parliament against English monarchy. The majority of the Commons, he told Halifax, were republicans. They used him like a dog. They were to reduce him to a doge of Venice, that seventeenth-century symbol of figurehead incapacity. His power, he felt, was becoming so illusory, that he felt like 'a king in a play'. But while William talked like a Stuart, he did not act like one. As he admitted to the marquis, his inclination to reject clauses of the bill of rights was overruled by 'the conditions of his affairs'.[33] The new king knew he was stuck with parliament. Needing finance to mobilise against France, he could neither dissolve his legislature, nor risk any major row with it. He therefore made no open moves against the bill of rights, and it passed into law.

This pattern was repeated through the rest of the war years. Having abandoned his evasion over the parliament's declaration, the king was forced further on the defensive, as principles he had defeated in 1689 came back to haunt him. Throughout the 1690s, legislators remained in a strongly 'country' frame of mind. Shaken by the excesses of royal power under James, and sensing that William's regime offered an opportunity for permanently curtailing the court, parliamentarians dusted off some of the suggestions which had circulated in the early days of the convention to reduce royal influence. For instance, there had been talk during the revolution of removing the king's right to prolong a parliament indefinitely. The idea had been to put an upper time limit on the sitting of a legislature so that general elections would occur frequently, and the court could not retain members whom it had corrupted. This suggestion had been dropped from the declaration of rights under William's pressure in 1689, but in the early 1690s the thinking behind it re-appeared. First, a series of bills were introduced to establish triennial parliaments. These would have guaranteed an election every three years to ensure legislators were 'fresh' (the MP Robert Harley's term), and accountable to their constituents.[34] Second, parliamentarians promoted a series of 'place' bills. These would have excluded anyone who took a job in the king's administration from the Commons, and so would have discouraged the court from bribing MPs with lucrative offices. Similarly 1689 campaigns to reduce the monarch's judicial influence were revived. Clauses restricting royal control over law courts had been abandoned as the declaration of rights had reached its final form, but in the 1690s the principle was taken up again. Specifically, MPs worked to regulate treason trials. Worried that government prosecutors had an unfair advantage when people were tried for plotting against the state, parliamentarians tried to redress the balance, insisting that the accused had proper counsel and that the evidence against them was sound.

As with the declaration of rights, William's initial reaction to these country campaigns was hostile He saw triennial bills, place bills and treason bills as unacceptable attacks on his influence, and worked hard to block them. His first tactic was to mobilise his supporters in the Lords and Commons to speak against the bills, or to introduce wrecking amendments. This was often successful. Treason trial bills fell this way annually in the early 1690s, and a place bill was lost in the Lords in the 1692–93 session. When persuasion failed, however, William was prepared to use his veto. Twice he rejected measures which had passed both houses when they were sent for his approval. Early in 1693 he felled a triennial bill, and did the same with a place bill early the next year. Unfortunately for William, surrender followed defiance just as certainly as it had with the bill of rights. The king's tussles with parliament took place during the most unsuccessful stages of the war with Louis. William consequently knew he would need continuing support from his legislators to avoid military disaster, and could not push them too hard. The turning point came with his 1694 veto of the place bill. When news came back to the Commons of the king's rejection of their measure, there was an explosion of anger reminiscent of the darkest days of the 1620s. Members railed that the king had no right to veto bills from a parliament which had voted him so much money. Evil courtiers must have tricked him into his policy to hide their corruptions. The debate ended with an address to the king, informing him that he had made a mistake, and should punish those who had advised him to it. For William, the most frightening thing about this debate were suggestions that the Commons block supplies of money if they did not get satisfaction.[35] Alarmed that the war effort was threatened, the king retreated. His reply to the address was conciliatory, and from this moment of averted crisis, his opposition to parliament was muted.[36] When a triennial bill came up for royal approval in the next session, William let it pass. Early in 1696 when the latest version of treason trials legislation arrived on his desk, the king approved it: government prosecutors now needed two believable witnesses to bring any case.

So far, the role of William's European focus in re-settling English politics has been pretty obvious. As historians have long pointed out, this king differed from his predecessors because of his interest in defeating Louis XIV. Whereas earlier Stuarts would have resisted parliamentary demands to the point of constitutional crisis, William saved the war instead. He surrendered prerogatives and so calmed tensions. It was difficult for even the most country-minded Englishman to believe in an absolutist conspiracy at a court which threw in the towel every time it faced a challenging bout. Yet this was not the only way in which the new king's foreignness helped stability in the 1690s. His Dutch-inspired commitment to working with parliaments also played a role. The picture of an authoritarian king forced to retreat because upholding his domestic power endangered his continental objectives is too simple. William eased relations between crown and legislature because his experience in the Netherlands had shown that rulers could successfully share power with representative assemblies. Although he sometimes stood on his royal dignity, the king imported a vision of a parliamentary system in which legislators played a constructive – and extensive – role in government.

The clearest evidence of William's new vision was his willingness to hold parliaments. Being 'always glad to meet' the two houses at Westminster, he called them to deliberate far more frequently and regularly than any of his Stuart predecessors.[37] Whereas all recent monarchs had had periods in their reign when they had not staged parliaments, and all had cut short sessions with business unresolved, William's approach was very different. No year of his reign passed without a substantive legislative assembly. After 1689, these meetings fell into an ordered pattern. They started in the autumn, sometime between the first week in October and the first week of December, and then sat well into spring. Not content with short sessions in which a basic statement of national concerns was swiftly followed by supply or angry confrontation, William refused to dissolve or prorogue until legislators had worked through lengthy programmes of business. Thus his first parliament had only two months' break in the whole period from January 1689 to January the next year. After that, the king insisted on a series of what were, by seventeenth-century standards, monster winter sessions. In the whole 1690s, the shortest of these lasted three months, while the session of 1697–98 dragged on for an exhausting seven months, right through to the heat of July. In fact, so peculiar was William's approach that it produced a reversal in rhetoric between king and legislators. In the earlier seventeenth century, it had been parliamentarians who had demanded to meet in order to control the court. In the 1690s, by contrast, it was the *king* who demanded sessions, and found himself apologising for calling MPs up from their constituencies so frequently and keeping them so long. On 19 October 1689 he admitted to the houses that 'it might have been more agreeable to you in your private concerns, not to have met so soon', but he regretted that the 'interest of the public lays an indispensable obligation upon me to call you together at this time'.[38] In a striking turnaround, it was a country-minded member, not the monarch, who became bothered by the endless sittings. Sir Christopher Musgrave, a tireless campaigner for place, triennial and treason bills told the Commons he looked forward to a time when 'there will not be such needs of annual sessions'.[39] Musgrave's hopes were vain. The 1690s were to mark a revolution in parliamentary history. Since William's accession, the legislature has met every year, and has held a substantive session. William had brought a transformation in the English political system, turning parliament into a standing institution.

Of course, much of the king's willingness to meet parliament stemmed from his need for money. Yet even so, it would be wrong to see William meeting the Lords and Commons solely because it was the only way to pay for the war. There were features of the king's approach to his parliaments which suggest he saw them as far more than a necessary financial evil. He appears to have wanted to meet them so often and for so long, because he thought they could help him govern. He seems to have thought it was important to keep in constant contact with his subjects' representatives, and that parliament could perform functions which his direct servants and office holders could not.

For a start, William treasured the legislature as a fierce financial watch-dog. Earlier Stuart kings had faced calls for Commons control over how the court spent money. Fears of corruption and extravagance in the royal household had sparked demands that parliament scrutinise and supervise public expenditure to ensure that all sums were used for the public good. Being Stuart kings, William's predecessors had resisted these calls. They had taken the traditional line that money voted for the king became his private revenue, and insisted that parliamentary comments on the king's finances were unwarranted intrusions into the mysteries of state. By contrast, William saw a use for Commons mistrust. He knew that parliamentarians suspected that money was wasted and embezzled at court. At the same time, he was determined that money his legislators voted for the struggle with France should actually be used for that purpose, and that it should not be dissipated in administrative inefficiency or corruption. He therefore reasoned that the Commons would make an excellent agent of royal policy. MPs' zeal in rooting out financial mismanagement matched his own commitment to full military mobilisation. Parliamentarians would almost certainly expose corruption more efficiently than investigations by the king's servants, since they were convinced they would find wrongdoing and had no reason to try to hide what was going on. All William had to do to harness this force for efficiency and honesty was to allow legislators in to examine his books. As we shall see in more detail in a later chapter, the king did just that. In a dramatic reversal of established royal attitudes, William permitted parliament close scrutiny of his financial affairs. He offered his accounts to the Commons to audit, and raised no objection when that House asked to see estimates for future expenditure so that they could go through them item by item.

William, therefore, saw a central role for parliament in ensuring financial probity. He also seems to have had wider views on the usefulness of his assembly. He appears to have had a vision of it as a source of information and counsel which could provide an alternative to his own circle. He apparently believed that a parliament which represented the nation and knew its condition should have a central role in formulating national policy. Peers and MPs were to be more than occasional vettors of approaches formulated by the king's servants. Under William, they were to have a role in shaping executive action, as well as in legislative scrutiny.

The clearest sign of this was that William asked the two houses for advice as well as money. In speeches – which unusually for a Stuart monarch he wrote himself – he constantly stressed he was a listening king, who would consider seriously any suggestions which the nation's representatives made. Take for example, his very first address to parliament, on 18 February 1689. Like many subsequent performances, it out-lined the situation facing the nation, but then made it clear that it was up to legislators to decide what exactly to do. Having talked of the threats to England's allies on the continent, and the dangers posed by the rebellion in Ireland, he said 'I must leave it to you ... to judge what forms may be most proper to bring those things to pass for the good of the nation, which I am confident are in all your minds'. The suggestion was that peers and MPs knew best how to mobilise for war, and that the monarch 'for [his] part' would 'be always ready to promote' their ends.[40] This style of dealing with parliament lasted through the early 1690s. In 1692 it went one stage further. Over the summer of that year, the war had gone badly and, when parliament met in November, the king invited it into the heart of policy formation by asking them what he should do next. In an extraordinary speech, which abandoned the old doctrine that military strategy was a matter for the royal court alone, the king asked not only for 'assistance' from his legislators in the form of tax, but also 'advice'. He told them he would receive suggestions – especially ones which would allow him to carry on the war without sending so much English money abroad – 'with all the satisfaction imaginable'.[41]

In seeking the opinion of parliaments like this, William was taking a risk. Asking the legislature for policy suggestions strained its capacities. The Commons had almost never been treated in this way, and had not set up mechanisms for formulating national strategy. As a result, it often lapsed into confusion or factional squabbles when asked for its views. On repeated occasions, William had to beg for dispatch from his parliamen-tarians, especially in deciding how they were going to raise the sums they agreed to provide in tax at the start of each session. He also had to inter-vene frequently to try to keep his legislators' minds on the issue in hand. The king's request for advice in 1692 was particularly disastrous. It led straight to a bitter wrangle between parties in parliament, and a spirited attack on the administration. Although initial reaction to the king's speech was positive, with members flattered to be included in policy making, the ensuing deliberations collapsed into battles over whom to blame for the disappointing campaigns of the summer. In particular, there was heated discussion of a committee report which seemed to accuse the king's lead-ing minister, Nottingham, of incompetence. William's requests for advice had thus resulted in partisan bickering, and an attack on his favourite ser-vant. No really useful suggestions about military strategy were made.[42] Yet despite such setbacks, the king persisted. Throughout the 1690s he continued to ask parliament to formulate policy on issues as diverse as raising revenue, helping French Protestants, suppressing vice and

encouraging the merchant navy.[43] William went on canvassing parliamentarians' views, even though the legislature lacked the true maturity
of deliberation and judgement to take on this counselling role. Perhaps
reflecting on the successes of the Netherlands' political system, the king
seems to have hoped that his representative assembly could prove a rich
source of policy ideas.

Obviously, William's Dutch-inspired vision of collaboration between
court and parliament helped to ease political tensions. It confounded any
fears of a royal conspiracy to rule without the legislature, and so began to
dispel the country paranoia which had destabilised England and Wales
for so long. When coupled with William's flexibility whenever parliament
demanded additional controls on his power, the new vision convinced
many that they were facing a very different kind of king. Even at
moments of tension, 'country'-minded members stressed that they were
on William's side. They were pushing ahead with their campaigns, they
explained, because the present reign offered a unique moment when initiatives to secure parliament's rights would not meet ultimate opposition
from the crown. Thus MPs would advance country measures citing
William's 1688 *Declaration* as evidence that the monarch backed their
cause.[44] They would insist that the king's rule offered a golden opportunity, a 'good reign' when protection could be secured against any future
'bad prince'.[45] As Robert Harley put it, advancing a treason trials bill: 'I
think it is the proper time to get good laws in a good reign, and therefore
I am for this bill now'.[46] William's co-operation with his legislature thus
appears to have dissolved the old Commons suspicion of the court. His
continental priorities and style re-established conditions for a successful
monarchical republicanism.

Much the same can be said of William's other main import from
Holland – his presentation of himself as a Protestant champion. After
1689 the king continued to portray himself as the embodiment and
defender of the reformed faith, and this went on easing the problems of
the English polity. As with William's propaganda campaign during the
Glorious Revolution, there have been attempts to deny that the monarch
centred his image on religion. These, however, primarily concern the way
in which the king explained his foreign policy to the English, and will be
dealt with in a later chapter. In the domestic sphere there can be no doubt
that William's Protestantism was central to his propaganda. Again and
again, the English were reminded that the Prince of Orange had saved
them from the horrors of popery at the revolution.

For example, the meaning of the 5 November thanksgiving was
changed in 1689. Every autumn since early Stuart times, the nation had

met together in its churches to thank God for his mercy in thwarting the Gunpowder Plot against James I. People had taken the day off work, and had attended religious services which reminded all of the perversions of Catholicism, and enthused all with the importance of upholding the reformed faith. After the revolution, these events were retained, but their purpose was altered. Exploiting the coincidence of the date, the days would henceforth thank God – not only for the deliverance of 5 November 1605 – but also for that of 5 November 1688, the moment when William had landed at Torbay. The new king's arrival was thus firmly attached to the providential protection of Protestantism which was seen to mark England's history; and an annual, and legally enforced, celebration was held to drive the message home. In this reorientation, the public liturgy of the day was rewritten to include a reference to the new king's work against popery, while a host of sermons praised the ruler for his defence of the reformed religion.[47]

Protestant propaganda soaked the rest of the year as well. Even outside the 5 November festivities, pulpit oratory praised William for his preservation of God's true faith in England. The English clergy used myriad occasions to preach up the virtuous religion of their new king, and to express near-millennial hopes that his reign might herald the final defeat of the popish anti-Christ. Meanwhile, Williamite poets, pamphleteers and balladeers celebrated the wholesomeness of the new king's faith throughout the 1690s.[48] Even the new king's artistic patronage was used to stress his religious credentials. The iconography of the new wings William built for himself at Hampton Court was saturated with images of Hercules. The figure appeared on Cibber's statue for the east front pediment, on Laguerre's painted roundels dominating the Fountain Court, on Verrio's murals for the King's Great Staircase, and on tapestries hung throughout the king's apartments. This Greek hero was often read as a symbol of Protestant fortitude. Hercules had chosen in his youth to use his strength for virtue rather than vice, and he had been a favoured symbol of Henri IV of France, the king who was not only William's ancestor, but had finally secured protection for the Protestants of France.[49]

Perhaps most importantly, William's court was presented as a powerhouse of Protestant piety. As we have seen, earlier Stuart courts had been seen as entry points for popery. The preceding four kings had all had popish wives; they had artistic and religious tastes which seemed to favour Catholicism; and misjudged royal policy seemed best explained by the machinations of popish conspirators near the monarch. By contrast, William's royal household was to be a beacon of the reformed faith. Queen Mary, at the very centre of the court, was celebrated as an appropriate

Protestant consort for the king. Under her influence, royal palaces were to promote right religion and to purge themselves of the corruption and extravagance which earlier popish tendencies had introduced. For example, Mary's household was portrayed as a powerhouse of Protestant preaching. In 1689, the new monarchs appointed as chaplains a dynamic group of London clergy who had led the clerical campaign against James II's Catholicising policies. The number of sermons these people were expected to give at court was increased by introducing a regular Wednesday afternoon service, and then the religious advice they gave the king and queen was advertised by publishing a very large number of their performances. For periods in the early 1690s, a court sermon was printed on average once a fortnight, advertising the fact that the monarchs regularly listened to Protestant oratory. At the same time, the reformed piety of the new rulers was broadcast. Mary reorganised court worship so that it was less ritualised, more regular and more visible, and as a result the monarchs were presented as enthusiastic adherents of a Protestant religious life. William, whose preference for privacy might have driven him away from such public performance of his faith, was effectively bullied into participating by one of his chief advisers on public relations, Gilbert Burnet.[50] Similarly, the court was placed at the centre of a drive for moral reform. This, it was made clear, was only possible now good Protestants had replaced debauched Catholics at the heart of the royal household. Accordingly a court-centred campaign for the reformation of manners became a central theme of the Williamite message. The monarchs issued a series of proclamations against vice which ordered magistrates to crack down – but crucially showed their household taking a lead by promising to debar all lewd and intemperate people from royal service. Similarly the queen sponsored local drives for moral reform in Middlesex and Tower Hamlets; her personal virtue and moderation were praised (especially in the outpouring of memorial literature which greeted her death in 1694); and the court sermons stressed the importance of holy conversation in a full spiritual life.[51]

In a later chapter, we shall see that such insistence on the court's Protestantism helped convince the English that they must support William's war against Catholic France, and so overcame their reluctance to build a modern state. At the moment, though, we should concentrate on its effects in solving constitutional difficulties. In this area, the obvious role of Protestant propaganda was to make suspicion of popish conspiracy at court untenable. It was hard to believe that papists were influencing William's policy, when he had come to rescue the country from Catholicism, and had stayed to defend it against the popish forces of

France and the Jacobites. It was ridiculous to worry about a nest of Catholic plotters at the heart of the royal household when the court was composed of staunch reformed Christians, and paraded both its piety and it moral virtue. It was, in fact, impossible to believe that the regime was in any way influenced by Rome, unless one thought that the whole campaign of Protestant polemic was some incredibly devious deception. William's propaganda thus cut to the heart of country fears. Of course, there were still things about William's court to worry the country-minded. As we have seen, he challenged parliament on occasion, and corruptions were sometimes revealed in the royal administration. Yet even though the old symptoms of popish debauch were still there, nobody could think the underlying disease was the same. As a result, when people complained about William's government, they did so without hysterical accusations of popery. The 1690s passed with a remarkable absence of religious panic: unhappiness with government action was expressed as simple political grievances, not as warnings of a terrifying evil at the heart of national life.

An example will make the new atmosphere clear. In late 1670s, Charles II had been accused of maintaining a standing army without parliamentary consent. The charges fed into the maelstrom of suspicion that erupted at the end of the decade. The army the king had raised was presented as proof of a Catholic conspiracy at the core of the administration, and the fears engendered by this led to calls for the future James II, as the arch-conspirator, to be barred from the throne. Twenty years later, William was in turn accused of maintaining a standing army without parliamentary consent. When the Commons met in the autumn of 1698 the house discovered, to its fury, that the king had not disbanded as many soldiers as they had resolved the previous winter. Yet, although the parliamentarians were angry, the course of events differed markedly from the 1670s. There was no anti-popish witch-hunt. Indeed, the pamphlets which attacked William's army constructed a new explanation for court ambitions which, for virtually the first time in the seventeenth century, did not rely on Catholic corruption. Pamphleteers such as John Trenchard and Walter Moyle accepted that the king and his servants were good Protestants: their warnings against government power were premised on long-term shifts in patterns of property holding which had weakened the subject's ability to resist the growth of the state.[52] The precise reasoning of such works was probably too abstract for most public opinion, but the lack of anti-popery did catch a general mood. In the army disputes of the 1690s, MPs did not level wild charges of Catholicism in the court. Nobody suggested the problem could be solved by cashiering Romish conspirators. As a result, rapid negotiation and compromise by the king could calm the situation. When the king agreed to disband the soldiers, most people thought the matter settled. William had overstepped the mark – but, once he realised his mistake, no one thought there was a Satanic cabal still to be tackled. Calmer politics returned after a moment of excitement.*

In the end, this rapid return to sanity was the pattern of the 1690s. At the start of this chapter, we explored how rival conspiracy theories had destroyed the delicate balance of monarchical republicanism in the Stuart age. Kings had been convinced that parliamentarians were plotting against them, parliamentarians had thought they were betrayed by highly placed plotters at court. Looking at William's record, we can see how his European focus and his Dutch experience dispelled these myths. The new king may sometimes have been as suspicious of his legislature as his predecessors, but his determination to defeat France meant he could not act on these suspicions because co-operation with parliament was too important for the war effort. Anyway, William's career in the Netherlands had told him that parliamentary mistrust of executives was neither insurmountable, nor entirely disadvantageous. Ultimately, he was prepared to work with parliament – or at least give way to it – so he never allowed royal irritation to end in constitutional breakdown. This behaviour, in turn, helped to soothe country nightmares. If William's continentally inspired co-operation with his legislature made it difficult to believe in a conspiracy at court, his continuation of the Protestant propaganda he had begun in Holland made it virtually impossible. In fact, the king's imported political strategies produced the extraordinary phenomenon of a 'country court'. Here was an executive which presented itself as everything critics of the executive had ever demanded. William's administration was Protestant, it was virtuous, it loved parliaments, it accepted checks on its actions, it was frugal – and it was willing to accept external scrutiny to ensure that it remained all these things.

William, then, exorcised the mutually reinforcing spectres which had destroyed English stability. Once he had done so, a form of functioning monarchical republicanism re-emerged. In the 1690s, the political nation worked well with monarchs. Parliamentary sessions became a regular part of the king's administration, not a portent of conflict; the legislature financed, scrutinised and suggested policy for a ruler who nevertheless maintained control over the broad strategy of the government. At no time did relations between the two sides become so strained that they made unacceptable, crisis-inducing, forays into one another's territory. Other monarchs would follow, who did not necessarily share William's European focus. Yet the strategies he had brought to England showed them how to make the system work. Court and country could collaborate so long as rulers put other things ahead of defending royal rights, so long as they sought ways to harness parliamentary energies in their administrations, and reassured the nation that they would preserve its Protestant religion. William's foreign origins allowed him to break a log-jam in constitutional thinking.

Notes

Two books provide the best political narratives of the 1690s. Henry Horwitz, *Parliament, Policy and Politics in the Reign of William III* (MUP, 1977) is a very dense account – but excellent on detail and with good analytical chapters. Rose, *England in the 1690s* is a more readable introduction. The constitutional battles of the seventeenth century are well handled in Coward, *Stuart Age*; with useful material on the clash of 'monarchical' and 'republican' principles in J.P. Sommerville, *Royalists and Patriots: Politics and Ideology in England 1603–1640* (Longman, 1999); and Glenn Burgess, *Absolute Monarchy and the Stuart Constitution* (Yale UP, 1995). There is a good narrative of the constitutional discussions in the 1689 convention in David L. Jones, *A Parliamentary History of the Glorious Revolution* (HMSO, 1988); while one of the clearest short guides to the issues involved can be found in Speck, *Reluctant Revolutionaries*. 'Protestant' presentations and understandings of William's rule are covered in Claydon, *William III.*

1 Charles I, *A Proclamation about the Dissolving of the Parliament, 2 March, 1629* (1629).

2 Andrew Browning (ed.), *English Historical Documents, 1660–1714* (Clarendon Press, 1953), p. 185.

3 The phrase was invented in Patrick Collinson, 'The monarchical republic of Queen Elizabeth I', *Bulletin of the John Rylands Library* **69** (1986), 394–424.

4 See Peter Lake, 'Anti-popery: the structure of a prejudice', in Richard Cust and Anne Hughes (eds), *Conflict in Early Stuart England* (Longman, 1989).

5 For example, *The Dutch Design Anatomized* (1688); *By the King, A Declaration given 6 November 1688* (1688).

6 See Lois G. Schwoerer, 'Propaganda in the revolution of 1688-9', *American Historical Review* **82** (1977), 843–74.

7 *A Paper Delivered to His Highness the Prince of Orange by the Commissioners* (1688); see also Jones, *Revolution of 1688*, p. 304.

8 E.g. William's declaration to the House of Lords, 28 December 1688, printed in Beddard, *Kingdom without a King*, p. 168; letter to convention, *LJ*, **14**, 101–2

9 See his messages to the convention: *LJ*, **14**, 101; *CJ*, **10** 12.

10 Anchitel Grey, *Debates of the House of Commons* (1769), **9**, 29–30.

11 Ibid., x, p. 32.

12 Robert J. Frankle, 'The formulation of the declaration of rights', *Historical Journal* **17** (1974), 265–79

13 *The Declaration of the Lords Spiritual and Temporal, and Commons Assembled ... with His Majesties Most Gracious Answer* (1689).

14 For doubts see Pincus, 'English nationalist revolution'.

15 *The Expedition of the Prince of Orange for England* (1689), esp. p. 3.

16 *To the Commanders of Ships and All Seamen who are now Imployed in the English Fleet* (1688).

17 *A Praier for the Present Expedition* (The Hague, 1688).

18 *True and Exact Relation of the Prince of Orange His Entrance into Exeter* (Exeter, 1688); *Expedition of the Prince,* pp. 7–8.

19 For example, Gilbert Burnet, *A Sermon Preached in the Chappel of St James' ... 23rd of December, 1688* (1689); *The Muses Farewell to Popery and Slavery ... A Collection of Poems, Satyrs, Songs* (1689).

20 S.W. Singer (ed.), *The Correspondence of Henry Hyde* (1828), **2**, 215; *LJ,* **14**, 102.

21 See, for example [John Whittel], *An Exact Diary of the Late Expedition* (1689), pp. 41–51; *Great News from Salisbury* (1688).

22 E.g. *A Copy of the Association Signed at Exeter* (1688); *The Duke of Norfolk's Speech at Lynn ... 12 December, 1688* (1688); *The Humble Address of the Lieutenantry of London ... December 17, 1688* (1688).

23 Grey, *Debates*, **9**, 27.

24 Ibid., pp. 1–83.

25 Quote from title of 1681 print, reproduced in Tim Harris, *London Crowds in the Reign of Charles II* (CUP, 1987), p. 126.

26 Mark Goldie, 'The political thought of the Anglican revolution', in Robert Beddard, (ed.), *The Revolutions of 1688* (Clarendon Press, 1991).

27 *CJ*, **10**, 15; *LJ*, **14**, 110.

28 *The Debate at Large between the Lords and Commons* (2nd edn, 1710), p. 15.

29 Browning, *English Historical Documents,* p. 127.

30 Grey, *Debates,* **9***,* 26–7.

31 For this view, see Jennifer Carter, 'The revolution and the constitution', in Geoffrey Holmes (ed.), *Britain after the Glorious Revolution* (1979).

32 *The Declaration of the Lords Spiritual and Temporal.*

33 Foxcroft, *Life and Letters*, **2**, 203–47.

34 William Cobbett (ed.), *The Parliamentary History of England* (1806–20), **5**, 760.

35 Ibid., **5**, 829–34.

36 *CJ,* **11,** 74.

37 *LJ,* **15,** 102.

38 *LJ*, **14**, 320.

39 Henry Horwitz (ed.), *The Parliamentary Diary of Narcissus Luttrell* (Clarendon Press, 1972), p. 406 – the irony is pointed out by Horwitz, *Parliament, Policy and Politics,* p. 88.

40 *LJ*, **14** 128.

41 *LJ*, **15**, 102.

42 Horwitz, *Parliament, Policy and Politics,* ch. 5.

43 See speeches of 12 November 1694 and 9 December, 1698 – *LJ,* **15**, 430; *LJ,* **16**, 312.

44 Grey, *Debates,* **10**, 375.

45 Cobbett, *Parliamentary History,* **5**, 760–6.

46 Ibid., **5**, 740.

47 *A Form of Prayer with Thanksgiving . . . 5th November* (1689); a model for later sermons was Gilbert Burnet, *A Sermon Preached before the House of Peers . . . 5th November* (1689).

48 Claydon, *William III, passim.*

49 S.B. Baxter, 'William III as Hercules', in Lois G. Schwoerer (ed.), *The Revolution of 1688–1689* (CUP, 1992).

50 Blencowe, *Diary*, **2**, 288.

51 Claydon, *William III*, pp. 93–100.

52 See, for example [John Trenchard and Walter Moyle], *An Argument Shewing that a Standing Army is Inconsistent with a Free Government* (1697).

Chapter Four

William and Political Party

The problem: the legacy of political division

On Christmas day, 1689, the comptroller of William's household, Tom Wharton, wrote a letter to his king. It was devoid of festive spirit. Although its opening sentence thanked the monarch for 'the protection you gave to our religion and laws', it went on to state 'I think it my duty to lay before you the desperate condition you are brought into, by the flatterers, knaves, and villains, you have the misfortune to employ'.[1] What followed must count as one of the most extraordinary tirades ever sent to a monarch by one of his subjects. Sparing William nothing, it painted an abject portrait of the state of the realm. It claimed the country was rent by corruption and division; it blamed the dire situation on the king's choice of servants; and included an emphatic attack on the ruler himself. 'The world was filled with your fame when you landed in England', Wharton opined. 'There was nothing wanting to declare you in the opinion of all mankind, to be the greatest and most glorious prince that had appeared for many ages, but your own resolution to give a finishing stroke to that deserved character. IN THIS YOU FAILED, AND FELL FROM A HEIGHT WHICH VERY FEW MEN EVER REACHED BEFORE YOU.'[2]

The passion of this letter reveals the difficulties William faced with parties at the start of his reign. Wharton was a staunch and partisan whig, who had hoped the new king would prove a close ally of his faction. The servants Wharton attacked were tories, whom William had included in his government to prove he was not a prisoner of one group. Wharton, however, refused to see the king's actions as a sensible balancing of his ministerial team. For him, employing tories could only be a suicidal pact with traitors. William had recruited 'the most obnoxious men of all England', whose 'experience was only in doing ill'. Keeping such people in court was personally as well as politically dangerous. 'With every bite you eat', Wharton warned, 'and every drop you drink, [they] may poison you.'[3] In one sense, the comptroller was exceptional. It was unusual for party hatred to drive men to quite such paranoid hysteria, and few members of the political nation were so full of bile against their rivals. Nevertheless, the sort of partisan sentiment which Wharton so freely disgorged posed a serious difficulty for William. The letter can only have confirmed that the king faced a dangerously polarised country.

The formal split between whigs and tories had occurred a decade before William arrived in England. The two parties had had their origin in the exclusion crisis of 1679–83. In that great controversy, the nation had been pulled apart by its contradictory 'monarchical' and 'republican' principles, and 'whig' and 'tory' had become the labels attached to the sides of the debate. On one side, those sufficiently worried by James's Catholicism to argue that parliament should exclude him from the succession had been called 'whigs'. This was a mocking name, intended to suggest the exclusionists shared attitudes with the 'whiggamores', a fanatical group of Scots Protestants who had terrorised the northern kingdom in the decades before. To mirror this, opponents of exclusion had come to be called 'tories'. Again, this label had started life as an insult. 'Tories' were bands of Catholic brigands in the south of Ireland, and exclusionists seized on the term to suggest the dangers of letting in the Roman faith by allowing James to come to the throne. As such name calling suggests, the contest had been bitter. The exclusion crisis had been fermented by battles in the street, in the press, at elections, and through mass petitioning, as well as in parliament. Once it was clear that the whigs would lose, some of them had plotted a violent overthrow of Charles II's regime. In 1683, several leading whigs were implicated in the 'Rye House Plot' to assassinate the king, and whig thinkers such as John Locke had constructed revolutionary political theories. At the start of James's reign, many whigs supported the duke of Monmouth's unsuccessful invasion of England, hoping that this Protestant might fight his way to the throne. Not for nothing had tory commentators feared that 1641 was come again. Party conflict over James's succession had brought the nation to the brink of civil war.

The arguments over exclusion had been frightening enough. However, two further factors aggravated the problems William was to face. First, debate over the succession seemed to feed on deeper and more long-standing fissures in English society. As the crisis wore on, it became obvious that whigs and tories were divided by more than the future of James. Perhaps most importantly, their disputes were fuelled by religious arguments about the nature of English Protestantism. To understand this, it is necessary to delve back to the mid sixteenth-century and the foundation of the church of England. The two parties of the late Stuart era were heirs of a spiritual argument which had its roots in the events which had given the nation its reformed faith.

In the 1560s, Queen Elizabeth had rejected the Catholicism of her predecessor, Mary. She had imposed an ecclesiastical settlement which, in doctrine at least, was definitively Protestant. The church she established rejected old beliefs in papal supremacy, transubstantiation and purgatory, and had thus aligned itself with the European reformation. The problem was that this doctrinal settlement was only part of the picture. In other elements of its constitution, the new church of England was more ambiguous. It retained features of the old Catholic institution, most notably government by bishops, a rich ceremonial life in worship and a fixed form of religious service which left relatively little time for preaching. As might be expected in a country easily gripped by anti-popery, these survivals caused controversy. While the queen and her supporters cherished the 'Catholic' features as signs of continuity with the ancient English faith, many others condemned them as popish infections in a church only half-reformed. Tension on this issue became the central political dispute of early modern England. It divided opinion under Elizabeth and the early Stuarts; it burst into open conflict in the civil war (royalists had fought for the traditional church establishment while parliamentarians had pressed for a more definitively Protestant settlement); and it destabilised the republican regimes which tried to govern after the execution of Charles I.

With the nation so divided about the church, it was unsurprising that ecclesiastical arguments fed the party disputes of the later seventeenth century. Victory for parliament in the civil war had spelt the end for bishops and introduced a more Spartan liturgy – but the return of the Stuart dynasty in 1660 posed the problem of whether the clock should be returned to the earlier, more mixed, settlement. Initially, Charles II had wished to compromise. He had wanted to cool passions by designing a church which could accommodate both 'Protestant' and 'mixed' sentiments – but he had been outmanoeuvred by some of his more intransigent supporters. In 1661, royalists in parliament imposed a full pre-war settlement, with the result that bishops, ceremony and liturgy flooded back. In reaction, the church split. Nearly 2,000 clergy found they could not swallow the 'popish' re-impositions. On St Bartholomew's day 1662, these ministers were ejected from their posts, and – together with their supporters – formed a 'dissenting' or 'non-conformist' community worshipping outside the church. From that moment, the issue of how to treat this body became the central dispute in English politics. It was this which reinforced the constitutional division between the exclusion crisis parties. As well as supporting James, tories argued that dissenters should be prosecuted with the full force of the law. They backed the series of statutes passed since the Restoration which persecuted non-conformists, and argued that dissenters were at least as evil and traitorous as papists. Whigs on the other hand, tended to see non-conformists as good Protestants, badly treated by an intolerant establishment. They argued that persecuting laws should be repealed, and that attempts should be made to meet the objections of dissenters so that they could be 'comprehended' back in the church.

Party argument over exclusion was therefore compounded by a religious debate fired by anti-popery. Unfortunately, however, it was not only the divisiveness of the issues which was to trouble William after 1688. A second factor – the growth of partisan organisation and sentiment – was to deepen disputes still more. As a consequence, whig–tory rivalry survived even changes in political circumstance which might have helped ease the conflict. This pattern was evident as soon as the exclusion crisis ended. From around 1683 it became clear that the whigs had lost on the basic issue. Charles II had effectively outfaced their threats, and most Englishmen got used to the idea that James would eventually succeed his brother. On the face of things, this tory victory could have eased rivalries. Whigs might have become demoralised, and have disbanded as a political movement when their cry of exclusion failed to mobilise support. Yet dispute did not fade. Tensions survived 1683 because the crisis had created forms of party organisation and identity. As whigs and tories had pressed their cases, sustained co-operation on either side of the dispute had produced political structures which continued to clash even once exclusion was settled. Thus MPs had got used to acting together to argue their case in parliament. Local groups of whigs and tories had organised to win elections, to stage street demonstrations, and to collect signatures for petitions. Writers and publishers had collaborated to form partisan propaganda machines, and activists had begun to meet regularly in particular taverns or coffeehouses to plan strategy and form political clubs. Above all, members of the political nation began to think of themselves as either whigs or as tories, and to dedicate their lives to the destruction of their rivals. In this situation, battle could persist, even though the formal issue which had split the parties died. After their victory in the exclusion crisis, tories used royal favour and partisan organisation to try to winkle whigs out of all positions of power. In the last years of Charles's reign they pumped out anti-whig propaganda, mobilised to control town corporations, and pressed for prosecution of dissenters. Under James, by contrast, whigs made the running. As the king discovered tories would not support his pro-Catholic policies, he turned to their enemies, and found many willing to use their party organisation to redress the political balance. After 1685, tories found themselves attacked in the whig press, hounded out of positions of power by their rivals, and prosecuted for supposed excesses in the years before.

The partisan history of the 1680s posed a serious problem for William. Wanting a nation which would unite to help him defeat Louis XIV, he faced instead, a country torn apart. Whigs and tories were estranged by their initial disagreement about the constitution, but they were rent asunder by their underlying disagreement about the church, and by the political organisation and loyalties which had sustained these disputes. As Wharton's letter made clear, they were in no mood to cool their passions in the new reign. This made William's task almost unmanageable. To govern his new realm he needed the co-operation of a large proportion of its inhabitants, but party rivalries stood squarely in the way. If William looked for support from one party, he was certain to alienate the other. If, on the other hand, he appealed across the political spectrum, favouring people from both parties, he risked chaos. The two sides were too hostile to work well together: sentiments like Wharton's could destroy effective and united administration. Given this, William had only one option. He would have to work to reduce the political temperature, so that rivalry could be contained within a stable political system. The rest of this chapter will demonstrate how the king achieved these aims. It will once again illustrate the role his Dutch priorities and experience played in the process.

William and the constitutional disputes between parties

As we have seen, the Glorious Revolution changed the English constitution fundamentally. It sacked a king, invented a novel joint monarchy, removed Catholics from the succession and limited the royal prerogative with the bill of rights. Amid this transformation, it might seem surprising that constitutional disputes between whigs and tories survived. The original argument had been whether parliament could deny James the crown. Now all had agreed he was unfit to rule, it might be hard to see the relevance of earlier constitutional debates. Yet in fact, whigs and tories remained almost as divided over the fundamentals of English government after the revolution as they had been in the 1680s. The issue of whether James could rule might have been settled – but the underlying tension between 'monarchical' and 'republican' principles remained, and could still be embodied in party conflict. Moreover, the tories, who had been forced to recant their support for the displaced king, needed to save face. They were reluctant to admit that their earlier royalism had been mistaken, and continued to insist that their position was very different from that of the whigs. As a result, William's time in England saw continuing constitutional tension. Tories and whigs expended much breath and ink denouncing the evil principles of their rivals.

Dispute arose as early as January 1689, in the constitutional convention. The whigs in that body had always been happy that subjects could alter the monarch if the rule of a particular king was dangerous. That is what they had argued in the exclusion crisis, so they were comfortable calling for William's immediate elevation. The tories on the other hand, still wished to resist this logic. In the early 1680s they had insisted that it was dangerous to question a monarch's hereditary right to rule as this might encourage the sort of rebellion seen in the civil war. Although they had been stung enough by James's attack on England's laws to admit he should not be allowed back as acting monarch, they sought solutions in the convention which would do least damage to the hereditary principle. In particular, tories were uncomfortable with the idea that the throne was vacant. For them, this questioned the unbreakable succession between a king and his heir, and opened the way for an elective monarchy. The tory majority in the Lords therefore rejected the Commons' resolution that the throne was empty, and instead searched for settlements which would do less to disrupt the succession. For example, on 29 January, the bishop of Ely suggested that the convention appoint a regent for James. This would leave the old king as nominal ruler, though it would place the actual exercise of power in safer hands. Similarly, in early February, a group around the earl of Danby resisted a popular election of the monarch through a slightly more involved set of ideas. They suggested that James's flight from the country constituted an abdication; they rejected the claims of his infant son because of his questionable legitimacy; and then they argued that James's next heir, Mary, should come to the throne. This would accept that a king could deprive himself of the throne by abandoning the kingdom – but would reject whig notions that subjects had the right to sack their monarchs and chose successors to suit themselves.

Unfortunately for the tories, whigs managed to defeat both their proposals in the convention. The call for a regency was rejected by three votes in the Lords. Even that tory-dominated house could see it would divide loyalties between the nominal king and the regent, and would merely perpetuate constitutional confusion. The idea of giving Mary the crown was damaged when it became clear William would not accept it, and it was finally scuppered when the princess herself said she would refuse coronation out of loyalty to her husband. All tories got to salve their hereditary consciences was the joint elevation of Mary to sit on the throne beside

William. Yet despite these disappointments, tories still refused to relinquish their monarchical reading of the constitution. A few became Jacobites, refusing to accept William's right to power, and hoping (or plotting) for a restoration of James. Far more were prepared to swear loyalty to the new king as the least bad alternative, but nevertheless denounced whig accounts of the revolution. In two areas in particular, Williamite tories went on questioning their rivals' interpretation of the constitution through the 1690s, and stoked political tensions as they did so.

The first dispute was about what had happened in 1688–89. For the whigs this was pretty simple. The English people, facing a tyrant, had exercised their right to resist such a monster, and had legitimately deposed him. For tories, however, this could never be the case. Subjects had no just way to remove a monarch, no matter how tyrannical. Granting them such a right would be a recipe for continued rebellion and chaos, since dissident groups could always claim a ruler had been acting despotically and use this as an excuse for subversion. Following this logic, Williamite tories had to find ways of accepting the revolution, without granting people an entitlement to rebel. Several complementary theories were advanced. These included the idea that James himself had abdicated (so change came through royal, rather than popular action); that William had gained the throne through right of conquest (he had not been a rebelling subject, but an independent foreign power who had triumphed through his own army); or that William was a providential monarch, brought to the throne by God's almighty hand. Almost any theory would do, so long as it denied that the will of the English people had any part in William's elevation. These ideas eased tory scruples about accepting 1688 – but they did little to calm party tensions. Whigs denounced their rivals' political thought as convenient logic chopping, and suggested it left the English with no rights against their rulers. Tories denounced whigs as dangerous radicals. Their enemies, they suggested, were not content with the extraordinary good fortune of the revolution, but wished to rewrite it as a charter for repeated rebellions. Especially in the early 1690s these two positions slugged it out in a pamphlet war of almost unprecedented ferocity. Mark Goldie, the modern bibliographer of this 'allegiance' controversy, counted nearly two hundred pamphlets arguing the rights of the revolution in the years down to 1694. He estimated these produced around 300,000 individual copies, catering for a readership of up to 100,000 people.[4]

The second area of constitutional tension under William was the king's exact legal title to the throne. Again, for whigs, this was simple. The revolution of 1688 had been fully legitimate, so William was an unequivocally legal king. Again, for tories, however, things were not so straightforward. For many of them, swearing that William was a 'rightful and lawful' monarch – as the traditional oath of allegiance would require them to do – came too close to endorsing a forcible change of king. Apart from the few Jacobites, tories *were* prepared to be loyal to the new ruler. However, they wanted to do so without accepting his full legal legitimacy. To do this, they drew a distinction between a de facto and a de jure king. They argued that James was still king in law (king de jure) – but that people owed loyalty to the man who was actually exercising royal power (William, the king de facto), because to refuse this obedience ran the risk of civil chaos. In their minds, William may not have been the legitimate monarch, but he had become the effective one. He was providing justice, public order and defence against foreign invasion, and to oppose him merely on the grounds that his title was questionable would undermine these vital functions. It was true that God had insisted on hereditary succession. However, the deity had done this to avoid political uncertainty and the risk of civil strife. To resist a ruling king to promote a rightful one would flirt with anarchy, and would therefore prioritise means (a hereditary succession) over ends (a peaceful and ordered society). This de facto argument allowed many tories to work for William: but, as might be expected, it enraged the whigs. For them, people who would only support the king on these grounds were barely loyal to the regime. The whigs claimed de facto tories were Jacobites in disguise. They were men with the thinnest commitment to William, who endangered his rule by claiming someone else was legally monarch. If the king ever faced a serious threat from James, the whigs pointed out, the de facto tories would be free to renounce their obedience as soon his power wobbled. Consequently, the whigs spent much of the reign attacking tories as secret enemies of the king. They also tried repeatedly to force all royal servants to swear to William's rightful claims. They knew many tories could not do this, and hoped such an enforced oath would sweep their rivals out of public posts.

For the king, then, constitutional dispute between the parties posed a continuing challenge through the 1690s. Once again, William's continental focus helped him find solutions. Because the king prioritised the defeat of Louis, rather than his domestic status, he was able to take a more farsighted view of party debate than his immediate predecessors. Most importantly, he did not particularly care what his position was in English law. To a man determined to rescue all Christendom, the English constitution seemed a parochial concern. He was therefore happy to adopt a conciliatory position on his precise legal title, even though it seemed to undermine his legitimacy.

To understand this, it is useful to reflect on the support offered to the monarchy by the constitutional principles of the two parties – and on the court's reaction to this – over the 1680s. Before 1688, tory thought had clearly been the most monarchical. While whigs claimed that parliament could alter the succession (and began to advocate resistance when they failed), tories upheld the rights of the king. They denounced rebellion, and insisted that succession should be by unchallenged hereditary descent. As a result, the Stuart kings backed the tories. Being concerned to consolidate their power, the monarchs promoted tory arguments (though James became alienated from the tory party itself when he discovered that its loyalty to the established church overrode its royalism). After 1688, by contrast, whig thought provided more comfort to the regime. While whigs declared William the rightful king, tories saw him only as de facto monarch and espoused accounts of the revolution (such as William's elevation by providence or conquest) which would legitimate James if he ever fought his way back to the throne. Given this, one might expect a switch in royal sympathies. William, it might be thought, would throw his weight behind the whigs.

In fact, however, William's concern to unite all Englishmen in the face of the continental threat defied these expectations. Surveying recent history, the new king realised that however logical supporting royal supporters looked, it actually alienated the estranged group even more completely and would prevent England uniting against France. William had seen that Charles and James had destabilised their realm by promoting tory royalism. In the early 1680s, whigs were already frustrated by the court's actions in the exclusion crisis: on seeing the kings' enthusiastic espousal of their opponents' case they were driven to desperate measures. After the revolution, William learned this lesson, and took a less blinkered view of his interests. If the new monarch had merely been concerned to confirm his claims to the English throne, he would have promoted his full legitimacy with whig arguments. However, as we know, constitutional glorification was not his prime aim. Rather he wanted to take all Englishmen with him in his battle with Louis, and so decided to appease – not to denounce – the group with most doubts about his authority. William made it clear he would not anathematise tory ideas. A monarch who was not bothered by his precise position in English law kept the tories loyal by accepting their grounds for obedience. So long as people were prepared to follow him in his European crusade, William decided he could not enquire too closely into their exact reasoning.

The policy emerged as early as the convention of 1689. In the immediate aftermath of deciding to make William king, this body began to debate the oaths by which office holders would swear loyalty to the new regime. At a crucial point in these discussions, the earl of Nottingham suggested a change in the wording, which he thought would allow many tories to work with the new government. Knowing that many of his party doubted that William would be a fully legitimate king (and sharing these doubts himself), the earl argued that the new oaths should drop reference to the new monarchs being 'rightful and lawful' rulers. In this way, those who believed that William and Mary were only de facto governors could promise to bear them true allegiance, even though they thought James wore the de jure crown. Nottingham also tried to soothe those who hoped that 1688 might mark a temporary diversion from Stuart legitimacy. The earl argued that when swearing loyalty to William, people should be excused from mentioning his heirs and successors.[5] These ideas were unwelcome to whigs, who believed that the new king was wholly legitimate. However, almost everybody recognised it was important to get the new regime off to an uncontroversial start, and Nottingham's rewording was adopted. As a result, the declaration of rights promulgated a new oath under which office holders would 'sincerely promise and swear, that I will be faithful and bear true allegiance to their Majesties King William and Queen Mary'.[6] Here there was no mention of rightful or lawful rule: no statement as to who should wear the crown next.

The important thing about the new oaths is that William acquiesced in them. Even though they seemed to diminish his claims to full monarchy, he showed no opposition to the revised versions, and accepted his subjects swearing by using the new wording as a full and satisfactory statement of their obedience. Moreover, William repeatedly resisted attempts to go beyond the convention's compromise. On numerous occasions, whigs tried to embarrass their rivals by re-inserting the phrase 'rightful and lawful' into oaths to the king. They knew the words would stick in many tories' throats, and that they might be able to eject their enemies from public posts if their victims could not make the promises required to qualify. For instance, in 1690, whigs attempted to change the rules for office holders so they would have to swear an oath abjuring obedience to James, and declaring the new monarchs 'rightful and lawful'. In 1692, the whig John Somers introduced a bill for 'the preservation of their majesties' which would penalise anyone using de facto arguments for William. After an assassination attempt on William in 1696, whig parliamentarians set up an 'association' to exact revenge on anyone who was successful in killing the king. Joining the association was to be compulsory for all office holders, and would require an open declaration that William was legally monarch. On all these occasions, however, the king opposed whig manoeuvring. Always publicly satisfied with the tories' reasons for obeying him, he exerted pressure to have the measures dropped. In both 1690 and 1692 he mobilised his friends in parliament to oppose whig arguments (even attending the Lords debate in 1690 to lend moral support) and, while the 1696 association *was* adopted in the atmosphere of panic following the attempt on the king's life, the threatened ruler himself told the earl of Chesterfield 'it was not a thing of his contriving'.[7]

William's tolerance of tory constitutional views seems exceptional. What is quite extraordinary is he promoted them. Mark Goldie's work on the 'allegiance controversy' reveals that the government spokesmen who took part in the exchange of pamphlets about the revolution's principles rejected whiggish arguments. In particular, they avoided theories which would excuse resistance, much preferring to argue the king to the throne by alternative routes. Gilbert Burnet is the best case in point. During the invasion of 1688, Burnet acted as the prince's chief propagandist, translating his manifesto into English and preaching in his favour as he advanced on London. In January 1689, Burnet took his publicist's duties further, producing *An Enquiry into the Present State of Affairs*, a pamphlet designed to influence discussion in the forthcoming constitutional convention. Boldly boasting on its title page that it was 'published by [William's] authority', this argued for the prince's elevation – but did so on grounds which gave no rights to subjects to rebel. For Burnet, James had lost the crown because he had abandoned the realm. He had therefore abdicated rather than been deposed. In these circumstances the *Enquiry* argued that Mary was the legitimate successor but, as she was married, her authority should rightly pass to her husband.[8] Burnet followed up this performance a few months later with his *Pastoral Letter*. Written to the clergy of Salisbury (the diocese to which William had promoted him bishop), this tried to resolve doubts about the new regime among churchmen by espousing strict de facto principles. Obedience, explained Burnet, was a tribute due to protection. William was now ensuring order, so he must be obeyed whatever the rights of his coming to power.[9] These types of argument were standard among those closely connected to the regime. They were embodied in the works of such government scribblers as Edmund Bohun, whose connections to the court were so close that many thought leading office holders had actually penned their works.[10] They were also the meat of arguments by the clerics whom William promoted in his early years in power. Such men as William Lloyd and Edward Stillingfleet preached that William was a providential monarch from their pulpits, and then argued abdication or conquest theories as they entered the allegiance controversy as pamphleteers.[11] When combined with

Goldie's evidence that the court was actively censuring radical resistance arguments as vigorously as it pursued the Jacobite press, we are left with the striking prospect of a tory-leaning official propaganda.

William, then, did more than accept the loyalty of men who would not accept that resistance to James had been legitimate. He made it clear he was happiest arguing for his right to rule in ways which avoided accepting such resistance. He was even willing to accept obedience on the bare grounds that he had somehow fought his way to control, and was now ruler in practice. Such willingness to have royal legitimacy dimmed can only be explained by the pressing need to unite the whole country against France. Remarkably, however, it did the trick. Whigs remained loyal because they had no real alternative. Although irked that William did not accept their arguments, they had to support him as the only basis for the limited monarchy they favoured. Tories too remained loyal. Able to work with the regime on principles they accepted, they did so, and a remarkably small number passed into Jacobitism. Although over three hundred clergy refused the oaths to the new monarchs, very few laymen did so, and even the non-juring churchmen tended to live quietly under the new regime rather than actively promoting the return of James. On constitutional issues, therefore, both parties were accommodated. William's continental focus ensured there was no repeat of the dangerous alienation which had driven groups to desperate actions before 1688.

William and the religious disputes between parties

Beyond continuing disputes over the constitution, whigs and tories were divided on religion in the 1690s. At first sight, this might again seem surprising. Just as the events of James's reign had altered arguments about the fundamentals of English government, they had transformed debates about the English church, and it might appear odd that old tensions survived the shift. The most important change in the late 1680s was that tory Anglicans came to realise how dangerous intolerance of dissenters could be. When James found tories would not help him ease the plight of Catholics, he exploited the bitter divisions in English Protestantism, and gained non-conformist support for an indulgence which would benefit Romanists and dissenters alike. Observing this, tories moved rapidly to reknit an anti-popish alliance. In the summer of 1688, William Sancroft, the previously hardline archbishop of Canterbury, began to advocate dialogue with non-Anglican Protestants, and assured them that the church of England had sympathy with their plight. When he, and six other bishops, were imprisoned for petitioning the king against his unparliamentary declaration of religious toleration, leading London clergy made contact with the capital's dissenting ministers and secured their support for protests against the extension of royal power. On the eve of William's invasion, therefore, it appeared that old ecclesiastical divisions were softening.

Unfortunately, however, the old tensions did not disappear. After the revolution, there was a general recognition that Protestant disunity had nearly led to disaster: but there was no consensus on how the old rivalries could be resolved. All agreed that a new religious settlement was needed to end damaging disputes, but there was no consensus on what it should look like. Whigs and tories polarised on three main issues. First, they disagreed on the extent of toleration. It was clear to nearly everyone that some people would have to be allowed to worship outside the church of England, since persecution had merely stoked resentment. Yet the terms of this toleration were controversial. While whigs argued it should be generous, tories felt it should have strict conditions. For tories the toleration should perhaps be temporary: it should certainly be limited to a bare freedom to worship, and closely supervised to ensure no sedition, immorality or blasphemy resulted. Second, whigs and tories disagreed about comprehension. While many whigs felt the church of England should offer compromises to dissenters to attract them back (particularly modifying its liturgy, and softening its line on the need for bishops to ordain ministers), opinion in tory circles hardened over 1689. Many came to feel that bare indulgence was all dissenters deserved, and that inviting non-conformists back into the establishment would readmit a headstrong and factious group. Finally, there was disagreement over the Anglican monopoly of public office. While some whigs felt non-conformists should be allowed to take up public posts, tories were adamant against this. They insisted on retaining the test acts of the 1670s, which had ruled that people could only be sworn into offices once they had attended Anglican communion. This, for them, was the only way to preserve the essential link between church and state; and avoid untrustworthy dissenters serving the king. Thus, although William benefited from some willingness to find a religious settlement as he came to power, he still faced parties bitterly divided over the faith of the nation.

In coping with these spiritual tensions, William had one great advantage over his predecessors. Again, this stemmed from his focus on the European continent. Earlier Stuarts had been immersed in English religious arguments, and had been brought up to believe the king's headship of the church of England was one of his most important roles. They therefore tended to come to strong religious positions, and had fuelled religious controversy as they tried to impose their own spiritual vision. William, by contrast, was an outsider – who knew little, and probably cared even less – about England's ecclesiastical arrangements. As with so much else, his prime aim in church affairs was to strengthen his alliance against France. This meant attracting support from across the whole religious spectrum in England, and also doing nothing to upset any of his confessionally diverse friends on the continent (after all, William hoped that Englishmen would fight alongside Calvinist Dutchmen, Lutheran Germans and even Catholic Austrians and Spanish). The new king therefore sought pragmatic accommodation in his religious policy, paying relatively small regard to his own religious beliefs.

It was *not* that William lacked spiritual convictions. He had been raised in the Dutch Reformed church, and there is more evidence than some historians have contended that he was loyal to its Calvinist doctrine, Presbyterian government and simple worship.[12] For example, William seems to have been uncomfortable that his wife worshipped according to Anglican rites when in The Hague.[13] Similarly, he sometimes let slip disparaging comments about the ritual and practices of the church of England; and as he disembarked at Torbay he joked with Gilbert Burnet, asking what the cleric thought of predestination now.[14] This suggested that the prince had earlier been defending Calvinism against Burnet's opposition. Moreover, there is evidence for a solid personal piety, based on frequent examination of conscience. Throughout his life he took counsel from such spiritual advisers as his boyhood tutor Cornelius Trigland, and his last archbishop of Canterbury Thomas Tenison; while personal prayers published soon after his death at least pretended rigorous preparation for communion.[15] William also had a deep religious conviction in his commitment to toleration. Although he presented himself as a Protestant champion, he did not believe God approved of persecuting fellow Christians (indeed it was Rome's poor record here which turned him against that faith); and he employed people from a wide variety of religious backgrounds in his personal service. This tolerance was further engrained by growing up in a Dutch society where freedom of worship was greater than almost anywhere else in Europe. Holland's success in uniting all its faiths in its struggles for survival – and the huge prosperity with which the country had been blessed – taught that there were at least practical, and probably providential, benefits in religious liberty.

William therefore had personal religious commitments at least as deep as his predecessors. In contrast to them, however, he did not try to foist these convictions on the English. Moved by his European priorities (which incidentally included a sense that God had chosen him to rescue the continent from a Satanic French king), he did what would help defeat Louis rather than follow his own spiritual tastes. He also reflected on his experience in Holland. There he had begun by supporting Calvinists like himself – but had later moderated his position as it became clear their intolerance of others was dividing Dutch society and making it harder for William to lead it against France.[16] The new king therefore sacrificed his own views. Unlike James I (whose independent forays into theological controversy had stirred bitter disputes); unlike Charles I (who had alienated many by his promotion of the Catholic remnants in the English church); and unlike the Restoration kings (whose sympathies for Catholicism had upset and divided Protestant opinion); William had a wider, European, view of his religious responsibilities which led him to a practical, moderate and calming line.

This balanced policy was evident even before the Prince of Orange invaded England. Surveying the religious disputes in his uncles' realm, William was personally attracted to the whig position. His own churchmanship was close to that of the dissenters, and his horror of religious persecution chimed with their calls for a wider toleration of religious disagreements. As a result, when whig exiles sought refuge in Holland after their defeat in the exclusion crisis, William gave them sanctuary and began consulting them on English affairs. He also endorsed their position in James's reign, making it clear it was his uncle's manner of promoting toleration, not the aim itself, which he opposed.[17] Given this, it was natural that many tories had doubts about William's faith. They feared that any advance by the Prince of Orange would damage their beloved church. What saved the situation, however, was that William recognised this potential opposition, and moved to allay it. Rather than state his own religious preferences, he kept his eyes on the broad anti-French alliance he wished to head in English politics, and did all he could to sooth tory anxiety.

This was partly why the expedition's manifesto avoided religious controversy. Instead of arguing the rights and wrongs of James's ecclesiastical objectives, it took its main stand on his violation of English law – something about which both whigs and tories had become concerned. Relations between Anglicans and dissenters were certainly handled in the document, but the prince deliberately neutered this issue, suggesting that church matters be discussed by the same 'free parliament' which would consider the constitution. In William's *Declaration* the uncoerced legislature was to promote 'such Laws as may establish a good Agreement between the Church of England and all Protestant Dissenters'. Moreover, tory fears about William's whiggish faith were calmed by the examples which established the illegality of James's rule. Whig exiles in Holland, who were consulted about the wording of the manifesto, suggested that tory excesses against dissenters in the aftermath of the exclusion crisis should be the meat of the case. Once the document had emerged from William's inner circle, however, all reference to these abuses disappeared. Instead, the *Declaration* cited only royal crimes committed after 1685 (the year in which James had turned against the tories), and it concentrated on the court's attacks on the church of England. The list of enormities which began the indictment included the fact that James had admitted non-Anglicans to public office in violation of the test acts; that he had suspended the bishop of London for not suppressing anti-popish preaching; and that he had imprisoned the leading bishops when they had protested about his religious policies. William thus presented himself as a close friend of the church of England. Hiding his personal distaste for the English establishment, he said he had come to protect it. This strain of propaganda continued during William's early weeks in England. He appointed the Anglican Burnet as his personal chaplain for the expedition; he made sure he was visible at Anglican services such as the act of thanksgiving in Exeter cathedral soon after his landing; he attended Anglican prayers and communion regularly once he was in London; and made early contact with the clergy of the capital to thank them for their opposition to James over the preceding years.[18]

This careful conciliation of tory opinion paid dividends during the revolution. It appears to have sufficiently calmed fears about William that the nation was willing to stick to his anti-French agenda. In the constitutional convention, members discussed how to fill the throne, and how to protect the nation against the threat from Louis. They did not descend, as they so easily might have done, into bitter rehearsals of their religious differences. Tories seem to have been reassured enough to accept a new monarch whom they had believed was a committed whig in church affairs. Whigs were reassured that they had a ruler after their own hearts – albeit one who had moderated his language for political gain.

Unfortunately, this success filled the new king with too much confidence. For a few weeks in early 1689, William's own personal religious preferences emerged in royal policy. The result was one of the most disastrous blunders in William's entire career: the ensuing political storm soon convinced him that his own ideals must be submerged again in the effort to keep the nation united for war.

In the spring of 1689, the new king's preference for a 'whiggish' approach to ecclesiastical disputes emerged in several ways. First, he supported an initiative by a group of more liberal London clergy to offer a generous settlement with dissent. Centred on such men as John Tillotson, Simon Patrick and Edward Stillingfleet, this group hoped to capitalise on the mood of reconciliation which had emerged at the end of James's reign, and were supported by their patron, the earl of Nottingham (a solid tory Anglican – but one who recognised that church persecution of dissent had weakened the whole Protestant cause). After a series of meetings in January and February, the group arranged their ideas into two parliamentary bills. One, for 'comprehension', would offer concessions on Anglican liturgy and on episcopal ordination. This, it was hoped, would allow moderate dissenters to rejoin the church. The other, for 'toleration', proposed that Protestants who could not be included in the broader church settlement would be allowed to worship outside the establishment. After Nottingham had finalised the details of the proposed legislation, the bills were introduced to the Lords in March, and received every sign of royal favour. William's second revelation of his personal preferences came in a speech to parliament. After consulting whig advisers such as Richard Hampden, the king decided to push for his own vision of religious inclusiveness. In an oration on 16 March he urged the 'admission to public office of all Protestants that are willing and able to serve'.[19] This may have been a throwaway line at the end of a speech about the importance of mobilising for war – but it had dramatic implications. It effectively suggested repeal of the tests which kept non-Anglicans from public office, and whose suspension by James for the benefit of Catholics had given rise to so much complaint.

The result of these royal actions was to undo the good work William had done reassuring tories over the winter of 1688–99. Anglican opinion in the Commons was so shocked by the king's questioning of the test that it instantly hardened and organised. On the evening of his speech, one hundred and fifty parliamentarians met in (what William might have thought the appropriately named) Devil's Tavern. There, over beers, they vowed to fight any further erosion of the church's position. They would not repeal the test, and would not accept the compromises with dissent suggested in Nottingham's bills. Quite how angry, and quite how effective, these MPs were was to be was revealed days afterwards as the Commons debated the oath which William was to swear at his forthcoming coronation. Against whig opposition, the tories successfully insisted that the king must not only promise to defend the church of England – but that he must defend that church 'as by law established'.[20] This would effectively set the liturgy and government of the establishment in stone. William could hardly support concessions to dissent, if the tories could force him to swear to uphold the church in its current form. The reaction against

William's speech erected sturdy parliamentary barriers in the path of the king's whole religious policy.

In such circumstances, earlier Stuarts might have pressed ahead. James I had warned parliament against discussing religious affairs. Charles I and James II had simply dissolved the legislature when it questioned their ecclesiastical policy. Charles II had twice retreated when parliament protested against his grants of toleration, but nevertheless went on pursuing his vision, hoping he could make his prerogatives stick. William, with his usual contrast to predecessors, surrendered. As always, he placed his European strategy above getting his way in England, and threw his church policy into gear-crunching – and permanent – reverse. After March, the king's priority was to avoid alienating tory opinion. He never mentioned a repeal of the test acts again. He also sacrificed the idea of comprehension by suggesting that any changes in the church's constitution be considered, not by parliament, but by the Anglican cleric's own legislative body, convocation. It was pretty clear that referral to this assembly would kill the measure. Preparations were made for a convocation over the summer of 1689, and a special commission met to prepare concessions to dissent, but when the body actually met in November, opposition to any change was so clear that none of the proposals even got to a vote. Most humiliatingly, perhaps, the king made a series of public statements praising the church. The institution whose worship he had detested in his wife was now 'the best constituted church in the world'. It was the 'greatest support' of the Protestant religion, and an 'eminent part of the Reformation'. The king would 'venture his life' in its defence, and had resolved to die in its communion.[21]

It is true that in one area, at least, William did not back down. Although he was willing to drop suggestions for a repeal of the test, and to sacrifice comprehension, he would not abandon a grant of toleration to Protestants who wished to worship outside the church. Recent historical investigation, especially by Jonathan Israel, has revealed that it was royal pressure which did most to get Nottingham's toleration act onto the statute book in April 1689.[22] Some tories opposed the measure or suggested it be temporary, but everybody at Westminster knew that intransigence would so anger the king that the fledgling regime would be endangered. Consequently, Protestant dissenters gained freedom to worship outside the church of England, so long as they registered their meetings with local magistrates, kept their doors unlocked during services and swore to uphold the doctrinal (as opposed to liturgical and episcopal) ideals of the establishment. Yet while the continued pressure for toleration might appear an exception to William's abandonment of his personal religious vision in 1689, it actually confirms the wider rule of prioritising European objectives over English ones. We should remember that the king had swung away from his whiggish policies because they weakened his continental position. They had so upset the tories that support for the war might wane. On close inspection, this concern for Europe lay behind the continued pressure for toleration as well. If there was to be no comprehension or repeal of the test, a basic freedom of worship would be the very minimum needed to safeguard William's continental aims. Without it, bitter religious dispute would go on, and could prove as disruptive to the war effort as Anglican alienation. Probably even tories recognised this. They accepted royal policy because they knew unresolved religious tension had weakened English Protestants under James II, and might weaken them again as they resisted the forcible return of that man. Moreover, Jonathan Israel has shown that toleration was vital to maintain the spiritually diverse alliance which the prince had built against Louis on the continent. If William was seen to accept religious intransigence in his new realm, some of his foreign allies might become restive. He therefore had to demonstrate he was no religious bigot. This not only dictated pressure for the toleration act, it also pushed against any continued persecution of those groups (such as Catholics and Jews) who had been left outside its terms. As a result, actual toleration in William's England went far further than the restricted terms of the toleration act might suggest.

By the end of 1689 the main lines of William's religious position were staked out. He may not have secured the generous religious settlement he would personally have preferred. There was no repeal of the tests, no broadening of the church to include non-conformists, and only a limited toleration which did not formally extend beyond doctrinally orthodox Protestants. Yet, despite these disappointments, he had achieved something more important. By pursuing a moderate and pragmatic line, and being prepared to sacrifice his own religious preferences for a greater goal, he had kept most strains of religious opinion behind his regime and his war effort. He had reassured the majority of the tories enough to keep them on board, and had granted just enough to the whigs to keep them happy. Having secured this difficult aim, the king determined not to jeopardise it. He removed himself from direct involvement in church affairs, while encouraging initiatives which might have appeal across the religious spectrum.

After 1689, William surrendered control of the church of England to solid Anglicans. He realised his Dutch Calvinist background made many of his subjects jumpy, and so abdicated his role as spiritual governor. While his wife was alive, she handled ecclesiastical patronage and policy.

Once she had died, control passed to a commission of bishops – most of whom had been promoted by the queen as she had filled vacancies caused by death, or by the deprivation of churchmen who could not swear loyalty to the new regime. In approach, these people kept up conciliation of tory opinion by trying to strengthen the church. Even though the promoted bishops were drawn heavily from the group of London clergy who had advanced comprehension in 1689, they dropped their open espousal of concessions to dissent, and instead tried to improve the pastoral provision, institutions and social standing of the establishment. Thus the new bishops were vigorous in preaching, confirming youngsters and disciplining errant clergy in their dioceses. They co-operated in writing Burnet's new manual for ministers – *A Discourse of the Pastoral Care* (1692) – which set out a strategy of intense clerical supervision of parishioners to restore the church to the heart of local communities. They also attempted to rebuild the system of church courts which judged parishioners' moral behaviour; and they issued a comprehensive set of injunctions in 1695 which tightened the application procedure for ordination, took action against non-resident clergy and bishops, and cracked down on clerical impropriety.[23] This soothing of Anglican opinion was balanced by some appeal to dissent, but this came in a form which was less likely to alienate tory support than formal concessions. Encouraging the campaign for 'reformation of manners' (action against such moral crimes as drunkenness, adultery, prostitution and profane swearing), the queen and bishops backed a long-standing non-conformist demand for a more godly society and made it clear that dissenters were welcome to join in this national campaign for religious renewal. As the historian Craig Rose has pointed out, they thus conciliated dissenters with assurances of their importance and of their belonging within a broadly conceived English Protestantism: but did this without resuscitating the divisive bogey of comprehension.[24]

This policy of moderation (and, on William's part, of virtual invisibility) in church affairs was remarkably successful. For the bulk of the reign, English politics was notable for the absence of hot religious controversy. While the status of dissenters had been the meat of dispute since the Restoration, religious issues lay relatively dormant after 1689, at least until the king's last years. From the mid-1690s, tories began to feel too much had been granted at the revolution. They complained that the remaining measures against non-conformists were not being properly enforced; and that non-Anglicans were too visible, powerful and rich. In response they began a campaign to revive convocation as the spearhead of a drive against unorthodoxy.[25] Yet even though this campaign put religion back at the centre of party controversy, it did not endanger

William's central achievement. Trying to conciliate both wings of English Protestantism to unite them against France, the king had gained the broad loyalty of both Anglicans and dissenters, and so removed the danger that religious dispute might result in revolt. He had granted non-conformists the bare liberties which were needed as a minimum solution to the problem of dissent, but rather than follow his own inclinations and go much further, he had reassured churchmen that he would back their privileged position. As a result, even the disputes of the late 1690s did not threaten the stability of the regime. William at first resisted the Anglican demand for a convocation, but then he fell back into compromise. He allowed the body to sit in 1701, though made it clear he would not permit a general witch-hunt against dissent. Probably only an outsider with continental priorities would have been as happy to play such a limited and pragmatic role as governor of the church. Probably, however, it took a king willing to be such a cipher to calm ecclesiastical politics.

William and party organisation

The king's obsession with France helped him ease party tensions over the constitution and religion. However, as with most political battles, it was less issues which divided whigs and tories in the 1690s than their personal enmities, and their organisational rivalries. At base, the two sides did not hate each other because of their nice differences on church and state, but because they had spent the previous ten years building up party machines with which to destroy each other. Unless William could calm these more visceral emotions, his achievements on points of principle would be chimeras. He needed to calm personal hatred and fears, and lead the political organisations into more peaceful pastures, or his realm would remain divided against itself. Once again, the king seems to have been successful. In the 1690s, the passion of party rivalry found bloodless expression, if it did not subside. Once again, it was William's European career which helps explain why.

A useful starting point here is to consider how Charles and James had treated party sentiment and organisation. Both William's predecessors had tried to harness partisan energies to strengthen the court. For instance, once Charles had found the courage to resist exclusion in 1681, he effectively entered into a pact with the tories. They would preach up the divine hereditary right of kings, and he would lend royal power to help them destroy the common enemy. In the period of the 'tory reaction', the king appointed tory ministers to national positions of power, and he packed judicial benches to ensure easy convictions of whig leaders for treason. He also collaborated with tories in the localities as they tried to root out their rivals. He used his prerogative to remodel borough charters in the tory interest; he drove whigs off commissions of the peace; and he supported prosecutions of non-conformists for worshipping outside the church. In this way, he hoped to harness the power of tory passions to his own cause. James's attitude was similar. At first aping his brother's alliance with tories (he used royal influence to help secure their landslide victory in the election of 1685), he later switched to wholehearted backing of the whigs when they seemed more in tune with his policy (at least in seeking greater religious toleration). For the bulk of his reign, James used whigs as tools to secure his aim of breaking Anglican power. He sacked Charles's tory ministers, backed judicial commissions to investigate the excesses of the tory reaction, reversed his brother's purges of local government, and tried to build up the whig interest as a way of securing a parliament which might dismantle the privileges of the church. Both kings therefore became party kings in an attempt to bolster their own position.

William, as in so many other areas, behaved very differently. Partly this was for the reasons already explored. He wanted to unite whigs and tories against France, and reasoned that using royal power to help one side destroy the other was unlikely to produce this result. More interestingly, though, William may have been applying lessons from his Dutch career. By 1688, he already had considerable experience of dealing with parties. The United Provinces were split between the prince's own supporters, and the more republican 'states' party, so William had already needed skills appropriate to partisan politics to wield influence in his native land. Most importantly he had learned that promoting one's vociferous supporters was not always the best route to real power. It is worth reviewing the history again, for it helps explain why he differed so much from his predecessors.

In the years immediately after he had come to power in the Provinces, William had behaved like his uncles. For a period in and after 1672, he had allied closely with the 'Orange' party in Dutch politics – benefiting from their promotion of him as he, in turn, promoted them to positions of power. He had systematically purged the old 'states' grouping from the magistracies of provincial towns and replaced them with his cronies. At first, this approach paid dividends. The prince's actions chimed with popular anger at the old guard's performance against Louis XIV, and public opinion cheered his takeover. Soon, however, the tide turned. As the Orange party came closer to domination, resentment grew at its monopolisation of power. William and his allies began to be seen as arrogant and corrupt, and their partisan approach was seen as excluding perfectly patriotic politicians from serving the republic. As a result, the prince's opponents organised against him, and one-time supporters defected. Men once enthusiastic for Orange rule became disappointed with the prince's factionalism, or resented that they had not scooped quite the booty secured by his inner circle. By the later 1670s this discontent was overwhelming. William lost control of the Provinces, and the Dutch made peace with Louis against his will.

After this setback, William thought more carefully about factional politics. He realised that trying to use a party to dominate a state could be counter-productive. Opponents could not be winkled out of all their bolt-holes and, sooner or later, they would gather other malcontents around them. In the 1680s, therefore, William tried a wholly contrasting approach. He moderated his party stance, making sure that he consulted and conciliated people from the states party as well as his Orange group-ing. As a result, he began to recover his political position. He found he could work with erstwhile opponents, and reduce their suspicions of him. The triumph of the new approach came in 1688, when the burgomeesters of Amsterdam – always the people most opposed to his domination of the Provinces – accepted the logic of his invasion of England. Thus by the time William arrived in London, his continental experience led him to very different conclusions to his uncles. He had been forced to realise how dangerous exclusive co-operation with one party was. He had seen the advantages of balancing political favours, and continuing to talk – even to people who had once seemed so opposed to him. Above all, he had learned he must avoid building up resentment against his own rule by helping one party destroy the other.

To see how William applied this lesson in England, it will be necessary to narrate his dealings with the two parties. The story of William's shifts of support between whigs and tories has been put off so far, because it is somewhat complex. However, it must now be told, because its complexity is much of its point. Although the exact details of the king's policy can be hard to remember, it was precisely because the king refused to follow a straightforward line, that he succeeded in managing party conflict.

On coming to the throne, William was determined to include both parties in his government. The first team of ministers he appointed was broadly whig (the prince had been working more closely with whigs in his plans for invasion) – but it included prominent tories to try to placate that faction. Among these was the anti-exclusionist earl of Nottingham, who was appointed one of the two secretaries of state; and Thomas Osborne, the earl of Danby who had been Charles's chief minister in the 1670s and who was now made Lord President of the Council. As can be imagined, such ministers made strange bedfellows with men who had suffered for opposing James's accession. Suspicion between the two sides began at once. Tories attacked the whigs for imagined plots to destroy the church of England; while whig members of the government accused the tories of treachery against the new king. By the winter of his first year William had realised that a mixed administration would not work. Especially horrified by the whig's factiousness, and impressed by the quiet and efficient loyalty of Nottingham, he swung towards the tories. In early 1690 an election was called to weaken the hold of the intransigent whigs in the Commons. Once it was over, leading whigs were eased out of the ministry until their leader, the earl of Shrewsbury, resigned.

Nottingham's ascendancy after William's first year promised saner government. The tory-led administration got down to the business of managing the war, and brought the nation through the king's first absences in Ireland and Flanders. Within a relatively short while, however, the new ministry was in trouble. Its chief difficulty was military. The years 1690–93 were some of the most frustrating in the conflict as Louis's armies advanced in Flanders, and as a series of projected 'descents' (or amphibious operations against the French coast) had to be abandoned to the ministry's embarrassment. To add to these woes, the court suffered an onslaught by country-minded MPs. Many backbenchers were hungry for place and triennial legislation, and were incensed by reports of mismanagement in public finance. By 1693, Nottingham's reputation was sinking fast. Hostile whigs scented blood, and began to intimate that the nation's trials could be attributed to the earl, whose de facto heart was not really in William's grand project. France's capture of a richly laden portion of England's merchant fleet as it sailed to Smyrna in Turkey was the last straw. Facing a clamour to dismiss Nottingham, William consulted the old political plotter, the earl of Sunderland, who advised him to swing back towards the whigs. Sunderland argued that a group centred on John Somers, Charles Montagu and Tom Wharton was more cohesive – and so would be more effective – than the current ministry. He also suggested that these whigs, unlike the tories, could never be accused of secret support for the Jacobite cause. In November, William reluctantly followed this advice. Nottingham was dismissed (albeit with a message of thanks for his 'fidelity' from the king); and a period of whig domination began.[26]

The remainder of William's reign saw the same switching between parties which had marked the early years. In the mid-decade the whigs remained triumphant. Members of the junto (the label rapidly attached to Somers's tight political grouping) organised a more successful stage of the war – in particular developing new instruments of public credit to finance the conflict, and benefiting from William's first major victory at Namur in the late summer of 1695. The junto also made gains in the 1695 general election, and exercised a tight discipline over their followers in the Commons. Certainly, they faced occasional difficulties. Attempts at improving England's debased currency by a wholesale recoinage caused economic hardship, and a group of country-minded whigs led by Robert Harley refused to support the junto once it became the court party.

Early signs of government weakness, however, were reversed at the start of 1696. Then, discovery of the assassination plot against William rallied public support around the ministry, and created an atmosphere of suspicion in which whigs could accuse tories of complicity with the conspiracy. Using the 'association' as a partisan weapon, the junto were able to dismiss many tories from local offices. They insisted that all public servants join this league to defend the regime, knowing that tories would be unable to swear its oath that William was a legal and rightful monarch.

This whig victory of 1696 was very nearly complete. However, as with all party advances in the 1690s, it proved temporary. Harley's group allied with and rallied the tories, and soon found an opportunity to humiliate the government. When it became clear that William wished to retain a large standing army even after the treaty of Ryswick, and that he expected his ministers to deliver this for him, Harley led opposition to the force. By lobbying a House of Commons which was sceptical of the king's motives, and launching an energetic campaign against the army in the press, the tories and country-whigs swept all before them. In this debacle, the junto earned the contempt – not only of the parliamentary majority who opposed them – but also of the king who resented their failure to save his army. From 1697, therefore, the whig ministry was in danger. It held its own well enough in the 1698 general election, but soon found itself mired in opposition attacks on the king's foreign policy (particularly his approach to dividing the Spanish empire), and on William's grants of land to supporters in Ireland. As a result, what little royal favour remained, evaporated. By 1700 the king had, once again, had enough of his ministers. On 27 April, Somers was sacked, and the junto administration terminated.

In this situation, William was reluctant to turn back to the tories. He blamed them for the destruction of his army, and had been soured by their attacks upon the partition treaties. Accordingly, he tried to build a non-partisan ministry, appointing minor stopgaps to the posts vacated by the junto. Yet within weeks, the monarch came to realise that Harley's party was not a bad bet as a government. Re-invigorated under its leader, the alliance of tories and country whigs began to take over the king's business as the junto disintegrated. For example, Harley and his allies had piloted money bills through the Commons in winter of 1699–1700, thus ensuring the court remained solvent. William soon surrendered to the logic of this situation, and rebuilt a tory ministry. In the second half of 1700 he opened negotiations which led to the appointment of tories such as Sidney Godolphin as first lord of the treasury, and the earl of Rochester as viceroy in Ireland. He also agreed to call an election for January 1701 which it was hoped would provide a majority for the new men; and to support Harley's bid for the speakership of the Commons when parliament re-assembled.

The new team got off to a good start. Most importantly, it secured the act of settlement which decreed that the protestant House of Hanover would succeed to the throne after the princess Anne. It thus ended the major uncertainty about England's political future. Yet as with most of William's ministries, Harley's men were soon in trouble. Their misfortune was to be in power as Louis XIV renewed his continental expansion. When the French king accepted the will of Carlos II of Spain, which presented the whole of the Spanish empire to a cadet branch of France's ruling house, William determined to stop him. Unfortunately, however, he found this was the one area in which his tory ministry could not support him wholeheartedly. The king demanded a rapid return to a war footing – but Harley's alliance had been built on opposition to an army which would now need to be re-created to satisfy the king's will. As a result, the ministry dragged its feet in military preparations. In the summer of 1701 an English force was sent to Flanders to help the Dutch ward off any French attack – but it had taken months to decide upon, and it was worryingly small. As might be expected, William became exasperated with his servants. Although hoping to avoid wholesale changes, and giving his men time to respond to the European situation, he also began casting his eyes back to the whigs who had managed his conflict so enthusiastically in the mid-1690s. Again taking the advice of Sunderland, the king began to negotiate with junto leaders. Somers urged that an election be held to cash in on public appetite for a new war with France, and to increase whig representation. William agreed. In November 1701, parliament was dissolved, and the construction of a second junto administration was probably only prevented by the king's death.

As the reader was warned, the history of William's dealings with the two parties is dizzying. Fortunately, however, the details of these rapid ministerial changes are probably less important than the overall pattern which they reveal. In particular, there are four trends in William's actions which should be noted, and illustrate his determination never to become a prisoner of one faction. All these trends show him keeping the political process open, refusing to allow parties to destroy each other, and always holding out the hope that the excluded might return peacefully to power.

The first thing to note is that William always tried to preserve a mixture in his ministries. Even though the experience of his first year had taught him the problems associated with a fully balanced ministry, he always did what he could to prevent one party monopolising every government post. This was particularly evident at times when government changed hands. In the account above, the shifts from whig to tory were condensed, so that they appeared to be sudden and complete switches of the king's administrative team. In fact, however, changes of ministry under William were always rolling processes. It took time for him to remove the outgoing party, and new men were appointed gradually over a period of months or even years. Often, indeed, the purge was incomplete by the time political tides changed. Consequently, some members of the outgoing party held on until they were the incoming party once more. At the start of 1690, for example, William did not swing absolutely decisively towards the tories. He had not wanted to lose the prominent whig Shrewsbury (the king was horrified when the secretary resigned), and many whigs stayed in post even after the minister had gone. Richard Hampden remained as Chancellor of the Exchequer; John Somers stayed on as solicitor-general; and – astonishingly – Tom Wharton continued as comptroller of the household. Wild accusations that the tories were trying to poison the king did not persuade William that Wharton could not serve alongside them. Similarly, the swing to the whigs after 1693 was gradual. Nottingham was sacked as secretary of state in November – but it was not until the following March that he was replaced by Shrewsbury; and the customs and excise commissions were not remodelled in favour of the whigs until the summer of 1694. Meanwhile, prominent tories stayed in place. Danby did not leave office until 1695; Sir William Trumbell remained until 1697; and the historian Henry Horwitz found thirty tory placemen in the Commons four years into the junto's dominance.[27] With the late-reign switches to the tories and back being similarly gradual affairs, William showed how reluctant he was to change his servants wholesale. As a result, both parties usually felt they had some stake in the ministry. They could certainly never conclude that the monarch had become their intolerant enemy.

The second important feature of William's handling of party was that he always kept his mind open to oppositions. Even when one party was dominating the government, they were unable to stop the monarch talking to the other side, and countenancing their return to power. We have an intimate insight into this royal flexibility through the marquis of Halifax's 'Spencer House' journals. Over the course of 1689, Halifax was one of William's closest advisers, and he recorded his frequent and frank conversations with the king in a political diary. This remarkable document traces a steady shift in William's loyalties over the course of the first year. At the start of his reign, the king leaned strongly towards the whigs. The journals reflected this, with comments in May that the king 'had heard something was doing against him by the Ch[urch] party', and an outburst that he would have the oaths of loyalty pressed on the House of Lords to flush out Jacobites among the tories there. Yet over time, William's political flexibility won through. He told Halifax he was a 'Trimmer' (the contemporary term for men who moved between the parties to prevent political extremes), and he gradually became politer about the tories as they proved faithful to the revolution. Thus by the end of July, the king was suspecting whigs of plots as well as the tories (Halifax noted that 'there seemed to be [a] turne in the K[ing]'s mind'); and on the 28th of that month he mentioned tory Jacobitism for the last time (a sign which the marquis thought 'sheweth he was then coming over to the Ch[urch – or tory] party'). By mid-August, William was considering whether 'he might rely upon' the tories.[28]

Such willingness to change horses and to explore alternative governments, lasted through the reign and is well illustrated in those shifts of royal allegiance which make the political history of the 1690s so confusing. In the summer of 1693, the king was publicly committed to his tory team of ministers – but he nevertheless opened negotiations with the whigs as his administration foundered. He went behind Nottingham's back to talk to the earl of Sunderland, who recommended the junto to him and brokered talks between the court and Somers's group. Similarly in 1701, the king first started considering the tories as the junto ministry was in its death throes; and then for a second time approached the whigs through Sunderland when disappointed with the tories he had appointed. At one level, of course, such behaviour stoked political tensions. It meant ministers were never quite secure in royal favour, and must have always been suspicious that their royal master was not true to them. At a more important level, however, the king's attitude probably calmed party suspicions. Just as excluded groups felt the king was not an inveterate enemy because they always had a least a few of their people in the ministry, they were also reassured that they might soon return to power.

William's third strategy in dealing with party was to refuse to help the groups destroy each other. Under his predecessors, as we have seen, royal power backed party power whenever the king formed an alliance with one faction. Both Charles and James had used their courts and prerogatives to help their favoured party eliminate their rivals from all levels of government – and, if possible – have opposition leaders prosecuted for treason or misuse of power. William resolutely refused to this. He disapproved of all campaigns of malice or vengeance, and – in total contrast to his uncles – used his powers to block any such vindictiveness.

Again, the year 1689 provides a fine illustration. After the revolution, whigs thought their Christmas had come. The new king, they thought, was one of them. He promoted their religious stance; he gave them the larger share of his first ministry; and they planned to exploit their new advantages against tories. Accordingly, they spent much of the first year of the new regime promoting attacks on their enemies. In particular, they attempted to punish those guilty of excesses in the 'tory reaction' which had followed the exclusion crisis. In early March, whigs began to demand investigations into who had advised Charles II on the policies of his last years. The idea was to identify the men responsible for the attacks on dissenters, for the purges of whigs from borough governments and for the execution of whig leaders after the Rye House plot – and then have them prosecuted for persuading the king to misuse his powers. Frequent references to the need for a 'blood' vengeance showed how far the whigs were planning to go.[29] In May, whigs pushed further. They persuaded the Commons that ten categories of offences from the 1680s should be examined to find out who had been guilty of them; while in June they pressed the king to sack all ministers who had served James II in his privy council, or had articles of impeachment approved against them by the Commons. This last move would touch no whigs, but it would affect prominent tories such as Nottingham and Carmarthen. In the winter of 1689–90, the intransigents launched their boldest initiatives. They set up a Lords committee charged with identifying those guilty of excesses in the tory reaction, and promoted a clause in a corporation bill which would have disqualified from public office all those who had collaborated in Charles II's remodelling of town government. Almost all tories, local and national, had supported this royal action to remove whigs: they would all have to go if the clause passed.

Yet to the whigs' horror, William would not help them in their campaign. Instead, he insisted it was important to forget the past, and to unite the nation by protecting people against old resentments. On 25 March, he sent a message to the Commons, urging that controversies over the 'disorders in the late times' be settled.[30] He proposed – not wholesale prosecution – but a generous and inclusive amnesty which would protect all but a few notorious offenders from any action against them for past crimes.

Over the next months, William followed this with repeated calls for progress on a bill of indemnity, and interventions to scupper the whigs' initiatives in parliament. The king sent his servants to the whig leadership over the summer to tell them to cool their campaigns; he made further calls for an act of grace in speeches to parliament on 19 October 1689 and 21 March 1690;[31] and stiffened tory resolve to oppose the hostile clause in the corporation bill. When this bill came up for debate in the Commons on 10 January 1690, messages were sent from court that the king would welcome rejection of the controversial amendment. Accordingly, it was voted down by an alliance of tories and of more independent MPs who did not want to upset the monarch. William's final action against whig factiousness came only a fortnight later when he surrendered to tory appeals and dissolved parliament. Although there were many issues which alienated the king from the whigs, one of the final straws was their repeated hampering of the king's indemnity. A vote on 21 January to investigate whole types of offence before granting an amnesty (rather than adopting the quicker route of simply excepting a few serious offenders by name) led the king to suggest a new parliament might be necessary. In many ways, therefore, the election of 1690 was royal punishment on the whigs for their partisanship.

Throughout the rest of the reign, William kept up his defence of parties assaulted by their rivals. We have already seen how he opposed whig attempts to sweep tories out of office by proffering unacceptable oaths of loyalty. In 1693, he was prepared to install a whig administration in Whitehall, but he refused to sanction the wholesale removal of local tories from county commissions of the peace which his new ministers demanded. Throughout the 1690s, he shocked his ministers with his lukewarm support of his servants at elections. In 1696, he was unhappy about whig attempts to use the association to remove tories: in the next couple of years the campaign against those who refused to swear to join relaxed rapidly, and non-associators were soon being re-appointed to commissions of the peace.[32] In all this moderation, the king may have offended bigoted party leaders – but he was again laying deeper foundations for stability. After 1688, excluded parties not only had men in the ministry and lines of communication with the king, they also gained a guarantee that the full force of court power would not be turned against them.

The final royal strategy in dealing with party was to reward responsible and effective government, whichever party was prepared to provide it. If close attention is paid to *why* William shifted allegiance at the moments he did, it was only ever marginally because he preferred the principles or the personnel of the new party. Rather, it was always principally because he believed the newly favoured faction would provide a more efficient executive: especially in what he saw as his ministers' prime function – countering France. In particular, two crimes seem to have dimmed William's love of his servants and to have led him to court the other side. First, putting factional bickering above national mobilisation would lead to rapid loss of favour. The whigs of 1689 found this. William had originally thought he would be their ally. He lost patience with them, however, because they attacked tories who were playing their part in organising the war. Similarly, tories lost royal support in 1701 by trying to impeach the junto lords. The king had been working well with Harley and his allies, but their factional vindictiveness at a moment of national emergency helped persuade William to turn back towards the whigs. An administration's second great failing was to lose control of the Commons. Whenever MPs' complaints against administrations grew loud, the king would fear for the war and would search for alternatives – however fond of his old servants he had become. The classic example here was Nottingham. Over the period 1689–93 William had come to see the earl as his most loyal and hard-working minister. Yet, as Nottingham's influence over the Commons waned, the king began looking again at the whigs. Although loathing their self-interest, he came to realise their tight parliamentary discipline would be useful if it could be harnessed to the war effort. He accordingly took Sunderland's advice to move them into office. In 1697–1700, the men brought in at this reverse suffered the same fate. William had grown to respect, and even like, Somers during his stewardship of the later stages of the war. He knew that the junto was committed to opposing Louis, and saw that they had tried to save his army after the treaty of Ryswick. When, however, Somers's group found themselves outmanoeuvred by Harley's tory–country alliance in parliament, these preferences for whig personnel and policy counted for little. Realising that having a government which could deliver a Commons majority for some resistance to France was better than having an administration which, although keener to stop Louis, was now in a minority, the king swung once again to the tory side.

William, therefore, demonstrated a multi-faceted neutrality in the 1690s. He preferred mixed teams of ministers; he kept talking to oppositions; he refused to allow one side to use official power to destroy the other; and he appointed the most effective ministers whatever their party allegiance. In all this, we see once again the paradox of William's use of power in England and Wales. He brought benefits to his new realm, even though the focus of his thoughts was not there. William behaved in the ways we have outlined because his objective was to unite all sides for his continental war. He was also guided by his Dutch political experience, and he quite possibly found it easy to work with both whigs and tories because his foreign upbringing meant he cared little which side won petty English squabbles. Yet, even though the king's approach was born of indifference to England and its party struggles, it transformed the way those battles were conducted. It guided partisan politics into peaceful channels, and established conditions in which a divided society could yet be a stable one.

This was achieved because William's strategy prevented backing either party into a corner. Under Charles and James, factions had sometimes despaired. Excluded from court, having no contact with the centres of power, and being pursued with the full authority of the state as well as the hatred of their rivals, they could easily conclude there was no way to survive but by illegal or violent means. That was why whigs flirted with rebellion at the time of the 'Rye House Plot', and why Monmouth invaded. It was also why many tories abandoned their doctrines of non-resistance under James and helped William plot his revolution. Under the new king, however, such desperation was unlikely. As we have seen, William never excluded any party completely. Everybody saw the monarch listened to both sides; they knew that the court would never become a weapon of party struggle, and that opposition parties had every chance of a rapid and peaceful return to favour. Violence and insurrection in the party interest were therefore unnecessary, and it is remarkable how quickly they ceased after 1688.

Moreover, the means of winning royal support also dictated calm action. Because the king disapproved of vindictive factionalism, and was prepared to work with any responsible government which controlled the Commons, the routes to power were now moderate and peaceful. Success against party enemies came not through plot, rebellion, impeachment or purge: it came through sober and efficient administration; it came from tight organisation of supporters in Lords and Commons; and it came from winning elections though local organisation, nursing of constituencies and production of persuasive propaganda. As a result, party men poured their energies into these activities. The dominant images of late Stuart politics were not conspiratorial cabals or show trials for treason. Rather they were pictures of men engaged in peaceful – if passionate – persuasion. Characteristic snapshots of politics in the 1690s might include Tom Wharton, the junto leader, drinking with a High Wycombe shoemaker's wife to secure his vote; Charles Davenant, the tory pamphleteer, inventing the paper villain Tom Double as the star of his satirical *Modern Whig* pamphlets; Robert Harley co-ordinating a press onslaught against the junto after the peace of Ryswick; John Somers carefully checking the arithmetic of division in the Commons and penning his own response to his critics in the pamphlet debates over the army.[33] Such strategies were essential under William because his continental obsessions and education meant they were the only way to influence the king. As these types of tactic were pursued, however, they calmed and ritualised party conflict. By 1702, England and Wales were well on the way to a functioning two-party system. Factions appealed to parliament and to public opinion, not arms; and they prepared to replace each other in ordered transfers of power.

William, then, achieved what seemed so impossible in 1688. He contained English party politics. In retrospect, the techniques he used did not seem very extraordinary. The monarch took a moderate line on the great principles of constitution and religion, and demonstrated that he would never become a prisoner of either party machine. In the preceding decades, however, it had been difficult for William's uncles to see how simple the trick could be. Being English themselves, they had been too involved in the people and policies in conflict; having grown up at a royal court, they could not accept the surrender of monarchical control which compromising between parties involved. William, focused on events outside England, and with an experience which came from a political system dominated by party and representative assemblies, *could* see the solution. Indifference to the kingdom once again had its benefits.

Notes

The birth of party politics can be followed in Mark Knights, *Politics and Opinion in Crisis* (CUP, 1994); and Tim Harris, *London Crowds in the Reign of Charles II* (CUP, 1987). The best general guides to constitutional argument in the 1690s are H.T. Dickinson, *Liberty and Property* (Weidenfeld & Nicolson, 1977), chs 1–2; and J.P. Kenyon, *Revolution Principles: The Politics of Party 1689–1720* (CUP, 1977), chs 1–6. The religious issues to the end of 1689 are covered in John Spurr, *The Restoration Church of England* (Yale UP, 1991) – after that they can be followed in Claydon, *William III*, ch. 4; and Rose, *England in the 1690s*, chs 5–6. The story of William's interactions with the parties is well told in Rose, ch. 3; it is told in exhaustive detail in Horwitz, *Parliament, Policy and Politics;* and is usefully summarised in E.L. Ellis, 'William III and the politicians', in Geoffrey Holmes, (ed.), *Britain after the Glorious Revolution* (Macmillan, 1969), pp. 115–34.

1 John Dalrymple, *Memoirs of Great Britain and Ireland* (1790), **2**, appendix to part 2, book 4, 187.

2 Ibid., p. 190.

3 Ibid., pp. 188, 189, 192.

4 Mark Goldie, 'The revolution of 1689 and the structure of political argument', *Bulletin of Research in the Humanities* **83** (1980), 473–521.

5 Singer, *Correspondence . . . Clarendon*, **2**, 261.

6 *LJ*, **14**, 119–20.

7 BL Add Ms 19253, f.35; Horwitz, *Parliament, Policy and Politics*, pp. 56, 96.

8 [Gilbert Burnet], *An Enquiry into the Present State of Affairs* (1688).

9 Gilbert Burnet, *A Pastoral Letter . . . Concerning the Oaths* (1689).

10 See [Edmund Bohun], *The History of the Desertion* (1689).

11 For the sermons, see Claydon, *William III, passim*. For pamphlets, see William Lloyd, *A Discourse of God's Way of Disposing of Kingdoms* (1691); [Edward Stillingfleet], *A Discourse Concerning the Unreasonableness of a New Separation* (1689).

12 For doubts about William's piety, see Jonathan Israel, 'William III and toleration', in Ole Grell *et al.* (eds), *From Persecution to Toleration* (Clarendon Press, 1980), pp. 129–70.

13 See W.A. Speck's entry on Mary in the forthcoming *New Dictionary of National Biography* (Clarendon Press, probably 2004).

14 Burnet, *History*, **1**, 789.

15 *A Form of Prayers Used by His Late Majesty K. William III when he Received the Holy Sacrament* (1704).

16 Israel, *Dutch Republic,* pp. 839, 857.

17 *Pensionary Fagel's Letter* (The Hague, 1687).

18 *The Expedition of the Prince of Orange* (1689), p. 57; Russell J. Kerr and Ida Coffin Duncan (eds), *The Routledge Papers* (private publication, 1928), p. 57; Simon Patrick, *The Autobiography* (Oxford, 1839), pp. 142–3.

19 *CJ*, **10**, 51.

20 Grey, *Debates,* **9**, 190–8, 200–4.

21 Narcissus Luttrell, *A Brief Relation of Affairs of State* (Oxford, 1857), **1**, 606; *LJ*, **14**, 320; *CSPD 1689–90*, p. 314.

22 Israel, 'William III and toleration'.

23 Gerald Bray (ed.), *The Anglican Canons, 1529–1947* (Boydell, 1998), pp. 830–3.

24 Craig Rose, 'Providence, Protestant union and godly reformation in the 1690s', *Transactions of the Royal Historical Society* (1993), 151–70.

25 The clarion call was [Francis Atterbury], *Letter to a Convocation Man* (1696).

26 Henry Horwitz, *Revolution Politicks: The Career of Daniel Finch, Second Earl of Nottingham* (CUP, 1968), p. 146.

27 Horwitz, *Parliament, Policy and Politics,* p. 217.

28 Foxcroft, *Life and Letters*, **2**, 203–47.

29 Rose, *England in the 1690s,* p. 74.

30 *CJ*, **10**, 64.

31 *LJ*, **14**, 320, 433.

32 Anthony Fletcher, *Reform in the Provinces* (Yale UP, 1986), pp. 27–8.

33 Richard Steele, *Memoirs of . . . Thomas .. Marquess of Wharton* (1715), pp. 33–4; [Charles Davenant], *The True Picture of a Modern Whig* (1701) and *Tom Double Return'd out of the Country* (1702); J.A. Downie, *Robert Harley and the Press* (CUP, 1979); [John Somers], *A Letter Ballancing the Necessity of Keeping a Land-force* (1697).

Chapter Five

William and the English State

The problem: the weakness of the English state in the seventeenth century

When the French attacked the Dutch in 1672, their English allies were supposed to play a major part in victory. As Louis's troops marched with terrifying force across the Provinces, Charles II's navy was supposed to gain control of the North Sea, to crush the Dutch fleet's resistance, and to land an invasion force on Holland's shore to trap the republic between two enemy forces. Unfortunately, the plan did not work out. Although the success of French troops meant the Dutch had few resources to deploy in the maritime conflict, and although the English did manage to dominate the open seas, the Stuarts were unable to make much of their advantage. Badly harried in an engagement at Sole Bay at the start of the conflict, England's fleet had to delay any decisive action until it could be refitted. Bad weather told against any operations for the rest of year, and then English merchantmen began sustaining heavy losses to Dutch privateers. When parliament met in February 1673 it undermined the war effort by using the crown's need for finance as an opportunity to complain about the king's religious policy. Consequently the public support, the planning and the preparation needed for an invasion of the Provinces was lacking, and Stuart will to continue the fight dwindled. Soon England began to negotiate with William for a way out of the battle. Thus even as France's blitzkrieg across the Provinces had shown the awesome power of its military machine, and as Holland's survival in the face of the onslaught had shown the robustness of its forces and administration, England's war effort had been a shambles. The Stuart realm had fallen far behind its rivals in developing an effective military capability.[1]

England had been having difficulties mobilising for over a century. Queen Elizabeth had sustained conflict with Spain for over fifteen years at the end of her reign – but the strains had soon begun to show. After her success in deflecting the Armada, she had few brilliant victories, and the burden of war taxation drew damaging protests from taxpayers. Viewing this, James I recognised peace was his only viable policy. He ended the conflict as soon as he came to the throne, and refused to get involved in the war which broke out on the continent in 1618, despite huge pressure to use England's forces to stave off a total defeat of European Protestantism. When conflict eventually came, the wisdom of James's caution was proved. In the late 1620s a series of military expeditions to the continent fizzled out in abject failure, and the financial demands of the crown fed the constitutional crisis of that era. Charles I regained some stability by making peace in the 1630s. However, when faced with an invasion from Scotland at the end of the decade, his regime collapsed. A tax strike deprived him of revenue, and the militia – his only land force – refused to march out of its respective home counties. In the ensuing civil war, parliamentary forces had mobilised successfully, and Cromwell's regime had shown how an effective standing army could be financed from innovations such as the excise. Yet these fiscal–military expedients had been unpopular, and their legality had been questionable. As a result, they had encouraged the monarchical restoration in 1660, which brought back military weakness as surely as it reimposed many other features of the old regime. Charles II was deprived of a standing army and sufficient revenue, so his wars were profoundly disappointing. Conflict with the Dutch in 1665–67 was humiliating, with the English fleet destroyed in its own harbour in the Medway, while the inglorious war of 1672–74 has just been reviewed. As this survey should make clear, there was an underlying problem with England's military efforts in the seventeenth century. She lacked the effective central government structures which could organise a war. She had no workable system of financing conflict; no administration capable of channelling resources to the armed forces; and no professional army or navy. In the language of historians, she had not established a sufficiently modern state.

There were, perhaps, two main causes of this weakness. First, England had become relatively inexperienced at warfare in the early modern period, and had not built up the financial, administrative and military structures which were needed to sustain it. While other powers such as France, the Netherlands, Sweden and Austria had been involved in almost continual struggle since the early sixteenth century, England had played only a marginal and occasional role in these wars. There are several reasons why this was so. Certainly the pacific temperaments of monarchs such as Elizabeth and James I played a role, as did reluctance by a commercial nation to encourage conflicts which disrupted trade routes. Most importantly, though, England's position on an island limited her engagement with foreign war. The Channel had always allowed the English some protection against European tensions, but in the early modern era it became an even more effective barrier because it prevented the country becoming involved in a new style of conflict. As a result of a series of changes in tactics and technology (often referred to as the 'military revolution'), warfare in the western world had ceased to be a matter of small and mobile cavalry actions. Instead, it had come to involve huge armies of foot soldiers, who spent most of their time besieging almost impregnable fortresses. This new sort of struggle was virtually impossible to conduct overseas. Whereas small cavalry forces could be easily shipped abroad, and sustained once in hostile territory, the logistical problems of moving huge armies across water, and then supplying them for prolonged actions were prohibitive. Consequently, English monarchs had not been able to conduct campaigns abroad, and foreign rulers had been dissuaded from attempting conquests of England.

This lack of war had meant a lack of war preparation. The English had never, for instance, established a standing army. Unable to deploy such a thing against rival powers, they had not bothered to construct a land force, and instead had relied on the militia. They had thus placed national defence in the hands of ramshackle bands of civilians who were unpaid and under-equipped, and would often go years without training, or even mustering. This lack of a standing army meant that there was no need to construct logistical or financial support for such a force. On the continent, states had been forced to build large and professional civil services to manage their huge military machines, and had needed to find secure ways of raising revenue to pay for their men in arms. In England, these pressures did not apply. The central civil service remained tiny, with most administration being done by local volunteers on town corporations, country commissions of the peace and parish vestries. The taxation system remained similarly rudimentary. In the early Stuart period, there were almost no full-time, dedicated, tax collectors and the main forms of Tudor wartime exaction – the 'subsidies', the 'fifteenths' and 'tenths' voted by parliament – were running into trouble. Since the tax burden on individuals was assessed by the same local elites who would have to pay most of the levy, these instruments yielded as little as one might expect. With crown lands sold to cover a deficit even in peacetime finances, the customs remained the only moderately reliable source of money until the excise was introduced in the mid-seventeenth century.

If relative peace had been the first major reason for the weakness of England's military state, the second was 'country' suspicion of the court. When we examined earlier why the political nation distrusted the king's rule in the seventeenth century, we fixed upon anti-popery. Here, it is important to flesh out the reasons for this country sentiment a little more fully. The English feared court Catholicism because of the marriages and religious policies of their rulers – but their horror was deepened as successive monarchs tried to remedy the weaknesses of the Stuart state in ways which reminded their subjects of Catholic regimes abroad. Throughout the seventeenth century, the court recognised that it would have to try to overcome its fiscal and military problems, or England would cease to count in European affairs. As it did this, however, it adopted policies which appeared to be modelled on France, Spain and Austria – countries where intolerant popery had triumphed. As a result, parliament and the wider political nation moved to block royal initiatives. Monarchs tried to establish secure finances, build up a civil service and improve the readiness of the armed forces, but each time they did this, they were accused of popish policy and their plans were frustrated by parliamentary and popular opposition. England, therefore, not only lacked the experience of war and the military need which would have established a more modern state, but her dominant political creed – country anti-popery – worked against any such progress.

Examples of the pattern can be drawn from all periods of Stuart rule. Before the civil war, James I and Charles I had tried to tackle the inadequacies of state finances. Recognising the uselessness of the old parliamentary taxes, they tried to secure steady sources of money which they could rely upon to keep the state solvent, and maintain a war capability. In particular, they tried to increase customs duties, and experimented with new forms of exaction – such as Charles's collection of a 'forced loan' in the late 1620s, and his extension of the 'Ship Money' levy to the whole country in 1635. The problem with such initiatives was that they provoked political opposition. Many Englishmen feared that the projects were attempts to bypass parliament's role in approving new taxes, and ultimately to govern without the legislature, as Catholic kings on the continent did. Thus disputes about money stoked the tensions between king and parliament which marked the early Stuart era. The Commons protested that new exactions were illegal because they had not approved them, and in protest started to deny requests from the king for the old parliamentary levies. On the ground, attempts to raise the money faced refusals to pay, and legal challenges in the courts. Resentment at the king's policy fed the horror of popish conspiracy at court which ultimately destroyed Charles I's regime. Royal attempts to build the state thus resulted in a backlash which actually kept it weak. In the later Stuart era, royal attempts to build a standing army provoked a similar pattern of events. Both Charles II and James II hoped to establish a paid, professional land force to supersede the inefficient militia; but both monarchs were accused of founding a popish instrument of absolutism. In the later 1670s, there was widespread anger that Charles had not disbanded an army raised for a war against France when that war had not materialised. In the late 1680s, James's standing force was seen as prime evidence of his evil intent. Resentment at his soldiers contributed to the collapse of his regime in 1688.

Thus William faced a daunting task. He wanted to mobilise English resources to confront Louis, yet his new realm had no recent experience of sustained military effort. It did not have the financial, administrative or military structures which would allow it to support such an endeavour; and its political culture was dominated by suspicion of any attempt to remedy this deficiency. The very earliest debates in William's parliament showed how deep the difficulties ran. When the Commons first met after resolving the constitutional issues of the revolution, it was obvious England would have to go to war to defend the settlement she had just made. It was equally obvious that William would need secure finances to organise this defence. In the discussions at Westminster, however, it was the danger of giving the court too much money which filled men's minds. Debating what revenues to grant the new king from customs and excise, parliamentarians argued that the court should be kept unsure of its funds – and the state kept correspondingly weak – to stop the executive becoming too powerful. As Sir Thomas Clarges put it in a debate on 27 February 1689: 'I think we ought to be cautious of the Revenue, which is the life of the Government ... If you give this Revenue for three years [only], you will be sure of a Parliament.'[2] Thus even as England faced its most pressing foreign threat for decades and needed urgently to boost its fiscal and military machine, the Commons fretted over the influence an increase in state resources might give the court.

William lost the debate in 1689. Despite the new king's appeals for an adequate, settled revenue, the Commons delayed deciding his income for a year – and then came only to a four-year deal, to be reviewed in 1694. Yet, in general, William's efforts to mobilise the English for war were unexpectedly successful. Despite all his problems, he expanded his tax base massively, and organised huge armed forces. By the mid-1690s, government's annual income had jumped from the £1.9 million under James, to nearly £5 million. New levies, such as the land tax, had been proposed and implemented; and older imposts, such as customs and excise, had increased and expanded in range. Government expenditure had exploded still more dramatically. Running just over £2 million a year under James, it grew to over £8 million by 1696. The difference between income and outgoings was covered by successful state borrowing. In 1696, William's regime borrowed £3.3 million – and part of this debt was covered by innovative instruments of public credit which will be described below. All this money financed a huge increase in the armed forces. By the peace of Ryswick William was paying for 75,000 troops and 323 ships. These figures represented 40,000 more troops and 150 more ships than James had commanded, and they meant that about 1.5 per cent of England and Wales's *entire* population (not just her adult male population) was fighting for the country. Such financial and military activity required extra crown agents to collect taxes and manage the logistics of war. James had employed around 4,000 people in the central administration of his state. In the mid-1690s, William had around 12,000 civil servants. England had thus caught up with the states of continental Europe in a remarkably short time. By the peace of Ryswick, the proportion of her people in the armed forces may still have been smaller than in Holland, Sweden or Austria – but it had surpassed France, the country which was the contemporary model of centralised government power.

Even more remarkable than William's success in growing the state, was the acquiescence of the English political nation in the process. The government's taxation and its borrowing were met with very little protest. Subjects willingly gave money in tax and loans, and parliament approved requests from the court for generous supply. Before 1697, there was no sustained concern about the size of the king's armed forces. Even as years without great victory on the battlefield mounted, and as English lives and English trade were lost, there was extraordinarily little questioning of William's basic policy, or of expansion of the state which it entailed. In this change of attitude William triumphed where his predecessors had failed. The new king had expanded his state machinery much more dramatically than earlier Stuarts, but had nevertheless kept it fighting for over eight gruelling years. The question, of course, is how William had worked this feat. Once again, his European objectives and expertise are crucial to the explanation.

William and the Dutch state

Looking at William's continental career prior to 1688, there is one obvious way in which his foreign experience could have helped England build her state. The new king had led the United Provinces. He had, therefore, headed one of the most organised and effective administrative systems in the world, and it is possible that he acted as a conduit for Dutch ideas and expertise in state building. To explore this possibility, it is important to understand the United Provinces' achievement. In the seventeenth century, the Dutch had been able to punch way above their weight in international affairs because their government had been extraordinarily efficient in mobilising the country's resources. For example, in the 1690s the Provinces paid for as many soldiers as England, despite having a population less than two-fifths of her ally's. This success was based on three main accomplishments, which even contemporaries recognised as the central pillars of Dutch power.

First, the Provinces had constructed a remarkably effective army. Founded in the war of independence in the late sixteenth century, this had been reformed and shaped by successive princes of Orange – particularly Maurice in the 1590s – into an unusually disciplined fighting force. Its central feature was that it was kept standing. Unlike the armies of many other states, it was not recruited only at the start of wars, and disbanded in peace, but was kept in a state of readiness, and was garrisoned throughout the republic. Keeping the army standing, of course, allowed better training and control. Full-time soldiers could be drilled in complex military manoeuvres, so the Provinces could pioneer new military techniques. Most famously, the Dutch perfected the 'counter march' in which successive lines of infantrymen would fire co-ordinated volleys of gunshot before retiring through their own ranks to reload. Keeping the army in being certainly posed problems – not least the danger of military coup or disorder. However, the solutions that were found merely made the force more professional. Because the republic was stationing large numbers of soldiers among its civilians, it had to make sure it had a controlled and ordered body. It therefore imposed strict codes of discipline and ensured its men were regularly paid, and so avoided the mutiny, riot and plunder which affected so many other early modern armies. Add to all this the constant experience of the forces (the Provinces were at war 1566–1609, 1621–48, 1652–54, 1665–67 and 1672–78) and the Dutch had an army which contemporaries credited with having altered the entire face of European warfare.[3]

The other two achievements of Provincial state building were financial. The Dutch found ways to make ordinary citizens bear a huge tax burden, and also found ways to secure the credit of government, so that people would lend to it readily. The key to taxation was the development of the excise. In response to the cost of fighting against their enemies, the Provinces had imposed a large number of heavy taxes on various items of consumption – a financial expedient which became one of the most remarked-upon features of Dutch life. Over the earlier seventeenth century, taxes were imposed on soap, beer, grain, spice, coal, iron, butter, candles, cheese, peat, wine, fine cloth and building materials. Sir William Temple was so astounded by the range of excises that he claimed over thirty were paid whenever the citizens of Amsterdam went to a tavern to eat fish and sauce.[4] Another visitor, William Carr, noted that penalties for evading these taxes were so severe that nobody dared bake his own bread, brew his own beer, or keep a hand mill in his house (for fear the authorities would suspect that coffee or mustard grinders were secretly used for grinding corn).[5] In hitting upon the excise, the Dutch found a way of raising huge sums with very little taxpayer resistance. Excises were heavy, but the consumer had no clear notion of exactly how heavy, since the tax was collected from manufacturers or retailers, with their cost disappearing in the general price of the product at market. Excises were also seen as just. They balanced land and property taxes paid mainly by the wealthy with levies which fell on everyone; there were no exemptions for particular ranks in society; and they hit everybody because they were levied on a range of goods from luxuries to staples. As Carr said, if such heavy taxes were imposed in England there would have been 'Rebellion upon Rebellion'.[6] In Holland, however, the method of raising revenue meant it was contributed without protest.

This success in taxation fed through into success in state credit. Because people who had money to lend could see that the Provinces had a steady income from which they might be repaid, they were very willing to advance cash to the Dutch state. They were also willing to charge reasonable rates of interest. In the seventeenth century, the Provinces could borrow at rates of around 6 per cent per annum. By contrast, the French or English crowns – both of which failed to repay loans on occasions – were forced to promise 10–15 per cent to secure sufficient loans. The Dutch eased the situation still further by dedicating the revenue from specific excises to interest payments (so lenders could see exactly where their money would come from), and by borrowing 'long-term'. Setting dates for repayment far in the future, and sometimes even raising 'permanent' loans which would never be repaid, they guaranteed the lender an income for very long periods and so increased the attractiveness of such an investment. As a result, the Dutch government secured a huge proportion of its society's financial resources. If it could not satisfy its hunger for funds through excises, it could always persuade its citizens to lend it the shortfall. Temple was so impressed he claimed that creditors of the Dutch state mourned whenever the government paid off the principal of a loan. Once they had got their money back, they knew not 'how to dispose of it to Interest, with such safety and ease'.[7]

Given the success of Dutch in state-building, it is tempting to suggest William applied the lessons of his homeland to his adopted country, and solved English problems with foreign expertise. This explanation is particularly attractive, as there is evidence of Dutch influence on England's fiscal and military miracle in the 1690s. For example, William's war effort often involved English soldiers being commanded by Dutch troops. Generals from the United Provinces were in overall strategic command of the war effort in Flanders (a situation which led to some complaint that foreigners were sending English troops to their deaths); and individual Dutchmen played important parts in building England's land forces.[8] For instance, William's Dutch favourite, Bentinck, took a crucial administrative role in the vital early months of 1689. He took charge as the army of James II was restructured to fight the war in Ireland and Flanders. The Secretary at War, William Blathwayt, was also vital to the organisation of the military. He may himself have been English – but he had considerable experience of the Netherlands. He had been secretary to the ambassador in The Hague in the late 1660s, and accompanied William to Flanders every year to oversee England's military effort.

In finance too, Dutch example appeared important. In the 1690s the English came to pay for their state in many of the ways the Provinces always had. The excise was increased and extended to cover more items; and the state began to borrow long-term, guaranteeing that income from particular taxes would be used to pay interest. Under William duties were raised on sales of salt, beer, tobacco, wine, spirits, tea, coaches and coffee, and the overall revenue from excise climbed from around half a million pounds a year to one and a half million by 1698. In January 1693 England conducted her first experiment in long-term funded credit, when parliament approved the issue of life annuities. These paid 14 per cent annual interest, the money being paid for the lender's lifetime, and being drawn from the revenue of an additional excise on beer and vinegar. This similarity with finance in Holland was no coincidence. The annuities expedient had been settled upon after consultation with financiers who had cited Dutch practice, and used Dutch terminology, as they advised on organising the loan.[9] In 1694, an even closer parallel was made when a royal charter incorporated the Bank of England. This body was designed along the lines of the Bank of Amsterdam, and played a similar role. It channelled subscribers' money into public debt, and widened the government's credit further by issuing banknotes (promissory notes chargeable to its deposits) which it lent to the crown in lieu of cash and which began to circulate as money. As a range of other financial projects drew on Dutch models in the 1690s, it seemed England was following the Provinces' model of state building.

Given the argument of this book, it would be nice to leave matters there, and claim the new king imported Dutch experience to solve the difficulties of English administration. Unfortunately, however, closer inspection questions whether this simple account of William's achievement holds much water. There are good reasons to question whether the monarch was actually bringing the Dutch solution to state building to his new realm. Most worryingly, there is rather little evidence of the king himself instigating the new policies, or of him employing invited Dutchmen to do this. It is, therefore, hard to see a *royal* conduit for Dutch ideas. For example, it is not clear that the newly enlarged English army really owed much to foreign commanders. England's soldiers might have fought under a Dutch king, and they might have had broad strategy decided by foreign generals, but their own command structure was staffed by natives. Although a continental soldier, the duke of Schomberg, was placed in overall control of forces in England in 1689, his knowledge of the details of the English army was limited. Consequently he relied on Lord Churchill (a leading English officer who had defected to William's camp during the invasion) to do the actual work of organisation. Further down the structure, the new king had far too few Dutch officers to head his English regiments. He therefore turned to local soldiers to do this work. At the start of the reign, a concerted drive was made to persuade James's old officers to switch allegiance to the incoming regime, and Englishmen who had been deprived of their commissions by the old king were reappointed to help organise the troops. It was thus local men – people like Sir John Lanier, Charles Trelawney, Percy Kirk and John Coy – who held the forces together and prepared them for their new challenges on the continent.

Similarly, while some of the financial expedients which paid for the 1690s conflict looked similar to those in the United Provinces, it was not William, or any of his Dutch servants who suggested them. As in so much else, the court stayed in the background as financial policy was formulated. The king told members of parliament that he needed money, and discussed exactly how much he wanted with his ministers, but he left it to those groups of people to determine exactly how the finance would be raised. As a result, the 1690s schemes for new taxes and new forms of public credit originated primarily with Englishmen (or at least with Britons). They came from individual ministers, from backbench MPs and from private projectors; and they were moulded in policy – often in a rather haphazard fashion – by discussions in the Privy Council and the Commons. The Bank of England provides a good example. The king may have been the first and largest subscriber to the Bank, but the idea to set it up had not come from him. Rather it had been the brainchild of William Paterson, the Scots farmer's son and freewheeling London merchant who had floated a raft of financial schemes in the early 1690s. Teaming up with another private projector, Michael Godfrey, he had approached Treasury Commissioner Charles Montagu with his idea, and persuaded him to put it to parliament. There it was discussed alongside alternative expedients to meet the government's growing debt, before MPs approved the scheme. Similarly, proposals for extensions of the excise tended to emerge during wide-ranging, and often unfocused, Commons debate, and were not instantly seized upon as cures for the nation's ills. For instance, on 18 January 1692 a Commons committee heard proposals which sounded like a close aping of the Provinces' fiscal practice. Colonel Henry Goldwell proposed excises on candles, soap and salt, explaining they would be easy to collect because they could be gathered at chandlers, boilers and salt-panners respectively. Yet this was no royal imposition of Dutch models. Goldwell had no close connections to the court, and his ideas got a rough ride. His proposals were rejected as too much like a general excise on all goods; other MPs suggested excises on other products, such as French red wine; and the Commons eventually settled on a quarterly poll tax to meet the king's needs, thus rejecting any extension of the excise that year.[10]

More generally, most of the steps towards a modern state which were made in the 1690s were extensions of English developments, rather than foreign imports. Although those involved may have been influenced by foreign models of how to build an army and establish a secure stream of revenue, they had some domestic foundations on which to build. The administration and military commanded by James II may have been paltry in comparison to his European neighbours, and to the later monsters created by William – but the English had begun to make some progress in state construction by the 1680s, and without major foreign input. In fact, once enthusiasm for finding Dutch parallels to English advances wears off, the extent of Holland's influence actually looks pretty meagre. In the 1690s, foreign ideas were never as important as the legacy of state-building from earlier reigns.

The case is perhaps most obvious with the military. Above, we saw that William used English officers to staff his expanded army. He was, of course, only able to do this because his predecessors had established an English force from which military experience could be drawn. By the end of his reign, Charles II had commanded over 10,000 soldiers. His brother had gone further, first expanding the army to meet the threat of Monmouth's rebellion in 1685, and then fostering it to help him impose his authoritarian rule. By 1688, he had nearly 40,000 men to defend himself, and had built up a corps of experienced and professional officers. It is true that James's force had been humiliated when William invaded. Demoralised by the king's flight, and by high-placed defections to the prince, it had descended into chaos over the winter of 1688–89. Enough survived, however, to form the nucleus of William's army. One third of James's officers were persuaded to stay on to serve a new master, and the new fighting units of the 1690s were built around the remnants of established regiments. William's army therefore looked very like James's. Certainly it was larger, and had been purged of those too committed to the old regime to transfer loyalty to the new but, as John Childs has shown, broad continuity of personnel spelt broad continuity of practice. William's officer corps perpetuated the army which had first trained them, so his forces never got a wholesale overhaul of organisation, discipline and methods, and they remained an English, rather than Dutch, style army.

William's navy was even more clearly a legacy of his predecessors. The English fleet had been steadily enlarged and improved under Charles I, Cromwell and Charles II – the last of these having enjoyed the talents of Samuel Pepys in organising administration and supply. By 1679, Pepys, the secretary to the admiralty, had built up a force of 76 ships and 12,000 men – and although this had declined in his political eclipse during the exclusion crisis, he had drawn up an effective recovery plan when returning to his office in 1684. Under James, £400,000 a year was spent on the navy, and repair to its ships and infrastructure was overseen by a special commission. Thus, when William invaded, he would have been opposed by a formidable fleet, had the wind not been against the English ships, and had not James delayed manning his force because he took so long to believe his son-in-law would actually attack him. On the old king's flight, the fleet's commander Dartmouth could surrender a force of over fifty ships to the Prince of Orange. In the months that followed, the navy was run down because of William's uncertainty about whether to berth or deploy it. In this case, the arrival of the Dutch king seems to have positively harmed English achievements in state-building, until an English admiralty commission could work on the remnants of Pepys's navy in the 1690s.

The pattern of extending domestic advances was repeated in government finance. The English had been making some strides in raising public money in the decades before 1688, and these advances were all ready for the Williamite regime to exploit. For example, the advantages of collecting money through an excise were realised as early as the 1640s and 1650s. The parliamentary and Cromwellian regimes had discovered that an impost raised at points of manufacture could be collected with little popular protest – and that the advantages were increased if it could be collected by a dedicated department, with expert, full-time and salaried staff. The new tax proved so successful that it was retained by the Restoration regimes. Under Charles II, further fiscal advances were made. Tax farming was ended (the state gathered its own money, rather than entrusting the task to private individuals who took a large cut of the proceeds); the customs office and other revenue divisions were remodelled on the efficient lines of the excise department; and the central administration of finance was rationalised by setting the Treasury over all other offices concerned with raising or spending cash. Early steps were also made to improve government borrowing (attempts were made to borrow from the general public via open subscription, rather than relying on cliques of bankers); and specialist civil servants took over from titled aristocrats in the central administration of finance. Taken together, these reforms solved the chronic shortage of public money which had plagued England since the early sixteenth century. By the 1680s, monarchs could command a financial surplus even without grants from parliament, so long as they stayed out of international conflict, and avoided personal extravagance. Charles II was able to outface the exclusionists, and James was able to advance his Catholic policies, because English financial evolution had ensured they were in surplus even without Commons taxes.

Of course, Charles and James had not faced sustained warfare. It is possible, therefore, that England's solvency could not have survived the 1690s without the importation of Dutch methods. Yet even during William's conflicts, the direct impact of models from Holland seems quite weak. The majority of the money raised after the revolution did not come from the methods of finance popular in the Provinces. For example, for every penny raised by long-term borrowing during the war, over four were raised in short-term loans. The English were thus coping with shortfalls in the official budget in broadly the same way that they had always done. Similarly, for every penny raised by extending the excise, nearly two were raised through 'assessed' taxes. These burdens on wealth – especially real estate – were not Dutch imports, but were modelled closely on earlier English forms of direct revenue. Like the assessments granted by parliament from the early 1640s (which in turn learnt many lessons from earlier imposts), they made estimates of people's worth, and then demanded payment of so many shillings in each pound of this sum. Moreover, the levies on wealth coped with the problems which had affected their earlier versions by drawing on specifically English experience. Any doubts about the legitimacy of the taxes were dispelled by requiring parliament to approve them; while fears that burdens might fall unevenly were soothed because they were collected by local officeholders who came from the same social classes as those who had to pay. These lessons were drawn, not from Amsterdam, but from Tudor tax-raising. Meanwhile, difficulties in getting the money into the central treasury were addressed by the administrative improvements made under Charles II, and the problem of under-assessment was solved by imposing a quota on each part of the country so that shires could not shirk their responsibilities. This last trick came not from Holland, but had been built into the sixteenth-century 'fifteenths' and 'tenths', and had been perfected in the experiment with Ship Money in the 1630s. Charles I's naval impost may ultimately have been defeated by political opposition but, before doubts about its legitimacy had led to a tax strike, its quota system had meant it had been collected very successfully. In 1697, all these advances were incorporated into a new land tax, which remained the core of English revenue through the eighteenth century. This tax was successful because its evolution had ensured it was adapted to English sensibilities and English circumstances.

In the light of this evidence, it is hard to argue that William's application of Dutch experience was the magical solution to the problems of English state-building. In the main, the English improved their military and administration in the 1690s by working out their own solutions, and developing trends which earlier English rulers had begun. Yet if the new king did not strengthen the state simply by importing Holland's solutions, the question arises whether his personal influence, and particularly his continental education and focus, played as crucial a role as has been claimed. The answer given below is that they did, but that they did in more subtle ways than a direct application of Dutch example. William's continental attitudes may not have built a new state directly, but they did help transform relations between the administrative machine and the wider political nation. By dispelling suspicion of the king's military and civil servants, they built a partnership between government and people which was essential in the smooth modernisation of govenment.

William's solution: the Protestant state

The key to William's state building was to secure consent. Earlier Stuart kings had realised that England's military, administration and revenue needed improvement, but they had blundered by trying to achieve this without taking their subjects with them in the project. By and large, they had used their prerogative to try to modernise their rule. This had raised suspicions of arbitrary power, and prevented co-operation in overhauling government. In this atmosphere, the English state had failed. Without popular or parliamentary backing, royal initiatives had not secured the finance which only Commons grants could bring, and they had been sacrificed to assuage the country's anger when the legislature met. Our earlier surveys of the seventeenth century showed this happening repeatedly. By contrast, William found a way forward. With his usual talent for a different and imaginative line, he persuaded the political nation to agree to state expansion. Parliament voted for the finance and armies he needed, and the people accepted the burdens of military mobilisation, because the king soothed the fear that big government would threaten their faith and liberties. The next two sections will explore how William managed this. At the end of the chapter, we will ask how much his success owed to his European experience and focus.

If we are seeking the central reason why the English accepted state expansion in the 1690s, the answer is clear. They thought it was essential for William's war. There was unease about the growing reach of the administration, but this was always moderated by the conviction that it was a necessary evil. Without it, people knew they would never defeat France – and they were utterly committed to that defeat. One of the most remarkable features of William's reign was the lack of an alternative foreign policy. Apart from the minority Jacobites, very few questioned whether fighting Louis was wise. Modern historians who have analysed parliamentary debate, or the press, in the 1690s find almost no suggestions that the conflict was a purely continental affair, or that England could stay out once the immediate threat of invasion had been contained.[11] Of course, concerns were expressed about the domestic effects of war. Speeches and pamphlets groaned under the tax burden, they cried against the size and conduct of the army, and dwelt in loving detail on waste unearthed in the administration.[12] Yet such doubts were nearly always accompanied by a determination to beat Louis, and by a recognition that some expansion of the state would be inevitable. For example, MPs readily questioned if William really needed all the money he had asked for. They went through his budget estimates carefully, trying to shave down expenditure on each and every item. They did this, however, because they knew big government would have to be supported for a long time. England, they pointed out, must husband her resources carefully because the battle with Louis had turned into a tedious war of attrition. As Sir Charles Sedley put it in when discussing how much to vote for the war in 1691: 'I am for going on as we may hold and not for precipitating matters. Not to ride at the same rate for 100 miles as a citizen does if he were going but to Islington. This is like to be a long war so that you must be saving as you can.'[13] Such attitudes reveal the central reason for William's success in state-building. William had persuaded even those with the greatest unease about the new machinery that it was essential if France were to be defeated. The key question thus becomes how the king was able to do this. How he had succeeded when earlier monarchs had never gained wholehearted support for war?

There is an important clue in those earlier failures. If we analyse why kings before 1688 had run into opposition when they tried to build their state, there appears to have been a consistent weakness in war propaganda. Earlier Stuart monarchs had never found arguments which convinced their subjects that their conflicts were worth the burdens of bigger government. Fears of oppressive taxes or armies had always outweighed fear of the enemy. Most remarkably, earlier rulers had not exploited the one English ideology potent enough to overcome doubts about an increased state. They had never successfully presented their struggles as defences of Protestantism against Catholic threat. They had therefore been unable to harness the powerful tradition of anti-popery to explain and justify the expansion of their military machine.

The failure was most stark with Charles II. His wars (of 1664–66 and 1672–74) had actually been against fellow Protestants. By attacking the Dutch, and even by allying with the Catholic French in the second of his conflicts, he had horrified his Protestant nation, and parliamentary opposition to the outrage had cut short both wars. In fact, in the 1670s conflict, anti-popery had been used against the war effort as William himself had co-ordinated a publicity campaign in England to undermine his uncle's attack on the Netherlands.[14] The early Stuarts had at least not made this basic mistake. Their wars had been against France and Spain, the leading Catholic powers, so they should have been able to sell their battles as a heroic defence of the Reformation. Unfortunately, however, circumstances surrounding the conflicts left subjects unconvinced that their kings really were godly champions, and worried that the superficial Protestantism of the wars hid some deeper and darker design. Although James I declared hostilities against Spain in 1624, his record on opposing the Catholic Habsburgs had been extremely poor. He had made peace with Madrid in the first months of his rule, and had then stood by as Spanish forces crushed the Protestant princes of Germany after 1618. His commitment to any anti-Catholic crusade was therefore suspect, and the joy which greeted his change of policy in 1624 was short-lived. Charles I had begun more promisingly, having agitated for war with Spain in the last year of his father's reign. However, events soon cast doubts on the new king's Protestantism. As part of his anti-Spanish policy, he first tried to ally with

France. This had led to his marrying a popish wife (Henrietta Maria, the French king's sister), and to the loan of English ships to the French regime. These vessels were promptly used to help the Bourbons suppress their own Protestant population. Thus, although Charles did declare war on France in 1627, his subjects had deep doubts about his motives, and these were compounded when an expedition to help French Protestants at La Rochelle ended in disaster. Consequently, parliament was not moved by anti-popish fervour to aid the war effort. Instead, the Commons spent the late 1620s denying supply as they attempted to root out a popish conspiracy which they believed was ensconced at court. Charles's later mobilisations were even more disastrous. His attempts in the late 1630s to suppress the Scots revolt were read by many as an attack on a good Protestant nation, and his campaigns fizzled out in general refusal to co-operate.

There were obvious lessons for William in these debacles. He must prevent anti-popery being used as a weapon against his mobilisation. If at all possible, he must do what Cromwell had managed to do, and harness this great ideological force to state-building. The parliamentary and republican regimes of the mid-century had had success in war as they had claimed to oppose the papist forces of Charles I, Irish rebels and the king of Spain. William might hope to follow their example, especially as his circumstances seemed to make this straightforward. The new king, after all, wanted to fight Louis XIV. He thus opposed a ruler who was not only the most powerful Catholic in the world, but who had consistently used this power against reformed Christianity. In his extraordinary career, Louis had attacked Protestant nations (as when invading the Netherlands in 1672); he had persecuted Protestants in his own realm (especially after 1685 when he had repealed the edict of Nantes which had granted them protection); and he had forced conversions to Catholicism in the Protestant cities (such as Strasbourg and Orange) which he had annexed during his expansion. Moreover, William had a proven record as a Protestant champion. He had saved the reformed faith in Holland in 1672, and done the same in Britain in 1688. He should therefore have found it easy to present his war as a Protestant crusade. Anti-popery, no longer the main stumbling block to the English state, might become its greatest support.

There is overwhelming evidence that William learnt from the experience of the seventeenth century. He and his supporters put huge efforts into explaining the Protestantism of his war to the English people. Expanding on the domestic rhetoric, which had presented William's court as an engine of reformed piety, the new regime set the king's international career in a similarly providential pattern. Here, spokesmen claimed, was a godly champion. The new king had been chosen by God to avenge the sufferings of true Protestants in Europe; to roll back the anti-Christian forces of the Counter-Reformation; and to make the world safe for godly worship with his arms. In their most apocalyptic moments, William's supporters even hinted his victory might herald the last days. It might set up the conditions where Christ himself might reign on earth – his enemies vanquished by his virtuous commander.[15]

As we might expect, the richest vein of such material came from Williamite pulpits. We have already seen how the royal court doubled the number of formal sermons preached in royal palaces, and ordered a high proportion to be published. In addition, the regime promulgated a large number of fasts and thanksgiving days to induce God to bless the war. These required the entire population to attend their parish churches (at least once a month over the summer of most early years of the war), and to listen to addresses which praised William as a providential saviour. In these, the king's military efforts against the French were attempts to protect reformed churches. The English must therefore support them out of loyalty to their religion. For instance, the solidly Williamite preacher Thomas Tenison told the House of Commons they were 'engaged in the evangelical cause against popish superstition'.[16] Similarly, the archbishop of Canterbury told the Corporation of London that England was the nation 'upon whom the eyes of all Protestants abroad are fixed, as the glory of the Reformation, and the great bulwark and support of it'.[17] This interpretation of the war lay behind almost all Williamite preaching.[18]

The clergy of the 1690s did not exhaust their protestant arguments in the pulpit. Each of the fasts and thanksgivings which they organised was accompanied by a specially composed liturgy for the church services. These promoted a Protestant crusade through the medium of public prayer. In particular, the liturgies revived a supplication 'for all the reformed churches' which had not been used since the 1620s. The various versions of this asked God to remember the persecuted Protestants abroad, and so presented the struggle with Louis as a war of religious liberation. All the prayers stressed how many reformed Christians were in a 'sad and mournful state' under 'superstitious and merciless men', and emphasised that the English were united with these foreigners 'into thy holy church, the mystical body of Christ'. The 1689 edition truly went to town. It painted a lurid picture of popish persecutions, and cried out to the deity to help William relieve them. 'How long', the prayers asked God, 'wilt thou forget thy people that prayeth!' 'Oh let the cry of the Blood of the Saints, and the sighing of the Prisons come before thee! ... Deliver thou those that are as Sheep appointed to the slaughter.'[19]

Naturally, the above quoted material came from the clerical allies of the king. They might be expected to stress confessional reasons for opposing Louis. Yet Protestant presentations of the conflict did not end there. William was happy to accept the mantle of godly redeemer in whatever material it was woven, and an anti-popish crusade was promoted well outside church services. For example, the Hercules iconography at Hampton Court stressed the martial valour of William for the Protestant cause. The Greek hero's use of strength for virtue was read as an allegory of armed struggled for reformed Christianity, while the icon's earlier use by Henri IV of France reminded all of that crusading friend of the Protestant religion. At the palace, the Hercules imagery was reinforced by displays of military hardware in the Guard Chamber and by warlike decorations on the King's Staircase. These reminded all of William's armed efforts for the godly cause. Similarly, the early 1690s saw an outpouring of pamphlets which set the war in a confessional context. The most moving of these described Louis's cruel persecution of reformed Christians in France, Orange and Savoy. By detailing the horrors of forced conversion, they perfected the portrait of Louis as the ultimate anti-Christ, and made at least tacit appeals for English intervention against the French king to end the suffering.[20] Some writers went further. The exiled French Protestant Pierre Jurieu detailed Louis's persecutions, but comforted his readers that such horrors were the dark days before a prophetic resurgence of Protestantism in Europe.[21] Other pamphlets had a more sober tone – but a similar purpose. Many productions provided strategic analyses of the state of Europe to explain why England must fight against France. As we shall see, these used an array of arguments to justify the war – but the need to defend a shrinking Protestantism loomed large.

It would be nice to wrap up our investigation of William's success here. We could simply argue that the king got support for his expanded state by ensuring anti-popery worked for the project. Sadly though, this explanation is open to serious challenge. The problem is William's Catholic allies. The king might have tried to present himself as a Protestant hero – but this publicity drive was hampered by pacts he had made as he tried to contain Louis. In the late 1680s, the Prince of Orange had sought the friendship of each and any nation who might have a quarrel with France. Consequently, the 'Grand Alliance' against Louis, signed in The Hague in the spring of 1689, included good Protestant allies such as England, the United Provinces and Brandenburg: but it also drew in the Catholic monarchs of Spain and Austria. Still more embarrassingly, it enjoyed the broad support of the Pope. His Holiness hoped William's strategy might reduce French influence in Italy, and made it clear he wished the Grand Alliance well. England's king was therefore somewhat caught. He knew a Protestant rhetoric would be the most effective way to sell the war to the English, but his European strategy ensured it would be hard to peddle this line.

Examining this dilemma, some historians have argued that William's justification of conflict did not, in fact, centre on anti-popery, or any form of religious polemic. Although there was some Protestantism in royal publicity, it is claimed the king convinced his new nation to fight using secular arguments. In particular, William pointed to the dangers French dominance would pose to English trade, or to the continental balance of power. According to Steven Pincus, the most vocal of these scholars, William encapsulated these concerns in a rhetoric of 'universal monarchy'. In an outpouring of propaganda which drowned any religious rhetoric, the English court accused Louis of aiming at total domination of the continent. He was, William suggested, an aspiring universal monarch who wished his writ to run everywhere, and who must be opposed by all other powers who wished to retain their liberties. This language, Pincus has claimed, solved the problem of England's Catholic allies. It explained that the war was not being fought for reasons of faith, so co-operation with Spain and Austria did not undermine its aims. Catholics and Protestants could come together, since the objective was to preserve national autonomies, not to launch an anti-popish crusade.[22]

There is much in this view. There was extensive analysis of universal monarchy in Williamite polemic after 1689, and the king often reminded his subjects that he had Catholic allies in the fight to preserve the rights of all countries. For example, a 1692 proclamation explained that England was engaged in a war against France 'together with most of the princes and states of Europe'.[23] Large numbers of contemporary pamphlets put the threat of France's universal monarchy at the heart of their analysis, using exactly this term to describe the danger. To cite one instance of very many, an author who took *A View of the True Interest of the Several States of Europe*, explained 'it would be requisite at present for the Christian Princes, carefully to observe how France aspires to the universal monarchy'.[24] Some material went as far as to denounce those who tried to present the war as a Protestant crusade. How, it was asked, could Spain and Austria be so central to the cause if it were. One author put the point in the very title of his work – *The Present French king Demonstrated an Enemy to the Catholick as well as Protestant Religion* (1689) – while many others asked how Louis could be a Catholic champion. He had tortured papists as well as Protestants in his invasions of Germany; and whilst pretending to be a champion of his faith, he had entered into secret leagues with Protestant rebels against the emperor of Austria.[25]

Yet, for all this, Protestant presentations of the war also remained vigorous. As we have seen, much Williamite propaganda insisted that the conflict *was* about saving the Reformation, whatever the state of the king's alliances. We must, of course, explain how the regime squared its treaties with its rhetoric, but we cannot do this simply by ignoring or playing down the existence of the Protestant arguments. The quantity and range of these was just too great. Instead, we should note that anti-popery was used alongside other discourses to sell the war. Many Williamite spokesmen appeared determined to exploit Protestant presentations of conflict as far as they would go, but would then grasp alternative arguments if their rhetoric took them to points where the help of Spain and Austria could no longer be glossed over. In short, they employed a blunderbuss technique. They would fire off all forms of argument simultaneously – hoping the audience would respond to each as appropriate for the needs of the moment.

William's speeches to parliament provide a good example. The very first of these used both secular and religious points to ask for funds for the war. The king stated that action was needed urgently because of the 'condition of our allies abroad'. This would have reminded MPs of the very varied alliance which William was constructing against Louis, and would have presented him as an enemy of *all* Europeans. Immediately, however, the new monarch became more confessional. He stated Holland was at the greatest danger, and reminded them of the rebellion in Ireland. He thus stressed areas where the battle between Louis and his enemies could most easily be presented as a struggle to contain popery. He went on to state that a good settlement was necessary 'not only for your own peace, but for the support of the Protestant interest both here and abroad'.[26] Later addresses took the same mixed line. The king talked of a broad front of princes and states in league with him, but also emphasised a religious cause in his warfare (see, for example, the speeches of 19 October 1689 and 23 May 1690). Many Williamite pamphlets were similarly schizophrenic. Even those which concentrated on universal monarchy, or analysed Louis's threat to Christians of all kinds, could lapse into Protestant crusading rhetoric. For example, the author of *The Most Christian Turk* emphasised that the French posed a danger to Christendom as a whole. As in response to the Ottomans (the Turks who had always threatened Christ's religion), all followers of Jesus must come together if they were to survive. Yet, despite appealing for Catholics and Protestants to unite, the same writer could breath Reformation zeal when describing France's persecutions of her Huguenot population. He claimed the cruelties were for the satisfaction of 'Jesuits and Popish priests', and linked recent events to those described in John Foxe's Protestant masterpiece when stating the numbers involved 'would fill a volume as large as those of the *Martyrs*'.[27] Similarly, the author of *The Means to Free Europe from French Usurpation* showed a split personality. He called Louis an enemy of all mankind, and called for princes of all stripes to unite against him. However, he also stressed the importance of England's deliverance from 'popish slavery' and reminded readers of the cruel fate of 'our Brethren of France' – the Protestant Huguenots.[28]

An analytical reader will wonder how William's supporters got away with this. Surely, propaganda could not work if it incorporated incompatible positions. The war was either about religion, or it wasn't. Difference of faith among William's allies would be fatal to a spiritual presentation of the campaigns. Yet to raise this objection may be to overestimate the consistency of audiences. A moment's self-reflection should convince us that people frequently hold contradictory beliefs. They can be moved by arguments which are logically inconsistent – even if those arguments are put immediately one after the other. It is therefore conceivable that late Stuart Englishmen believed *both* that they were engaged in a godly struggle against popery *and* that Catholic allies were acceptable because Louis was an aspiring universal monarch. So long as no pedants pointed out their confusion, they would not have spotted it. Also, objecting to the contradiction in Williamite propaganda misses rhetorical techniques through which its danger could be reduced. There was, after all, no need for propagandists to dwell on the inconsistency. People could defend the war as a Protestant crusade without mentioning the Catholic allies. Propaganda which concentrated on blackening Louis as a persecuting anti-Christ, and upon England's spiritual duty to stop him, could whip up Reformation fervour and hope it would sweep away thoughts about Spain and Austria. This was how most of the sermons worked. They stressed England's duties against popery, but avoided geo-political analysis of the state of European alliances. William's supporters could also rely on a domestic/European division in their audience. Obviously they had to play down Protestant enthusiasm in material meant for, or easily seen by, their Catholic allies. Formal declarations of war, or position papers meant for international consumption, stressed Louis's secular danger to other powers.[29] Material directed for internal consumption, however, could be more anti-popish. Preaching, prayers and many cheap pamphlets were unlikely to be studied in Vienna or Madrid, and they dressed the French king as a Catholic Satan. Thus the division seen in William's 1688 propaganda was repeated throughout the 1690s. Legal and political arguments were directed outwards, spiritual ones were deployed for home consumption.

So, anti-popery *did* play a central role in William's justification of the war. There were difficulties with it – but these could be overcome, and there is a strong argument that William's successful deployment of Protestantism made the difference between his ability to secure support for an expanded state in wartime, and his predecessors' miserable failures. Here was a king who argued that his battles were for England's favourite cause. His vigour in attacking the leading Catholic power of the day meant his taxes, armies and administrations could be accepted as a price worth paying for the defeat of anti-Christ. If doubts persist, it is worth reflecting that William's vigour and cogency in asserting his Protestant crusade was the only significant difference between his war propaganda and that of his unsuccessful predecessors. Of other possible defences of conflict, most had been used by the earlier kings. In particular the discourse of universal monarchy had been deployed with enthusiasm during Charles II's conflicts, which were presented as essential to stop the Dutch dominating the world.[30] Only when these arguments were combined with anti-popery, however, did they seem to convince. William tapped into what was still the deepest English ideology, and at last persuaded his subjects to overcome their doubts about sustained, state-building war.

William's solution: the parliamentary state

Whatever the controversies surrounding William's Protestantism, there can be far less debate about his other technique for securing consent to state-building. In marked contrast to his predecessors, the new king involved parliament in managing government. By inviting the nation's representatives to help organise and scrutinise the machinery of state, he avoided any sense that the administration would be an alien imposition, or a tool of royal absolutism.

The king's first step in creating this new atmosphere was to ensure that his war was parliament's as much as his own. Although William had invaded England in order to bring its forces into the conflict with Louis, and although he was ordering the English fleet to take operations against the French even before he became king, he was careful to ensure that the formal declaration of hostilities came only after a request from the Lords and Commons. In fact, given the urgency of the continental situation in the spring of 1689, it is surprising how long William allowed this nicety to delay the start of the war. He did not use his royal prerogative to begin the conflict, but instead described the international situation to the legislature in his first speech (18 February), and waited for peers and MPs to respond. Most of parliament's time in March was taken up debating the king's financial settlement, and the future of the church of England, so it was not until 25 April that the Commons addressed the king suggesting that Louis should be restrained with English force. Despite this loss of momentum, the king remained calm. He knew that much of the delay came from disputes about what exactly should be in the address (whigs, up to their usual tricks, hoped to implicate tories in Louis's evil by including a clause blaming the French for bribing members of Charles II's court), and he knew that parliamentary support for his foreign policy would be better if it were unanimous. Consequently William was happy to wait for a consensus to emerge. As a result of this patience, the monarch was able to present the conflict as a parliamentary one. Responding to the 25 April address, he told the Commons 'I have no doubt of such an assistance from you, as shall be suitable to your advice to me, to declare war against a powerful enemy'.[31] He had thus involved his subjects' representatives in initiating the conflict which would demand a growth of his state, and he would ever after remind them that he had entered into it with their encouragement. As he explained to his third parliament as it met on 23 November 1695: 'I was engaged in this present war by the advice of my first parliament ... The last parliament with great cheerfulness did assist me to carry it on, and I cannot doubt that your concern for the common safety will oblige you to be uniformly zealous in the prosecution of it.'[32]

Capitalising on this initial coup, William ensured that parliament was involved, and so implicated, in all aspects of wartime state-building. The case was most obvious with finance. The declaration of right had provided a useful starting point here, by declaring that all forms of unparliamentary taxation were unlawful. When William acquiesced in the declaration, the nation's representatives could be assured that they would have the final say on all fiscal burdens. As in several other areas, the new king explored whether he had any wriggle room in his early days in power. In February 1689, members of his court consulted leading English lawyers, asking if the grant of customs and excise to James II could simply be transferred to the new monarch without Commons confirmation. The men approached expressed their enthusiasm for the new regime by suggesting that it could, but it soon became clear that a majority at Westminster thought this flew in the face of the ban on unparliamentary taxation, and that the revenues would have to be voted to William anew. In the face of this opposition, the court – as usual – backed down, and reassured everybody that no attempt would be made to collect money until it was approved by the Commons. William waited patiently for his revenue to be settled by parliament, and even surrendered the lucrative hearth tax because there were doubts about its full legality. From this point on, the king was scrupulous in observing the principle announced in the declaration. He only taxed once the Commons had allowed him to do so, and so killed suspicion that a large income would allow him build a tyrannical state.

Moreover, William ensured parliament controlled the level, type and method of taxation, as well as giving its basic approval. Despite the urgency of his financial needs in the 1690s, the king left detailed deter- mination of how much money to raise, and exactly how to raise it, to his subjects' representatives in the Commons. He obeyed the old convention that 'backbench' MPs initiate suggestions for tax measures; and he gave little lead as his legislators dithered over various proposals. The history of the spring session of 1689 set the pattern for the reign. When William first asked the Commons for financial assistance, he had a shopping list of immediate demands. He wanted around two and a half million pounds to make preparations for an expedition to Ireland, and to meet the expenses of the Dutch forces in England. Beyond making his broad needs known, however, the king stepped back. He left it to MPs, first to approve a pre- cise sum, and then to decide how to raise it.

Both processes took some time. The Commons took over six weeks to sanction the various heads of expenditure, and did little to settle the details of which taxes it would raise. As late as 25 April, the House had still only approved £420,000 worth of revenue. On the 26th, money started to flow more freely, but the process of meeting the king's needs remained falter- ing and haphazard. A poll tax was agreed, and the crown was allowed to collect customs and excise (so long as £700,000 of the first year's takings were dedicated to the war). However, a considerable shortfall remained, and the Commons had no clear strategy to make it good. Rather, MPs debated myriad schemes suggested by individual members in committees of the whole house. By the end of the month four of these had emerged as front runners, but two of them (a building tax in London, and fines on those who had taken office under James II without taking religious tests) quickly ran into difficulties. The overly complex schemes were therefore dropped, leaving only an additional poll tax, and new excises on drinks, which did not plug the hole in William's finance. It took an initiative by the country backbencher Sir Christopher Musgrave to save the day. On 10 May he suggested an additional shilling assessment on land, and the house gratefully seized on the idea. In all this chaos, William had remained calm. He had left parliament to come up with its own suggestions for public finance – only occasionally reminding it that his war needs were urgent.

Such royal stoicism in the face of Commons distraction caused problems for William's administration. It left the king living hand-to-mouth, never knowing whether enough finance would be granted in time. Frustration at this sometimes emerged in king's speeches to his legislature (see, for example, the speeches of 19 October 1689, 21 March 1690, and 23 May 1690). In the end, however, the tone of royal reprimand was mild because the king knew the situation had advantages. Commons control of finance might be exasperating, but it also calmed MPs, making them less likely to fear the growth of an independent, absolutist state. The nation's representatives were further reassured as the king's tolerance extended to a series of restrictions imposed by legislators on tax grants. Through the early 1690s, William made no protest as the Commons tied his financial hands. He did not object when MPs demanded information on how money was likely to be spent before agreeing to vote taxes. For instance, in the autumn of 1692, he acquiesced when the lower house wanted to see his international alliances, and records of recent naval campaigns, before granting supply. Similarly, William sat by as parliamentarians ring-fenced money. Traditionally, the spending of tax revenue had been the monarch's sole affair once it had been granted. In the 1690s, however, revenue came to be awarded only on condition that it was spent on particular purposes. In fact, in the 1690–91 and the 1691–92 sessions *all* the taxes which were approved were voted on this understanding. They were either appropriated for specific services, or were at least earmarked for the conduct of the war in general. This prevented the king redirecting funds to civil administration or personal expenditure.

So far, William's handling of finance might appear sensible, but not particularly imaginative. He had dealt with fears that a heavy taxing state might oppress its subjects, but he had done so simply by surrendering control of tax policy to those subjects' representatives. Given that his desperate need for money weakened him in the face of parliamentary demands, his approach hardly seems visionary. Far more impressive, however, were William's initiatives to reassure the Commons by allowing them to audit his accounts. In the early years of his reign, he ran ahead of parliamentary opinion by recognising that his legislators would worry that public funds might be misspent, and realising that they were more likely to be generous if they could satisfy themselves of the administration's honesty. Rather than obscuring his financial affairs, therefore, he broke with Stuart precedent and made public expenditure transparent.

The new audit culture was announced in William's speech to parliament on 28 June 1689. Warning the Commons that the money they had so far granted to the war would be unlikely to cover expenses, the king implicitly acknowledged that the huge sums demanded might be misdirected, and suggested that his legislators check for themselves that it was actually needed. William said 'that you might make the truer judgement of the matter, I am very willing you should see how the monies have hitherto been laid out ... To that end I have commanded that those accounts be speedily brought to you'.[33] As an offer, this was so far ahead of its time that the Commons did not know how to respond. They had rarely been permitted, and absolutely never invited, to look at royal finances before – and they seemed to have little idea how to organise such an examination. In fact, in the first half of 1689, parliamentarians had not been asking for closer scrutiny of the king's accounts. Rather, their strategy had been the cruder one of restricting the king's income by delaying the customary grant of customs and excise revenue, in the hope that this would control court corruption. As a result, it took another prompt from the king to get the Commons to examine his financial record. Opening parliament in October, he told it 'that you may be satisfied how the money has been laid out ... I have directed the accounts to be laid before you, when you think fit to call for them'.[34] Only then did the Commons take up the suggestion. They received the accounts on 1 November, and constituted a committee to go through them item by item. Later, parliament was emboldened to go further. It asked for estimates of future expenditure, so that it could subject proposed budgets to the same scrutiny as past payouts. Yet although the Commons finally took the initiative in financial scrutiny in the 1690s, it is important to see these examinations as part of a *royal* vision. William agreed to provide estimates with no hesitation; he went on offering accounts year after year; and he calmly accepted savings and criticisms which the Commons made when going through his books. Above all, it is important to remember that his original offer of the accounts had been far more radical than anything the legislators had been demanding. William should therefore receive much of the credit for establishing the modern annual cycle of parliamentary budget setting, and financial scrutiny.

The Commission of Public Accounts presents a similar picture. This body, first established in 1691, was a committee of MPs, charged by parliament with investigating the management of public money. In some descriptions of the 1690s, it is seen as the core of a 'country' opposition to William. It has been argued that, as the commission produced its annual reports on public accounts, it brought together a group of politicians who were confirmed in their suspicions of the court, and began to co-ordinate wider country campaigns.[35] To an extent, this is true. Some of the leading lights of the campaigns for place and triennial legislation – people like Sir Thomas Clarges, Paul Foley and Robert Harley – had been political rivals in 1689, and it had taken common service on the accounts commission to bring them to co-operate. Yet, while the commission could be a forum for developing anti-court ideas, it was also an instrument of court policy. It had been suggested and set up by the king, who had hoped it could weed out incompetent and corrupt public servants. According to Gilbert Burnet, the idea for an investigative body was first floated by the court in the early months of 1690.[36] The bill launched in the spring of that year to empanel nine MPs thus seems to have had – not only royal support – but royal sponsorship. When this bill was lost at the adjournment of parliament in May, court enthusiasm persisted. The king used his own authority to try to set up a body with the same functions and membership as the spring proposals.[37] This royal design to establish an inquisition on finance was frustrated by a factional dispute between the whigs and tories named in the summer, but William got another chance once parliament had reconvened in the autumn. The king gave his assent to an act establishing the commission in January 1691.

Royal support for the new body continued once it had been set up. Even though the group of MPs began publishing damning annual reports on the use of public money, the king showed them every co-operation and encouragement. Individual ministers, perhaps frightened of being exposed, did not always welcome investigation, but their master ordered them to open their records to the commissioners. For example, at the end of June 1691, the court wrote to the earl of Suffolk to warn him against any attempts to frustrate the MPs' enquiries into the cost of Dutch forces in England.[38] Similarly, William provided logistical support for the commission. He put them on the public payroll and met all their expenses. In fact, the commissioners found themselves in the embarrassing position of being king's placemen. Even though many of these people were promoting legislation to ban those who held public office from parliament, it was possible these measures would boomerang on the commissioners themselves as they were technically royal servants. The close relations between court and the commission continued right through to the publication of the reports. The first of these, produced in 1691, catalogued a series of corruptions and extravagances in the king's administration, but the monarch himself was not dismayed. Robert Harley, the rising star of the commission, recorded that the king received him and his colleagues graciously after the presentation of one of their findings, and thanked them for their efforts.[39]

If openness, and ceding ultimate control to the Commons, were William's ways of calming fears about heavy taxation, the techniques worked equally well with the military. In the 1690s, the king built up enormous armed forces – but he kept parliament on board by reassuring MPs that they would determine the size and shape of the army and navy, and that they could scrutinise these bodies in the most intimate detail. As with money, the king's first trick was to assure the legislature that he could raise nothing without them. Again the declaration of rights provided a starting point with its ban on peacetime standing armies unless they had parliamentary consent. William's acceptance of the document guaranteed that he would not raise a force like James's. His army would not be deployed in England without the nation's agreement, nor would it be used to threaten internal coercion against the legislature. Soon, however, the new king showed he would go further than the declaration's terms. He was to allow parliament considerable control, even in wartime, and even over the forces sent abroad.

Much of this control was ceded through the systems of financial supervision which we have been examining. At a very basic level, William's surrender of tax raising to the Commons meant fundamental surrender of military policy, since large armies and navies could only be afforded if parliament agreed to vote the money to pay for them. Although the king remained in control of war strategy, and had absolute command on the battlefield, decisions made in Westminster about how much revenue would be available obviously affected what operations were possible. Beyond this essential fact, parliament gained considerable control over the detailed structure of the military because the king allowed it to examine as well as set his finances. The Commons, after all, did not simply vote sums for the war. It scrutinised the estimates for the army and navy head by head; and it went through the forces' accounts to see what had been spent where. By the early 1690s, debates over army estimates had the Commons deciding exactly how many men were needed. For 1692, for example, it resolved that 64,924 troops were required for the summer's campaigning – not a man more or a man less. The House also decided what the ratio of officers to men should be (MPs tried to maintain the overall size of the army but cut its costs by having fewer commissions); and discussed the exact numbers to be deployed in each theatre of war. Discussions of navy estimates, meanwhile, resolved the exact size of the fleet (33,010 men in 1692); they decided whether marines should be included in this number or not, and they determined what new vessels should be built at public expense. Retrospective auditing of expenditure gave the Commons similar power over the forces. Reports by the Commission of Public Accounts demanded changes in military practices as they uncovered waste, fraud and inefficiency. The first report in 1691 told parliament there were too many officers in most regiments, that musters were inefficient ways of recording how many effective men each part of the army had, that the newly introduced system of agents to organise logistics was expensive and corrupt; and that the forces were buying supplies such as clothing far too dearly.[40] All this, of course, affected military policy and capability, and meant the king had to manage the military parts of his state under tight parliamentary constraints. It also meant parliamentarians were likely to feel less threatened by the military, and even, perhaps, have a sense of ownership of it. These were forces their votes for money had approved, right down to fine organisation.

Nor did parliamentary influence stop with the financial. The king's openness to legislative enquiry ran beyond regular scrutiny of expenditure to permit wholesale investigations of the military. These began as early as the summer of 1689, when peers and MPs became concerned at the slow progress the king's forces were making in Ireland. As William's commander Schomberg became bogged down in his campaign to defeat the Jacobite rebels, people at Westminster began to suspect that corruption, or even treason, in parts of the army were to blame. An extensive investigation of the military supplies began, and eventually unearthed the activities of a Commissary John Shales. This man was an old servant of James II, who had been charged with organising horses and arms for the soldiers in Ireland, but who had instead pocketed many of the funds granted for these purposes. By November, the enquiry had reached the heights of military command. Parliament addressed the king to demand that Shales be sacked, and to know by whose advice he had been employed in the first place.[41] In response, William baulked at disclosing confidential discussions in the Privy Council. Otherwise, however, he accepted the legislature's right to investigate and raise concerns, telling the Commons that Shales was being arrested and his papers seized so the affair could be examined even more closely.[42] Other enquiries were to follow, and the king kept up his broad co-operation with them. When, in 1692, parliament was disappointed by the failure of the fleet to follow up its victory over French ships in the Channel, William allowed the Commons to examine the orders which had been sent out from the Admiralty, and to grill his leading naval commanders. The Commons questioned whether the tactics pursued had been realistic, and whether commanders at sea had followed them appropriately.[43] In 1695, a Public Accounts Commission investigation into abuses committed by regimental agents escalated into a major scandal. Although it had started as a set of local concerns about billeting in Hertfordshire, the parliamentary inquisition uncovered corruption in increasingly high places, until it claimed the scalp of Treasury Secretary Henry Guy.[44] William's attitude thus gave parliament considerable control over the army and navy. His willingness to let parliamentarians scrutinise and censure took them to the heart of the war machine.

Parliament even came to have a considerable influence on military strategy. Because William knew the Commons would need to approve the general handling of the conflict if it were to continue voting funds, he proved willing to shape the general direction of the war effort to suit their prejudices, even if he himself doubted the wisdom of what MPs wanted to do. The series of planned 'descents' in the early 1690s provide a vivid example. These descents were supposed to be amphibious operations against the north French coast. The idea was to win control of the Channel, and land large forces in France's ports to divert Louis's troops from the front in Flanders. William was always sceptical that descents could work, but the Commons liked them because they imagined they could bring a quick end to the war, and because they did not involve using English troops to preserve Dutch borders. In response, the king sacrificed his own sense that Flanders must be the prime theatre of conflict. He planned a descent each spring, even though the preparations interfered with the war to defend the Netherlands. In fact, parliamentary scrutiny locked the court into this strategy. Each summer the practical difficulties of massive amphibious operations meant they were abandoned, or went off half-cock: each autumn MPs demanded to know what had happened. Ministers were then forced to apologise, to explain the failure, and to promise a bigger effort next year, as a way to get through the session. In the end, a successful descent was never launched, but the king had accepted parliamentary influence over one of his most cherished areas of policy.[45] Even in his function as commander in chief, he had one eye on Commons opinion.

Of course, the most dramatic exercise of parliamentary power over the military was the great disbandment of 1697–99. As has already been described, the Commons refused to accept royal arguments for the maintenance of a strong army after the peace of Ryswick, and instead insisted on a massive demobilisation. It is easy to see this as William's greatest political defeat, and in many ways it was. It drove the king to the brink of abdication, and it seemed to spell a complete unravelling of his approach during the war. Down to 1697, he had built up the army by ceding control over it to his MPs. Now that same parliamentary control worked to destroy the army. In the face of this reverse, the king fumed. As we have seen, he tried to deceive his legislators about the number of men he had in arms, and he threatened to retire to Holland. Yet while the disbandment defied William's will, in the end it represented a triumph of his logic. If

the army could only be built on the trust of legislators, it was more important to retain that trust than to insist on a huge military in peacetime. So
long as parliamentary confidence was maintained, and even if the price of
this was to send the army home, the forces might – one day – be expanded
again. If, on the other hand, the Commons' confidence was lost, so too
would be any future mobilisation.

William's actions in the later 1690s reveal he understood this.
Alongside his ranting, he pursued policies which attempted to preserve
his alliance with parliament. First, he tried to persuade his legislators that
his was a new sort of army. Through his spokesmen and pamphleteers he
reminded MPs that these were their forces far more than the king's. His
principal minister, John Somers, wrote a widely circulated paper which
explained that parliament controlled the army through its votes for its
funds.[46] The force could never, therefore become a monstrous burden or a
threat to Englishmen's liberties. When this case failed to convince, the
king – with great reluctance – surrendered. Going to parliament on the
first day of February 1699, he told them he would cut the forces to 7,000
men as they had asked. The words of his capitulation are significant. He
said he had given in because a breach between monarch and legislature
was 'even more fatal' than the demobilisation.[47] He thus recognised that,
before he could have an army, he must have the consent of parliament. To
forfeit the latter to try to keep the former would be to sacrifice an underlying cause for a temporary effect. In this light, William's particular defeat
was actually a victory for his more general approach. Its reward came less
than two years later. When the king's warnings about Louis's untrust-
worthiness proved wise, the Commons wearily began to reconstruct the
army they had so recently sent home. In the next decade, under Anne, it
would reach still greater size.

William's state and Europe

On 19 November 1691, Sir John Lowther rose to tell the House of
Commons why it should be generous in granting soldiers to William. His
fellow MPs, he told them, now had a king 'entirely in your interests and
one whom you may confide in will prosecute this war heartily'.[48] Drawing
a contrast with both William's uncles, Lowther reminded his audience
that previous parliaments had been desirous of a war with France, but had
had just reason to fear that the government had not been so inclined.
Although this speaker held a government post, and was therefore not
unbiased in his presentation of the world, Lowther's words do seem to

indicate why William succeeded in building a state, when earlier kings had failed. He had presented himself as a monarch in the nation's interest, who would fight a war they wanted. The last few sections have tried to show how he accomplished this. He fought a Protestant war, and sold it as a Protestant war. He reassured the political nation that neither taxes nor military would rob them of freedoms by ensuring parliament controlled both. By involving the legislature in the details of the state's machinery, he ensured they felt they owned this machinery and were implicated in its growth. The question which remains is how far these royal strategies were determined by William's European experience and focus. We have seen the English state owed little to direct importation of models from the Netherlands. Did it, nevertheless, owe something to political objectives and lessons from abroad?

In one very basic way it did. It is important to remember that it took William's continent-born determination to attack Louis to produce the sort of conflict to which the English were willing to consent. For a century, there had been public enthusiasm for a war to stop the advance of Catholicism across Europe. From the 1670s, this had crystallised into calls to contain France. Yet before 1688, these popular demands had been thwarted because reigning monarchs had not shared their subjects' bellicose aims. Fixed on their domestic position, kings had refused to fight the French. They had either remained neutral to avoid the costs of war, or had – like Charles II – actually allied with Versailles because the Bourbons had become a source of secret pension money. The result was either that England did not engage in the conflicts which would have built her state, or withdrew from them rapidly as popular opposition stalled any war effort. Only when William arrived was the log-jam broken. A king with a European desire to defeat France finally shared the objectives of his people, and engaged in a conflict they were willing to sustain.

Other aspects of William's achievement also had foreign origins. His presentation of the war as a Protestant crusade certainly did. To secure the agreement of the English to war, it was not enough simply to attack the leading Catholic power of the day. The battles had to be explained and justified as a religious war, or anti-popery could not play its part. Arguably, William had learned how to tap into Protestant fervour in Holland. His war propaganda had stressed the defence of reformed Christianity since 1672, and much of this material was available for translation across the Channel. It is true that the majority of the publicists who sold the war in England were English, and that they drew on indigenous strains of opposition to Catholic advance. Nevertheless, important media and messages were imported, and many individual propagandists had been active in the

Provinces before they sold William's Protestant crusade in England. For example, many of the men who wrote accounts of Catholic persecutions in Europe had initially penned their works for a Dutch, or a wider continental, audience. Similarly Dutch pictorial printers such as Romagne de Hooghe, who had chronicled William's Protestant triumphs in Europe, had their wares distributed in England. Perhaps most importantly, Gilbert Burnet, the new king's leading religious spokesman, had been employed by the prince's press officers in The Hague since 1686. While on the continent, he had witnessed what he thought were the absurdities and cruelties of popery, and had begun to write about these in support of the Orange cause.[49] The sermons and pamphlets he produced in England after the Revolution were therefore extensions of works produced in Holland for a continent-wide audience.

If William can plausibly be said to have imported the Protestant part of his state-building strategy, the parliamentary part can also be read as continental in origin. The new king, after all, came from a country where representative assemblies were sovereign. In the Provinces, consulting these bodies before military mobilisation was more than advisable: it was essential. William also came from a country which had seen the benefits of building the state machine on explicit political consent. The Provinces had been able to organise so many of their national resources into a war machine precisely because the people felt they had been consulted. Contemporaries explained that the Dutch were willing to sacrifice so much in warfare and taxes because they knew these burdens were needed to preserve their liberties (including their government by representative assemblies). Modern historians, agreeing, have explained that resistance to the state was lowered by the belief it was under popular control. City councils, provincial states and the federal estates general provided forums in which the military could negotiate with civic elites for funds, and in which those elites could advance their cities' interests as the price of providing money.[50] Close scrutiny by the nation's representatives also helped. The knowledge that officials would have to account to the assemblies for their use of funds kept them honest, and produced a slimline administration which ordinary citizens were more likely to support. As William Temple explained, the Dutch were oppressed by harder taxes than any nation ever had been. Yet did not rebel because there was little waste or corruption. 'No great riches are seen to enter by Public Payments into private Purses . . . all Public Monies are applied to the Safety, Greatness or Honour of the State.'[51] In all this, there were clear inspirations for William's approach in England. His willingness to allow parliament such an influential role in finance and the military looks like a lesson from Provincial government.

Moreover, William had learnt a hard personal lesson in Holland, which would have convinced him of the need for parliamentary consent even without the established traditions of his homeland. In 1683, he had tried to boost the Dutch state through his own prestige, prerogative and power. He had demanded that the army be enlarged, and that the province of Holland, and particularly the city of Amsterdam, pay for this. As we recall, the incident led to humiliation by the mobs and magistrates of the Netherlands' greatest city. By contrast, after William had spent five years mending fences and using the constitutional systems of consultation, he got a greater military capability than he could have dreamed possible. In 1688, the Dutch, with the Amsterdam magistrates in the lead, agreed to supply the prince handsomely for his renewed war with Louis. By the late summer, the estates general had agreed to pay for around 80,000 troops, and a navy of 20,000 men. There could be no starker illustration of the difference working with representative assemblies could make in state-building. William was unlikely to have forgotten this as he began to deal with the parliament in Westminster. Unlike his predecessors, he had had a continental career that taught him to see through the paradox of royal power and the state. He knew that if rulers gave up some of their control over finance and the military, they could be more than compensated by a vast increase in the size and capability of the machine they still headed. They may no longer determine the precise scale, structure or even strategy of the state: but that state could go to war for royal objectives, and sustain the struggle over many years.

Earlier in this chapter, we said that the English state of the 1690s owed rather little to European models. Now, however, we might reassess. It is true that there was little direct borrowing of detailed structures or solutions: but this perhaps misses the point. The precise political and economic circumstances of two countries are rarely close enough to allow simple exchanges of military, fiscal or administrative practice; so it was probably always a mistake to look for those. Broad principles of state-building, on the other hand, may be more transferable – and here Dutch and British parallels seem clear. The Dutch had proved a state could be built by securing consent through Protestant warfare, and allowing representative assemblies to control and scrutinise the fiscal–military machine. Under William's guidance the English applied that insight. The new king used his continental experience to bring fresh thinking to English state-building. He acted as an important conduit of foreign wisdom after all.

Notes

Most of the general material in this chapter on the long-term development of the English state comes from M.J. Braddick, *The Nerves of State* (MUP, 1996); John Brewer, *The Sinews of Power: War, Money and the English State, 1688–1783* (Unwin, 1989); and J.R. Western, *Monarchy and Revolution: the English State in the 1680s* (Blandford Press, 1972) chs 5–6. Israel, *Dutch Republic* has useful material on the organisation of the Dutch state, but a deeper analysis is provided by Marjolein t'Hart, *The Making of a Bourgeois State* (MUP, 1993). For the 1690s, Rose, *England in the 1690s*, pp. 132–51 provides a useful summary. Government taxation, spending and borrowing are well handled in Henry Roseveare, *The Financial Revolution, 1660–1760* (Longman, 1991), and P.G.M. Dickson, *The Financial Revolution in England* (Macmillan, 1967). D.W. Jones, *War and Economy in the Age of William III and Marlborough* (OUP, 1988) provides analysis and statistics. The military is well handled in Childs, *The British Army of William III*; and John Herman, *The Navy in the War of William III, 1689–1697* (CUP, 1953). Rose, *England in the 1690s;* and Horwitz, *Parliament, Policy and Politics* provide respectively a clear, and a highly detailed, guide to politics in this area (as in so many others) – while many of the detailed discussions in parliament in the early 1690s can be followed in Horwitz, *Parliamentary Diary ... Luttrell.* Robert McJimsey, 'Crisis management and political stability, 1692–1719, *Albion* **32** (2000), 559–88, provides a nuanced account of parliametary management of the war machine in the 1690s – I am grateful to Professor McJimsey for helping me find this article again after I had neglected to note its details on first reading.

1 For an account, see J.R. Jones, *The Anglo-Dutch Wars of the Seventeenth Century* (Longman, 1996), ch. 8.

2 Grey, *Debates*, **9**, 123.

3 William Temple, *Observations upon the United Provinces of the Netherlands* (5th edn, 1690), pp. 248–9.

4 Ibid., p. 251.

5 William Carr, *An Accurate Description of the United Netherlands* (1691), p. 49.

6 Ibid.

7 Temple, *Observations*, p. 253.

8 For complaint, see Horwitz, *Parliamentary Diary,* pp. 243, 304.

9 Dickson, *Financial Revolution,* pp. 50–2.

10 Horwitz, *Parliamentary Diary*, pp. 137–9.

11 See, especially, Robert D. McJimsey, 'A country divided? English politics and the Nine Years War', *Albion* **23** (1991), 61–74.

12 Such concern dominated the discussions covered in Horwitz, *Parliamentary Diary*; and Commons addresses – see Cobbett, *Parliamentary History*, **5**, 462, 892, 1196. Some print complaints were Jacobite productions hiding sedition in country criticism – but a flavour of

Williamite concern can be got from *Plain English: or an Enquiry into the Causes which have Frustrated Our Expectations of the Late Happy Revolution* (1691); *Some Short Considerations Concerning the State of the Nation* (1692); or the many writings of Robert Crosfield.

13 Horwitz, *Parliamentary Diary*, p. 53.

14 K.H.D. Haley, *William of Orange and the English Opposition* (Clarendon Press, 1953).

15 Gilbert Burnet, *A Sermon Preached at the Coronation of William III* (1689), p. 20.

16 Thomas Tenison, *A Sermon against Self-love ... 5 June, 1689 being the Fast Day* (1689), p. 23.

17 John Tillotson, *A Sermon Preach'd at St Mary le Bow ... Wed 18th June ... a Day Appointed for a Solemn Monthly Fast'* (1690), p. 33.

18 Claydon, *William III* – esp. ch. 4.

19 *A Form of Prayer to be Used the Fifth Fay of June* (1689).

20 See, for example, *The History of the Persecution of the Protestants by the French King* (1689); *The French King's Decree against Protestants ... to which is added a Brief and True Account of the Cruel Persecutions* (1689); *A Faithful Account of the Renewed Persecution of the Churches of Lower Aquitaine* (1691).

21 For a taste, see Pierre Jurieu, *Seasonable Advice to All the Protestants in Europe* (1689).

22 Pincus, 'English nationalist revolution'.

23 *By the King and Queen a Proclamation for a General Fast ... 24 March, 1691/2* (1692).

24 *A View of the True Interest of the Several States of Europe* (1689), p. 3.

25 See, for example, *Nero Gallicanus* (1690); *The Intrigues of the French King at Constantinople* (1689).

26 *LJ*, **14**, 128.

27 *The Most Christian Turk* (1690), p. 78.

28 *The Means to Free Europe from French Usurpation* (1689), epistle dedicatory.

29 See, for example, *A Memorial Drawn up at King William's Special Direction, Intended to be Given in at the Treaty of Ryswick* (1707).

30 Pincus, *Protestantism and Patriotism*, esp. part 3.

31 *CJ*, **10**, 101.

32 *LJ*, **15**, 599.

33 *CJ*, **10**, 200.

34 *LJ*, **14**, 320.

35 See, for example, J.A. Downie, 'The Commission of Public Accounts and the formation of the country party', *English Historical Review* **91** (1976), 33–51.

36 Gilbert Burnet, *History of his Own Times* (2nd edn, Oxford, 1833), **4**, 116–17.

37 *CSPD, 1690–1*, p. 29.

38 Ibid, p. 428.

WILLIAM III

39 HMC, *Report on the Manuscripts of His Grace the Duke of Portland* (1894), **3**, 507.

40 HMC, *House of Lords, 1690–1* (1892), pp. 404–8.

41 CJ, **10**, 298.

42 Cobbett, *Parliamentary History,* **5**, 501.

43 Horwitz, *Parliamentary Diary,* pp. 222–3

44 See *A Collection of the Debates and Proceedings in Parliament* (1695).

45 Howitz, *Parliament, Policy and Politics*, pp. 88, 103–4, 118, 135.

46 [Somers], *Letter Ballancing*.

47 *LJ*, **16**, 372.

48 Horwitz, *Parliamentary Diary*, p. 29.

49 See, for example, [Gilbert Burnet], *Three Letters Concerning the Current State of Italy* (1688).

50 See t'Hart, *Making of a Bourgeois State,* Conclusion.

51 Temple, *Observations*, p. 130.

Chapter Six

William and the 'Three Kingdoms': England, Scotland and Ireland

The 'British problem' in the seventeenth century

In the early hours of 13 December 1688, there was an unnerving conclusion to the disorder which had gripped London for the previous day and a half. Ever since news of James's flight had spread on the 11th, mobs had vented their anger on papist targets. The embassies of Catholic powers had been torched by angry crowds; the king's Catholic printer, Henry Hills, had seen his works go up in flames; and the night sky had been lit by a huge bonfire on Lincoln's Inn Fields fuelled by the furnishings and ornaments of Romish chapels. Now, past midnight on the second evening of rioting, rumours began to spread that a huge band of Irish troops had destroyed Uxbridge and were marching on London to slaughter its inhabitants. Within half an hour, nearly 100,000 people were on the streets. Panicking, banging drums, and running backwards and forwards with no plan or organisation, they enforced an illumination of the town by demanding that all householders fill their windows with candles and barracking those who did not do so immediately. It was, one witness recorded 'the greatest uproar that ever perhaps was known in London'.[1] The disturbance did not subside until a group of peers meeting at the Guildhall took vigorous action. They sent horsemen along the road to Uxbridge to verify the reports of an Irish army, and then arranged to calm the populace down when these outriders found no such force. By dawn, Londoners who had spent the night racing along the city's thoroughfares, or nervously guarding their own front doors, began to retire to bed. From then, tiredness took its toll. The following days were more subdued as overexcited crowds found they could no longer throng without proper sleep.

This story obviously illustrates the high tension of the south-east of England during the revolution. It also, however, points to an underlying problem with Stuart rule. What had disturbed Londoners so much had been the thought that *Irish* troops were coming to massacre them. They had thus shown concern that one of the Stuart kingdoms was destabilising, even invading, another. This was a fear rendered all too plausible by decades of dangerous entanglements between England, Scotland and Ireland. Ever since James VI of Scotland had become James I of England in 1603, the different kingdoms over which his descendants had ruled had plunged each other into suspicion, conspiracy, rebellion and war. The details of this history are complex. Because it is always hard to be clear when relating tales of multi-layered interactions, confusion has been an unfortunate hallmark of the scholarship which has focused on these relationships in recent years. To make things simpler here, we will restrict ourselves to a few sampled periods when 'the British problem' (as the disrupting interactions of realms has come to be known) was severe. We will then analyse the fundamental causes of the 'problem of the three kingdoms' (as it is also known) and so try to establish exactly what difficulties William needed to solve to bring stability to his new lands.

Probably the most dramatic example of the British problem in the seventeenth century came in the years before the English civil war. In fact, it is perfectly possible to argue that this conflict only happened because of Scotland and Ireland's impact on their larger and richer neighbour. Rebellion against Charles I, after all, started, not in England, but in Scotland. In 1637, much of the northern nation had risen against the court's religious policy: the road to revolt in the south began only when the king proved incapable of suppressing the Scots, and found his English subjects more in sympathy with the rebels than with their sovereign. When, in 1640, the Westminster parliament refused to aid Charles in his peril, the scene was set for a Scots occupation of England's northern counties which guaranteed the English parliament's power. Charles could not dissolve his London legislature while a Scottish army threatened further advance, and this gave MPs the chance for their first assaults on the king's prerogatives. By itself, parliament's Scot-based advance created tensions. Conflict, however, was not certain until a further rebellion, this time in Ireland, sealed it. In October 1641, the Catholics of Ulster rose in revolt, disastrously claiming that one of their objectives was to free Charles from enslavement by the radical party in the English Commons. This blew apart any hopes of compromise, since it raised the question of who could be trusted to suppress the Irish rebels. The king said he would do it, but leading parliamentarians claimed some courtiers might not want to, since the revolt claimed to be in the royal cause. In response, court and legislature squabbled over command of the English army. This issue was the formal – perhaps even the substantive – cause of rupture.

The years 1637–42 demonstrated the most tragic effects of the entanglement of the three kingdoms – but the horror extended well beyond them. If England had been alone, her civil wars would almost certainly have ended with parliament's triumph in 1646. She was not alone, however, and this ensured continued bloodshed in the island kingdoms until 1652. Problems began because Scotland became mistrustful of the victorious forces in England. Although the Scots had allied with the parliamentarians before 1646, they came to reject the religious radicalism of the winners in England, and swung back to support the Stuart crown. In consequence there was a second civil war in 1648 when the Scots allied with English royalists. Later, in 1650, the English general Oliver Cromwell was forced to invade Scotland to discipline a northern regime which had not accepted the execution of the king in London; and in 1651 a Scots army led by Charles II penetrated as far south as Worcester before the English forces defeated it. In Ireland, meanwhile, the parliamentarians had not won. Forces loyal to Charles (incorporating many of the 1641 rebels) gained control, with the result that the English regime had to fight to close a backdoor to royalist influence. In 1649, Cromwell staged his notorious invasion of Ireland, which included the massacres of Drogheda and Wexford. Similar cross-national disruptions dominated the years during and after the Restoration. Charles II only regained his throne because a Scots army marched south; religious dissidents in the three realms encouraged each other in the 1660s and 1670s; and – as Tim Harris has begun to show – the exclusion crisis in England (1679–83) was aggravated by fears of what was happening in both Scotland and Ireland. While whigs pressed harder because they believed the authoritarian regimes in Edinburgh and Dublin would soon be applied in London, tories were driven by fears that whigs had dangerous alliances with advanced Protestants in both kingdoms.[2]

This potted history demonstrates the depths and dangers of the British problem in the Stuart period. Its fundamental cause was simply that it was difficult to control all the realms from one centre. This was not just because of the distances involved (although these were important factors in an age of slow communications, and of personal, face-to-face, rule): it also involved points of political principle, political reality and religious diversity.

The political principle was the constitutional independence of Scotland and Ireland from England. In the case of the northern kingdom, freedom was almost complete. When James VI of Scotland had taken the English crown, he had hoped to unite his two realms into a more organised whole, but opposition from the parliament in Westminster had scuppered these plans. This had left the two kingdoms almost completely autonomous. Scotland happened to have the same monarch as England, but it had its own laws, its own parliament, its own policies and its own government (a Privy Council in Edinburgh appointed by the king independently of his English ministers). The Irish situation was not quite as bad, since Ireland had been tied more closely to the English crown in the Tudor period. The monarch of England was automatically the ruler of Ireland; no new law could be proposed in the western kingdom until it had had the approval of the English Privy Council; and Irish government was headed by a lord lieutenant appointed from London. Beyond this, however, the Irish enjoyed their own parliament which had to approve all new statutes and taxes, and were governed by their own executive based in Dublin Castle.

The political reality making rule from London harder was the internal decentralisation of both Scotland and Ireland. Unlike England, where the power of the royal court had been strong in the outlying provinces since the Middle Ages, the two other kingdoms had powerful regional aristocracies which controlled affairs in their particular parts of the realms. In Scotland, provincial autonomy was reinforced by the clan system which ensured people were more loyal to their extended kin, its lands and leader, than to the Scots crown. In Ireland, the court's authority only truly extended to the 'Pale' – a small defended area around Dublin. The rest of the country, 'beyond the Pale', was still dominated by great lords who, like their Scots counterparts, retained the allegiance of local inhabitants. In both kingdoms decentralisation was preserved by mountainous terrain which made communications difficult, and by a lack of urban or gentry classes who might look to the centre rather than the local aristocracy. As a result, both Scotland and Ireland were alliances of nobles rather than closely co-ordinated states. Rulers had to bargain and accommodate these magnates if their writ was to run at all.

Added to these difficulties of central control, was a religious diversity, stemming from the varying fortunes of the sixteenth-century Reformation. Because the three kingdoms had been so independent of each other, and because it was hard for the central authority to impose its orders on the provinces in two of them, the brands of Protestantism introduced in the decades after the 1520s had been different, and their imposition had met with varying success. In Scotland, the new faith had been enforced – not by the crown – but by some of the magnates who dominated Scots politics. This meant both that Catholic remnants had remained in areas controlled by nobles who took against the Reformation, and that Scots religion was rather different from the Protestantism of England. The Campbells, and other enthusiasts for the new faith, had favoured a more thorough-going reform than the Tudors to the south. The Scottish church – or 'kirk' – therefore retained far less ceremony, it adhered to a far clearer statement of Calvinist doctrine, and was far cooler about bishops. Episcopal government (with bishops) had been imposed by James VI, but many Scots still preferred the alternative presbyterian system (where the church was controlled by assemblies of ministers). In Ireland, the Reformation *had* been introduced by the same authorities as in England, but it had been almost entirely unsuccessful. A church similar to the English one had been established by the official government – but it had not been adopted in the independent lordships outside Dublin. Ireland therefore remained a predominantly Catholic country. The only substantial population of Protestants were Scots who had begun settling in Ulster in the early seventeenth century, and who shared the more advanced Protestant view of their homeland. Such religious diversity increased the difficulties of central control. For early modern rulers, the church was a vital adjunct of the state. The clergy had close contact with all the populace, and so should have been useful tools of administration and propaganda for monarchs who claimed to be spiritual as well as political heads of their society. Yet with such differences in religion through the three kingdoms, the court in London found it hard to reap these benefits.

This problem of central control was the first dangerous fact about the three kingdoms. A second was that the different realms constantly destabilised each other. The key reason for this was that each was internally divided, especially on religion. As we have already begun to see, Scotland, Ireland and England had minorities who did not share the views of most of their countrymen, and who wished that the settlement – particularly the church settlement – in their nation was different. In this situation, the fact that other realms, close by and under the same monarch, had alternative arrangements was a standing encouragement to these minorities. Cross-border alliances formed easily. Minorities in one place teamed up with groups in one of the other kingdoms who enjoyed more influence, and persuaded them to use their power to interfere in the first realm's affairs. Thus, the English puritans, who wanted England to have a more thorough-going Protestant church, saw a model for their desires in Scotland. When, in the late 1630s, the Scots rebelled against royal attempts to impose a more English-style church, leaders of that rebellion entered into treasonous co-operation with English puritans to sustain the revolt and keep the cause of robust Protestantism alive. Other instances can be cited. Those minority groups in Scotland opposed to radical Protestant domination looked to the majority Catholics of Ireland to help them. The result was a series of rumours that an Irish army was to land in Western Scotland, and actual Irish help for Scots royalists in the first civil war. After 1646, Scotland's leaders feared the majority of English parliamentarians had become too religiously innovative even for their own tastes. They therefore allied with moderate opinion in England, resulting in the Scots incursions of 1648, 1651 and 1660. The three realms thus bounced endlessly against each other, in a manner which has been likened to billiard balls on the green cloth.

A third, and most tragic, fact about the three kingdoms stemmed directly from the first two. Because the king lacked tight control from the centre, and because the kingdoms constantly destabilised each other, there was no obvious strategy which rulers could follow to halt the endless round of crisis and bloodshed. They could not, for instance, simply accept the diversity of their realms. They could not govern each with different policies according to its own circumstances, and hope that this accommodation would make the tensions go away. Both James I and Charles II tried this flexible approach, but it soon became apparent that they had merely stored up trouble for successors. Within years of their deaths, it was clear they had merely preserved the differences between the kingdoms which encouraged minorities to form cross-border alliances, and so had made it more likely that nations would interfere in each other's affairs. On the other hand, trying to impose uniform policies on the three kingdoms was even more instantly disastrous. It was tried on several occasions: but each time it collapsed because people read imposed uniformity as an attempt to force the traditions of one kingdom on another and erode their own national liberties. Thus when Charles I tried to end the British problem by increasing royal control over magnates in Scotland and Ireland, and reducing Scots and Irish religion to the English model, the results were terrible. His efforts led to the civil war, as the policy stoked the resentments which led to revolt in Scotland in 1637, and rebellion in Ireland in 1641. James II's promotion of Catholicism in the three kingdoms could be read as another attempt to bring about uniformity – this time by encouraging universal conversion back to the ancient faith. The approach bred huge opposition in Scotland and England, however, not least because it looked like an attempt to make these British realms more like papist Ireland. The London panic on 13 December 1688, stemmed directly from these fears.

The interlacing web of problems we have just surveyed meant there was no easy resolution of the relationships between the Stuart realms. If there was a way forward, it was clear it would have to be far more subtle than crude attempts to harmonise the kingdoms, and rather more active than benign negligence. The nations would have to be edged towards each other and encouraged to co-operate, but this would have to be done with sympathy for their particular laws and elites, and without blatant exercises of central power which were too easily read as threats to national autonomy.

Given this, William's continental career might have provided grounds for optimism. The new king was not enmeshed in the failures of earlier Stuart policy, and he had experience in the United Provinces of balancing requirements which were not dissimilar to the islands' circumstances. In the Netherlands, after all, he was already a ruler of multiple states. He was stadholder of Zeeland, Utrecht, Overijssel and Gelderland as well as in the central province of Holland. He had therefore had to respect a diversity of local constitutions and local politics, while lining all these units behind his overarching opposition to Louis. In meeting this challenge, William had been quite impressive. He had held each province by working within its traditions and with its elites; but had nevertheless pulled all together by stressing a common cause. In Holland, for example, he had used his diplomatic skills to build anti-French sentiment among the burgers of Amsterdam. In rural Gelderland, by contrast, he had employed different tactics, stressing his position as a military aristocrat to appeal to the nobles who dominated the province. Meanwhile in Zeeland he had used the traditional strength of the Orange party in the towns to whip up support for the war. After 1688, this achievement might seem of relevance to Britain and Ireland. William might be expected to use the flexibility and accommodation he had learnt in the Provinces to deal sympathetically with the different leaders of England, Scotland and Ireland.

Disappointingly, however, William seems to have made a hash of the British problem. Even in modern popular consciousness, his failure looms large. If people today have one image of William, it must be as the badge of stern Ulster unionism. This is the man whose image upon a rearing white horse dominates gable ends in loyalist parts of Belfast, and whose livery is displayed in Orange Order parades. William, therefore, has become a symbol of the difficulties the British and Irish still have in reconciling their entangled jurisdictions and religions. Even for academic historians, William's record in dealing with his three realms looks poor. His continental experience and focus helped him resolve a crisis at the very start of his reign, but as we shall see, he soon provoked resentments which threatened to shipwreck the union of the isles. Most damagingly for the argument of this book, it seems to have been William's European enthusiasms which led to this. Distracted by Flanders, he gave too little attention to the dangers of his interacting kingdoms.

The initial British crisis: William, Scotland and Ireland, 1688–91

The British problem loomed very large at the start of William's reign. In fact, it posed the most immediate and most dangerous challenge to his rule. Although the Prince of Orange gained the crown very easily in London, the looseness of the union between the Stuart realms ensured his task would be harder in Edinburgh and Dublin. In Scotland, the difficulty was constitutional. The Scottish monarchy had remained technically autonomous: there was no reason for the Scots to follow suit if the English decided to break the hereditary succession to their crown. William, therefore, would have to get himself accepted in Edinburgh quite separately from his southern triumph. In Ireland, the problem was religious. Constitutionally, the Irish crown *was* linked to that of England, so William became king in Dublin the moment the English promoted him. This meant little, however, as confessional considerations spelt the collapse of England's authority on the western isle. The Irish were overwhelmingly Catholic; they had been benefiting from James's pro-Catholic policies; and they were not prepared to forgo this advance by supporting a new Protestant regime. James's governor in Ireland, the earl of Tyrconnell, declared loyalty to the displaced king and Ireland went into full rebellion against William's authority.

In coping with this initial 'British' crisis, William's continental focus and resources stood him in good stead. Within three years, he was in full control in all three kingdoms, and the danger that the Stuart union might disintegrate was averted. To take Scotland first, William succeeded through the tact he had learned from Dutch politics. In the northern kingdom he applied the lessons of 1672, just as he had in England. He avoided alienating support by refusing to seize power, and by waiting for a properly constituted representative to offer him rule.

As in Holland and England during his earlier coups, William's actual position in Edinburgh was quite strong. Once news came that James had fled London, the old king's control in the north evaporated. Scots nobles and privy councillors were anxious to get in with the new power in Britain, and so scrambled over the border. This left Scotland bereft of its natural leaders. By January 1688 the council in Edinburgh could not raise a quorum, tax collection ceased, and local administration devolved back to whatever private men of influence were left. Meeting in London on 7 January, the Scots council – and indeed most of the rest of the Scots political nation – put temporary authority in William's hands. They asked him to call a convention, constituted in the same way as a Scottish parliament, to decide the future of the land. Events in Scotland, therefore, seemed to be racing towards a Williamite monarchy.

Yet, as in Holland and England, the prince himself was cautious. He knew he could weaken his claims by highhanded action; and, when the convention met in Edinburgh in March 1689, it was clear that many – indeed nearly half the representatives – still wanted James to remain king. In this situation, the prince used his old trick of flattery, and of leaving the formal decisions to the representative assembly. The success of his approach was dramatically demonstrated on 16 March. Split down the middle, the convention decided to read out letters which both James and William had sent to the body. William's was a model of diplomacy. Making no direct claims, it assured the convention that 'it lies to you to enter upon such consultations as are most probably to settle you'.[3] James, by disastrous contrast, suggested treason trials for all who forsook their natural allegiance. This sank the old king's cause. As an observer noted, the bulk of the convention was unimpressed by James's blustering 'threats and promises'.[4] Most of James's supporters realised such intransigence could never be a basis for a settlement, and sadly left the meeting. On 11 April, the Williamites who remained declared the prince and his wife joint monarchs of Scotland. The new king's path was smoothed further by his accustomed lack of protest as representative assemblies cut back on his powers. The offer of the throne was accompanied by a 'claim of right' which declared Scotland to be 'a legal limited monarchy', and by 'articles of grievance' which protested at many of the crown's traditional prerogatives. Despite the radical nature of these documents (rather more radical in fact than the English declaration of rights), William said nothing immediately which suggested he rejected them.

This Dutch tact did not secure Scotland completely or immediately. Some Jacobites left the convention to rebel. Romantically, Viscount Dundee raised an army in the Highlands, and scored a worrying military victory at Killiecrankie on 27 July. Yet William's accommodating treatment of the Scots elite ensured him support where it counted. He won over most of the nobles of the rich and populous Lowlands, and he enthused the many radical Protestants of Scotland by appearing to promise an abolition of the bishops who had been re-imposed on the Scots church at the Restoration. The claim of right and articles of grievance cited these 'prelates' as unacceptable instruments of oppression: William's apparent acceptance of these documents suggested he would be prepared to see them go. In consequence, the Orange cause in Scotland was well armed and well funded. Dundee himself had been killed at Killiecrankie. On 21 August, his troops were defeated at Dunkeld – the gateway to the Lowlands – by a regiment of rigidly Protestant Cameronians. After that, it took three years of skirmishes in the north to quell the last of the Jacobite clans, but the new regime's control in the heartlands was secure. When the war ended with the massacre of Glencoe in 1692, Scots sympathies could safely lie with the victims, even though they had fought for the exiled James. Enquiries into the incident were launched because the murdered Macdonalds had posed no real threat in a solidly Williamite Scotland. Once the victors were secure, they could afford to deplore the fate of the slaughtered clansmen – who, it emerged, had been trying to surrender to the king's officials, and had been offered hospitality by their Campbell assassins immediately before the fatal hour.

Across the Irish sea, the new king tried to be as accommodating as he had been in Britain. He sent an envoy, Richard Hamilton, to Tyrconnell – presumably making assurances about the position of Catholics in a Williamite Ireland, and hoping these might persuade the lord lieutenant to his side. Unfortunately, the situation in Dublin was beyond any such diplomacy, even if Hamilton had not rapidly deserted to the Jacobite cause.[5] Hearing of anti-popish hysteria in England, and still loyal to the old king who had shared their religion, most Irish Catholics believed they would gain most from supporting James. Accordingly, Tyrconnell began organising the local population into a Jacobite army. By the early spring of 1689, he controlled all of Ireland, except parts of Ulster, where the Protestant city of Londonderry refused to admit his officers, and was besieged from April. On 12 March Tyrconnell was joined by James himself. The old king brought with him 3,000 French troops whom Louis had sent in hopes of trapping William in a battle for Ireland. James set himself up as king in Dublin, and began planning to link up with the Jacobite forces in Scotland.

In dealing with this threat, William once again relied upon his European advantages. What he brought to bear this time, however, was the very opposite of political tact. It was an efficient army, built around a core of professional Dutch troops. Once it had become clear that William would need to secure Ireland before he could turn his attention to the continental war, the estates in The Hague had agreed that they would help their captain-general by supplying experienced troops for the enterprise. In May 1689, they allowed William an extra 5,000 men. When added to the soldiers left over from the original invasion of England, this meant the king commanded 17,000 Netherlanders in Britain, who were supplemented by a force of 2,000 French Protestants. William's continental connections thus ensured he had a rare advantage for a London-based ruler trying to control Ireland. Unlike most of his predecessors (Cromwell was the exception), he could back his claims to sovereignty with a modern, trained and battle-hardened military.

In the summer of 1689, this army began to be transported to Ireland. In August, 10,000 troops, commanded by the Protestant Frenchman Schomberg, landed in the north and made good progress. They took back Ulster, capturing the vital port of Carrickfergus and benefiting from the relief of Derry by an English naval squadron after the city's four-month ordeal. Admittedly, there were setbacks over the winter. Schomberg camped just north of Dundalk, where his forces became literally bogged down in the local marshes, and died in their hundreds from dysentery. The next summer, however, continuing support from Europe allowed the Orange army to push forward. On 14 June, William himself arrived with 15,000 fresh troops, nearly half of whom had been hired from the king of Denmark. Marching south from Dundalk, this mixed continental army engaged with Tyrconnell's forces at the Battle of the Boyne (1 July), and defeated it soundly enough to open the road to Dublin. The victory did not immediately end Jacobite resistance. Irish Catholics fought on in the west, and some French forces stayed to stiffen their resolve. The Boyne was, however, the decisive point in the war. It prompted James to flee the country; it secured Orange control of the vital areas closest to England and Scotland; and it allowed William to return to London after some unsuccessful raids on remaining Jacobite territory. The next summer, Godert de Ginkel, the Dutch general whom the king left in charge (Schomberg had been killed at the Boyne), was able to complete the pacification of the country. He defeated his enemies at Aughrim on 12 July, and drove them to Limerick where he surrounded them in their last stronghold.

Ginkel's success underlines the European nature of William's war effort in his western kingdom. Even though the battle of the Boyne has forever after been celebrated by Irish Protestants as the salvation of a *British* Ireland (why William's image is still paraded through northern streets), the victory is best understood as part of continent-wide war. The king had been determined to snuff out Irish Catholic resistance so he could turn his attention to Flanders. He had therefore deployed his best foreign troops and commanders to end this irritating side-show. Yet, while these European priorities spelt an efficient suppression of Catholic resistance up to the summer of 1691, William's continental perspective began to play a different role that autumn. After Aughrim, it was clear it would only be a matter of time before the Irish were completely defeated. Yet, with the Jacobites holed up in the formidable fortress of Limerick, it was clear this time could be a long one. William therefore feared that he would have to divert forces from the Dutch border to Ireland for many months. Consequently, he ordered the men on site to negotiate lenient terms for his opponents. Under the 'Treaty of Limerick', agreed on 3 October, the

Jacobite soldiers who surrendered were offered a choice. They could, if they wished, depart with the French forces and join the armies of Louis XIV. 12,000 of the 15,000 men in the garrison took this option. If they preferred to stay in Ireland, the Jacobites would be disarmed, but they – and those under their protection – would be treated very well. They would be pardoned for rebellion, they could keep their lands, and they could exercise the wide freedom of worship they had enjoyed under Charles II. With this extraordinarily generous offer, the new king extricated himself from Irish conflict.

Taken overall, William's handling of his initial 'British' crisis demonstrated some possible advantages of European experience, perspectives and resources. He had persuaded the Scots to alter their succession in line with the English one by using tactics learned in Holland. He had speeded his acquisition of power by prioritising the simple acquisition of the throne (which would ensure he had his hands free to act on the continent of Europe) over preserving the parochial prerogatives of the Scots crown. At the same time, he had reconquered Ireland with continental resources. He had, however, ensured warfare would not be prolonged by preferring the defence of Flanders over any unconditional surrender by the Catholic Irish. This sort of Dutch pragmatism, backed by military strength and the unifying purpose of William's European alliance, might seem exactly the recipe to solve the more general tensions between the three kingdoms. Unfortunately, though, William's continental finesse with the British problem did not last beyond 1691. Soon relations between the three realms were deteriorating back to crisis, and the king's obsession with Europe was to blame.

William's failure in British politics: Scots and Irish resentment

In earlier chapters, this book has insisted that William's continental focus eased the problems of English politics. Its main message has been that it took a man unconnected with old political tensions, and caring little about England itself, to free the log-jam which had afflicted public life under the Stuarts. As we turn our attention to the British and Irish dimensions, however, William's disengagement suddenly seems dangerous. In Scotland and Ireland, the king's attitudes worsened internal difficulties, and put relations between the three Stuart kingdoms under strain. Partly, this was because William's neglect of his western and northern realms was more complete. The English may have worried that their king was obsessed with Flanders, but at least they saw him for several months every winter. By contrast, William only visited Ireland for the Boyne campaign in 1690, and never set foot in Scotland at all. The Irish and Scots thus still suffered from an absentee monarch, and William was unable to deploy directly the skills of negotiation with political elites which he had gained from the United Provinces. Even more damaging was the underlying reason for the king's preference for England. William spent time in London because he wanted to persuade the English to lend their resources to the continental conflict. He certainly wanted Scots and Irish resources too, but he knew that these relatively poor realms had little to offer. William therefore concentrated on London, rather than Dublin or Edinburgh, and would sacrifice Scots and Irish interests to English ones if they ever clashed. The result was growing resentment in Ireland and Scotland as the king listened to the demands of the Westminster parliament over the complaints of the other national legislatures.

The pattern is clearest in Ireland. Problems in the western kingdom started with the Treaty of Limerick. Of course, the Irish Protestant elite who dominated the Dublin parliament were grateful to William for rescuing them from James. Yet their delight soon turned to horror when they saw where the king's European fixation led. By granting such generous terms to the garrison at Limerick, the monarch had freed his own hands for Flanders, but he had not punished people whom the Protestants were convinced were extremely dangerous. Catholics whose fathers had slaughtered reformed Christians in the 1641 rebellion – and who themselves had tried to starve the defenders of Derry – were to be allowed property, free religion and a peaceful life. William, it seemed, had sacrificed the Irish Protestants' interests for those of the Dutch.

Reaction was swift. It burst forth in the parliament William called in 1692 to gain revenues from Ireland and to ratify the Limerick treaty. As soon as the legislature met, the depths of anger were apparent. The parliament was an exclusively Protestant body (Catholics had been denied the vote during the Tyrconnell rebellion), and it had been elected in an atmosphere so anti-court that many ministers in the Irish administration had found it hard to gain a seat. Unsurprisingly, William's lord lieutenant, Henry Sydney, found the Commons unmanageable. The house delayed financial supply, and threatened impeachments against ministers whom they accused of corruption and collaboration with Jacobites. As for the treaty of Limerick, the king's servants dared not even introduce it. After four weeks the parliament was dissolved with almost nothing achieved.

When the Irish legislature next met, in 1695, things had improved, but only because William had surrendered to his enemies. A new lord lieutenant, Henry Capel, made contact with the leaders of the 1692 opposition and offered posts in the administration in return for help in managing the Commons. These men – who became known as 'undertakers' – secured supply, but their price was a rolling back of the concessions granted at Limerick. A series of 'penal laws' were added to the Irish statute book, which limited Catholic worship, and so directly contravened the promise of religious toleration in the treaty. In 1695, Catholics were prevented from holding arms, sending their children abroad for their education, or owning houses worth more the £5 a year. In 1697 all Catholic bishops were banished from the land, as were all monks, Jesuits and friars. When the court finally mustered the courage to attempt to ratify Limerick, it had to sit by while the Irish Commons butchered the text. As the treaty finally emerged from parliament in 1697, it still granted *some* concessions to the Jacobite forces – but the more general leniency for Catholics had gone. The clause promising freedom of worship had vanished. The pardon and property rights were still there, but now they were granted only to those who had still been in arms at the surrender. Those who had stopped fighting, or had been civilians under the Jacobite force's protection, were no longer covered by the terms. This meant their land was vulnerable to forfeiture, or illegal occupation by rapacious Protestants. By the end of the Stuart age, the proportion of Irish land owned by Catholics had dropped to 15 per cent. Nearly a tenth of the country had changed hands after Limerick had been neutered.

William's determination to concentrate on the Flanders battlefields in 1691 had thus caused great problems for his government of Ireland. First, it had weakened his power. He had been unable to manage the Dublin parliament; he had lost the direction of Irish policy to the undertakers; and he had had to suffer the personal dishonour of reneging on a treaty. Second, William's rule deepened internal divisions in Ireland. The Catholic majority had been cheated and forever after repined at the 'lost clauses' of Limerick; while much of the Protestant community had become alienated from the administration, and had formed themselves into a vocal 'country' opposition. Third, and perhaps most worryingly, William had worsened relations between his realms. Angered by the executive's policy, the country group in the Irish parliament began to question links with England. They began to interpret the pro-Catholic policy of the king's administration as an English imposition, and began to speak a 'patriotic' language, arguing that their kingdom should be more independent of London. In the 1692 legislature some Irish MPs insisted the Dublin Commons had the sole right to initiate supply bills (in contradiction of the convention that legislation should originate in the English Privy Council); and the lord lieutenant was to claim some troublemakers were talking as if the Dublin assembly should have full legislative autonomy.[6]

This Irish separatism was fanned to a flame in the later 1690s when the king once again put his European strategy above the feelings of Irishmen. The background here was William's difficult relations with the Westminster parliament after the treaty of Ryswick. As we have seen, the king effectively lost control of the English Commons in the disputes over the standing army, and was only able to restore his influence by capitulating to its demands. Unfortunately for Ireland, William's need to regain the favour of the London parliament (vital if any future war against France were to be properly financed), meant sacrificing the western kingdom. On two key occasions, the king allowed Westminster to impose its will on Ireland. In 1699, English MPs became worried about sheep farming in their country. Convinced that the industry was suffering unfair competition from across the Irish sea, they sent William a bill to ban imports of wool. With his eyes on the continent, the king assented to the measure, even though it would devastate Ireland's economy. The very next year, the English Commons delved still deeper into Irish affairs. Investigations into profits made by certain of the king's favourites culminated in a resumptions act, which re-confiscated lands in Ireland originally forfeited by Jacobites but then granted by the crown to its followers. Again, the king agreed, even though this meant Westminster interfering in internal Irish policy, and taking property from many Irish Protestants who had gained it after the revolution.

As can be imagined, reaction in Dublin to these events was apoplectic. Without regard for Irish interests, and without the consent of the Irish parliament, the English had regulated Ireland's affairs. Most Irishmen rejected Westminster's right to do this, and in a stream of pamphlets and petitions the nascent nationalism of the opposition burst into demands for greater independence. At its most eloquent, the new Irish patriotism could appeal for a wholesale re-negotiation of the constitutional links between Ireland and England. William Molyneux's famous tract, *The Case of Ireland* (1698) became a rallying cry – and it argued for the full equality of the Dublin and Westminster parliaments. The Irish, Molyneux argued, were not a conquered people and so should not be treated as subservient. In the Middle Ages, Irish chieftains had come willingly under Englishmen to gain the rights and liberties the invaders enjoyed, so modern Irishmen deserved the same consideration. One way to secure this would be to merge the Dublin and Westminster parliaments. Molyneux thought such a solution would be 'a happiness', but recognised that self-interested Englishmen would reject any representatives from Ireland interfering in their rule on the mainland. He therefore called for Irish autonomy as the best alternative. In his scheme, the crowns of the two kingdoms would still be linked; but the Irish parliament would have full sovereignty over Irish affairs (there would be no repeat of the woollens or resumptions acts); the English Privy Council would lose its right to initiate legislation in the Dublin assembly; and the lord lieutenant would have to enjoy the confidence of the Irish political nation – not simply be appointed by the administration in London.[7] With the triumph of such sentiments, William had to abandon any further thoughts of meeting the Irish parliament. By the end of his reign, the king's continental need to placate the English Commons had bred a full-scale crisis in relations between his western and his south-eastern kingdoms.

Tragically, almost exactly the same story can be told of Scotland. Again, anti-court sentiment built, and then festered into calls for the wholesale removal of English influence. At first, it is true, opposition had little to do with William's European policy. In the late Stuart era, Scotland suffered from a structural weakness which would have made it hard for anyone to establish a stable government, whether they had distractions in Flanders or not. The difficulty was the fractured nature of Scots political life. Unlike the nation south of the border, Scotland was not polarised into two clear parties but was dominated by a number of factions, each clustered round a great aristocrat. The battles of these factions for power made political management complex, and ensured an almost automatic majority for parliamentary oppositions. If the king appointed a member of one faction to a juicy job in the administration, all its rivals would become jealous. The monarch could not placate these rivals by offering other posts, since every group wished to monopolise influence and would bicker with competitors in government, so all but the dominant faction went into opposition. Once there, they would fix on popular causes which criticised their rivals in the administration, and would band with other groups (people always found it easier to co-operate outside government) to control the Edinburgh parliament. The result was an inherently unstable regime. No team of ministers could be appointed who could enjoy the confidence of the legislature.[8]

This pattern emerged even during the 1689 constitutional settlement in Scotland. As we have seen, William eased his path to the throne in Edinburgh by saying nothing against the claim of right or the articles of grievance which accompanied the offer of power, and which attempted to curtail the prerogatives of monarchy. Yet as we would expect from his attitudes in England, William was actually unhappy about these documents. In particular, he disliked their demands that the Lords of the Articles be abolished. The lords were a committee of the Scots parliament, dominated by ministers, which could approve the executive's actions when the full legislature was not sitting. William was also horrified by the suggestion that the monarchy lose its headship of the Scots church; and he wished to moderate the documents' attacks on episcopacy, since bishops had always been good supporters of crown power. To try to save his influence over Scots politics, the monarch turned to the duke of Hamilton, a seasoned statesman and influential regional magnate. William appointed Hamilton his parliamentary commissioner, and charged him with toning down the claim and the articles. From what has already been said, the results were predictable. All Hamilton's enemies united, and took up the original restrictions on the crown as their slogan. The summer of 1689 was therefore a stormy one in parliament. The united opposition – soon known as the 'Club' – brought together magnate rivals of Hamilton with rigid presbyterians determined to secure religious change. Together, these groups had a majority in parliament, and denied the crown revenue unless it would enact the claim and the articles. Before long, it was clear Hamilton would have to go. The king dissolved the legislature in disgust in August, but when it met again in the spring of 1690, George Melville headed the Scots executive, and William accepted he would have to surrender to the Club's protests. Lords of the Articles, royal headship of the church, and bishops: all came crashing down. Unfortunately, the king's concessions solved little. The structural problem with Scots politics persisted, so parliament remained in the grip of 'country' oppositions, using plausible anti-court issues to undermine ministers.

In these calamities, there was no immediate 'British dimension'. However, as crises piled up, there were increasing signs that Scotland's internal conflicts were developing into a wider tension between Edinburgh and London. As in Ireland, constant attacks on the ministry grew into criticism of English influence. One of the easiest ways to discredit a government in Edinburgh was to suggest it was in the pockets of the executive in Westminster. Accusations of toadying to the English became central to Scots country rhetoric, and resentments at the ties between the two British kingdoms grew. The early 1690s were therefore marked by a series of brief ministries, each of which was brought down by factional opposition, and each of whose life was shortened by the perception that they danced to an English tune.

It was at this point that the damaging role of William's European obsession became clearer. Surveying the political instability of the northern kingdom, the king's advisers in Scotland suggested William himself come to Edinburgh. His political skills must forge an alliance which could control parliament; factional leaders must be persuaded into government by the flattery and sense of influence that only face-to-face dealings with their monarch could produce. The idea of a royal journey north was circulating in the Scots privy council at least as early as the winter of 1689–90 – and persisted right through to the end of the reign.[9] William, however, never came. In this refusal to travel, the king's continental priorities began to contribute to his difficulties in holding Scotland. As has been shown, the king thought only two activities worth much time. The first was leading his armies against Louis, the second was negotiating with the Westminster parliament for resources to supply the fight. The first had taken him to Ireland for a few months in 1690 – but neither ever enticed him to his northern realm. Rule in Scotland was a struggle, but its local difficulties were never as pressing as the battlefields of Flanders or the English Commons. Thus, despite repeated begging from ministers in Scotland, his administrations there did not enjoy his bodily support. They went on falling to parliamentary votes: attacks on England grew more severe.

In the later 1690s, the king's European focus plunged relations between the British realms even deeper into crisis. The immediate catalyst was an attempt at Scots commercial expansion. By the end of the seventeenth century, many Scotsmen were coming to feel they had been left behind in the development of world trade. While England, and many European countries, had set up trading posts and colonies in America, Asia and Africa, Scotland had done very little. Given that contemporary theories suggested that a vigorous commercial empire was essential for national power and prosperity, this was extremely worrying. In 1695, a group of Scots merchants, initially encouraged by the executive in Edinburgh, resolved to do something about the situation and founded the Company of Scotland. This was a joint stock venture – modelled on the Dutch and the English East India Companies – which would sell shares, and would use the money to develop Scotland's international trade. Within months, the directors had fixed on a scheme in central America as its main project. Dazzled out of practicality by the ever-persuasive financier William Paterson (fresh from his triumph with the Bank of England), the company decided to establish a trading post on the Darien isthmus, near the present-day Panama Canal. The hope was to build this colony into a hub of its operations in the western hemisphere.

Sadly for the company, its plans fell foul of two sets of interests. Worse, William was forced to support these opponents out of consideration for his continental war. The first shatterers of Scotland's dreams were English merchants. Many of these, particularly those in the East India interest, saw the company as a potential trading rival, and protested to the Commons. As a result, the Westminster parliament passed motions condemning the venture, and preventing it raising money in England. The Scots' second great opponent was the king of Spain. He made the reasonable point that central America was Spanish territory, and that the Darien adventurers intended to settle it without his permission. In the face of these objections, William sacrificed Scotland's ambition. He did not want to upset the revenue-granting English parliament, and could not afford a row with Spain, as this Habsburg monarchy was one of his most important allies in the struggle with Louis. The king therefore moved to clip the company's wings. In 1695 he sacked the ministers in Edinburgh who had approved the venture, muttering he had been 'ill-served' in Scotland.[10] He similarly disrupted the company's attempts to raise money on European stock markets (informing investors in Hamburg that the scheme was 'an affront to his royal authority'); and he ordered the governors of England's colonies in the West Indies to do all they could to thwart Scots plans in the Caribbean.[11]

The Darien project was a self-inflicted fiasco. It was ill-conceived, badly organised and incompetently led. Although a township was founded in Darien in October 1698 and called New Edinburgh, it was sited in a disease-infested area and the colonists soon fell to feuding among themselves. The settlement was abandoned after a great loss of life, and although it was re-inhabited by a fresh expedition from Scotland in 1699, its fortunes did not improve. A Spanish fleet and army converged on New Edinburgh to root out the illegal squatters, and the colonists were forced to surrender in March 1700. Overall, 2,000 men had been lost, and investors saw no return on 153,000 English pounds' worth of their stock (this was nearly a quarter of Scotland's liquid capital). Yet despite this comedy of error, few people back home could believe it was the Company's absurd ambitions and total mismanagement which had led to national humiliation. Rather, most of them thought they had been betrayed by the English government. Scotland's arrogant neighbour had snuffed out her best chance of becoming a first-division power, and of joining other European nations in imperial expansion.

In reaction there was an explosion of anger against English influence. This was exploited by the duke of Hamilton, who hoped to use the issue to lever the new chief minister, the duke of Queensberry, from power. Hamilton brought together a wide coalition – from radical presbyterians to Jacobites – to press for the Company's interests, and to question England's right to scupper Scotland's foreign policy. This opposition addressed the king to call parliaments which would bring ministers to account; it organised boycotts of foreign goods to reduce the administration's customs revenue; and hampered court business in the legislature. By the time the almost-unmanageable parliamentary sessions of 1700 and 1701 were complete, it was clear there was a crisis in relations between the British kingdoms. Ministers in England began to conclude that the Scots were intent on a course which would lead towards independence: people both sides of the border began to discuss radical constitutional changes to transform the nature of the Stuart union.

Thus in Scotland, as in Ireland, William's continental concerns had led to disaster. At a time when the strains of war, and the political structures of the northern and western kingdoms would encourage 'country' opposition to the local administrations, William's absences in Flanders meant he had no time personally to placate these opponents. His inevitable preference for the views of the Westminster parliament meant it was easy for country spokesmen to dress their complaints against the court in 'nationalist' garb. By 1701, there were many in both Dublin and Edinburgh who saw English interference as the root of all evil, and it was clear to almost everybody that the old Stuart relations between the three kingdoms could not be maintained. As many Scots questioned whether they should follow their southern neighbours in accepting a Hanoverian dynasty once William and his sister-in-law Anne had died; many other people – both north and south of the border – began to promote the idea of full parliamentary merger of the two kingdoms. Alongside supporters of Molyneux's call for full legislative autonomy for Ireland were others – including majorities in the Dublin legislature – who wanted their kingdom fully absorbed by England and Wales.[12] William himself had given up hope of managing his non-English realms in the traditional way. He had ceased to meet his Dublin parliament, knowing that its opposition would stymie all government; and from 1700 was openly proposing that the Edinburgh legislature be abolished so that the whole British island could be governed from a single point.[13] Far from solving the problem of the three kingdoms, the king had presided over the final impasse between them.

Yet for all the severity of the crisis at the end of William's reign, the difficulties proved surprisingly easy to resolve in the years after the king's death. In fact, the high eighteenth century was to mark one of the quietest and most successful periods in England's rule over the other realms of the archipelago. After parliamentary union in 1707, Scotland caused little difficulty (apart from doomed Jacobite risings in 1708, 1715 and 1745). There was to be little further overt separatism north of the border until the later twentieth century. Conditions in the west improved too. After further rounds of penal legislation to reassure the governing Protestant interest, Ireland settled down to almost total calm until the American rebellion in the 1770s re-opened debates between Westminster and other assemblies. In this light, the crisis of the late 1690s looks serious, but nowhere near desperate. Solutions to the problems turned out to be straightforward. In the last section of this chapter we will ask whether William – despite his disappointments – had helped pave the way for these settlements. Under the gathering storms, had this European ruler been sowing the seeds of eventual consensus?

William's success in British politics: religious moderation and parliamentary government

When we examine how stability came to the three kingdoms in the early eighteenth century, it is clear it emerged from two converging developments. The first of these has been brilliantly analysed by David Hayton.[14] It was simply that the English administration found a way to hold Scotland and Ireland by using local men to manage the realms. Rather than following the earlier Stuart experiments in direct rule from Westminster, eighteenth-century ministries cultivated a group of statesmen in each country who would be granted powers of patronage and a say in policy, in return for making the king's government work. These politicians would construct pro-court majorities among Scots or Irish legislators, and would deliver votes for revenue and for any legislation which English ministers wanted. In this way, the London administration harmonised Scotland and Ireland with England's interests, while allowing the elites of Dublin and Edinburgh to gain rewards. Constitutional crisis between the countries was avoided: both English and non-English secured their essential needs.

We have already seen the start of this process in Ireland. When lord lieutenant Capel made contact with the opposition in preparation for the 1695 parliament, he was initiating the system of 'undertakers' who would manage the Dublin parliament for the English for the bulk of the Georgian age. It is true that Capel's system was blown off-course in the outcry over the woollens act in the late 1690s. By Queen Anne's reign, however, it was functioning again; and, under the Hanoverian kings, it was perfected. After 1714, the Irishman William Connolly became chief manager of the Irish Commons. He helped the London ministry control his homeland – but he built himself an electoral empire from the patronage he could bestow once the English had granted him control of the Irish customs house. In Scotland it was harder to put together a stable team of under-takers, since factional jealousies denied a parliamentary majority to any-one favoured by the crown. The solution here was union with England. If the Edinburgh and Westminster parliaments were merged, the hostility of excluded Scots magnates would matter little, since they would control far too few votes in the new united legislature to bring proceedings to a halt. This trick was openly advocated from the last years of William's reign. In 1707, a mixture of persuasion and bribery pulled it off, and the Scots parliament voted itself out of existence. When the amalgamated body met, Scotland had only 45 MPs in the Commons, and 16 rep-resentatives in the Lords, which meant she had only around a twelfth of the numbers enjoyed by England and Wales. Scots opposition had thus been neutered, and the ministry in London was able to govern its north-ern kingdom much as it now ruled in the west. A few great magnates were granted patronage and a role advising on policy in Scotland. In return these men whipped the Scots representatives at Westminster behind the ruling party's line. Classic examples included Queensberry, who master-minded the union in Scotland in 1707 and gained his reward in the years afterwards; and the duke of Argyll, who ran the northern kingdom as a quasi-autonomous fiefdom in the 1720s.

Converging with this discovery of the means of parliamentary man-agement, was a second development which aided England's rule in the north and west. This was a calming of religious tensions – stemming from the moderate ecclesiastical settlements made in Scotland and Ireland in the wake of the 1689 revolution. After changes in church structure, and in the treatment of those who worshipped outside official institutions, much of the passion of Scots and Irish politics drained away. In a more temper-ate atmosphere, Westminster's new government techniques got a chance to work.

At first glance this may seem surprising. To modern eyes, there was nothing particularly moderate about the ecclesiastical settlements. We have already seen how the generous offers to Irish Catholics at Limerick were thwarted in the 1690s, and gave way to persecuting penal laws. In Ulster, the Scots Protestants who could not bring themselves to worship in the Anglican-style church of Ireland were also disappointed. Proposed measures to tolerate their churches were introduced in the 1692 and 1695 parliaments, but failed in the face of overwhelming opposition. This left dissenters as second-class citizens, still excluded from public office by reli-gious tests. In Scotland too, things seemed little improved. The episcopal establishment was abolished in 1690, but what replaced it was no more tolerant. Scots Catholics were as badly off in law as they had been under the restoration kings, while the newly instituted presbyterian church proved hostile to any other form of Protestantism. The Edinburgh parliament did not follow Westminster in granting toleration to non-conformists, and the court was forced to accept an act allowing the new ecclesiastical authorities to deprive clergy they judged 'scandalous or erroneous' (categories which came to mean the same thing as episcopalian). Nearly half the ministers of the kingdom were purged from their parishes in the next seven years. The range of opinion among Scots clergy was narrowed still further when lay patronage was abolished. This last measure ensured clergy were appointed by kirk sessions, which could be relied upon to promote rigid Calvinist presbyterians. In all this, there would seem to be room for considerable religious tension. Sizeable communities of faith were still excluded from the official churches of Scotland and Ireland: many suffered severe discrimination to boot.

Yet, for all this, there *was* a lessening of religious resentments in the years after 1689. It is a mistake to judge the post-revolution settlements by modern standards. In comparison to the prevalent intransigence of churches in the seventeenth century, the situations in Ireland and Scotland after the revolution were generous. In Ireland, for example, non-Anglican communities were probably more secure under William than they had been before. The radical Protestants of the north had certainly made progress. Under Charles and James, they had been allowed periods of toleration, but these had been interspersed with surges of vicious persecution. In the 1690s, the Ulstermen may not have gained a full right to free worship, but the Catholic resurgence of 1689–91 frightened Anglicans into greater acceptance. They now realised they must hang with fellow (if presbyterian) Protestants if they were not to hang separately. In practice, therefore, no prosecutions were brought for non-conformity, and the northerners flourished. Under William they could vote, they could take a full part in economic life, and they came to dominate their region. Nor, surprisingly, was existence so bad for Catholics. Certainly they lost some of the freedoms they had enjoyed under Charles II, and their interest declined hugely from its heyday during the Jacobite rebellion. Yet, considering their cause had been so decisively defeated at the Boyne and Aughrim, they were treated extraordinarily well. The Dublin parliament did not completely vandalise the Limerick treaty (surrendering Catholics were allowed to return to and retain their lands), and there were holes in the penal legislation. For example, although Catholic bishops and regular clergy were banished, Catholic worship per se was not illegal. Ordinary parish priests were suffered to remain, and the 1697 act sending some clerics into exile was only patchily enforced (many monks and several bishops hung on by registering as ordinary clergy). Similarly, although there were tight restrictions on Catholics holding real estate or entering the professions, not all economic life was closed to them. They were allowed to be manufacturers, shopkeepers and merchants; and, if they wished to farm, they could become very substantial tenants, even gaining some of the powers (if not the title) of landlords by sub-letting much of their rented land. Another way to avoid discrimination was to convert. The moment a person became Protestant, all legal disadvantage ceased, and many Catholic families took this option. Sometimes the conversion was sincere, but perhaps more often it was undergone simply to avoid penalisation. In these cases, the head of the family might become a nominal Protestant to protect the clan's property: all other relatives stayed loyal to the ancient faith.[15] Given all these concessions, Catholics had relatively little reason to complain. They had been treated far better than a militarily defeated community usually would have been in contemporary Europe, and – paradoxically – their position was more dependable than it had been under the Catholic monarch. James had helped them, but his actions in doing so had so angered English opinion that the gains proved illusory.

In Scotland too, the post-revolution church settlement was more generous than at first appears. One obvious point is that the advent of a presbyterian establishment liberated a substantial number of Scotsmen. The Anglican-style church imposed at the Restoration had never gained broad consent north of the border. Although it may have had the adherence of a bare majority of Scots, many people had stayed loyal to their more advanced vision of Protestantism, and in consequence had been extremely badly treated. Under Charles II, preaching outside the official church at 'field conventicles' had been punishable by death; receiving the ministrations of a non-conformist minister had incurred harsh financial penalties; and there had been several attempts (most notably in 1678–79, and after 1681) to snuff out religious radicalism with executions and military occupation of its heartlands. The advent of a presbyterian establishment therefore ended a particularly nasty persecution. It is true that the newly triumphant churchmen wished, in their turn, to suppress their rivals. However, they had less success than they had hoped. The act setting up the new church stopped short of declaring presbyterianism to be by 'divine right' (in other words it did not declare that presbytery was the only valid ecclesiastical form), and this set the tone for more tolerance in ecclesiastical affairs than had initially seemed likely. For example, while Roman worship remained illegal in Scotland, Catholics actually enjoyed considerable freedom. Upholding the legislation against popery had always been difficult in the wild Highlands. After 1690 enforcement was, in practice, abandoned. Similarly, the supporters of the old episcopalian church did surprisingly well, especially considering that so many of them supported the Jacobite cause. In 1693 and 1695 acts were passed in the Scots parliament to give some degree of relief to the old clergy. If they would swear allegiance to William they would evade the contemporary purges, and be allowed to keep their livings. Religious diversity was increased still further when the most radical wing of the Protestants refused to join the new establishment on the grounds that it had failed to declare divine right presbytery. From 1690, 'Cameronians' formed their own kirk, which existed alongside the offical one.

Taken with the new methods of parliamentary management, the moderation of the ecclesiastical settlements in Ireland and Scotland quietened the British problem for the bulk of the eighteenth century. By employing undertakers, English administrations found a way of securing control in the peripheral nations, while the chief cause of the nations interfering in each other's business – namely their bitter internal divisions over religion – was being soothed. Given the argument of this book, the question arises of how much this success owed to William and to his European perspective. Despite all his problems in controlling the three kingdoms, can this ruler be seen as the author of the new ideas and conditions which rapidly led to contentment?

Probably, there are ways in which he can. First, we have to acknowledge that the system of undertakers only emerged because Scots and Irish parliaments were being held regularly, and were being taken seriously. It was only because the court in London decided to try to rule through legislatures that it became clear it needed local leaders to whip up parliamentary support. In addition, it was only because substantive parliamentary sessions were held that monarchs began to see who were the most effective operators in those sessions, and so could choose those who might be approached to manage the assemblies. To take an obvious example: Capel would not have selected local men to manage the Dublin assembly until the 1692 parliament had shown the crown could not control affairs on its own, and he could not have picked particular people until he knew whose opposition must be subdued. Similarly, the eventful sessions of the Edinburgh estates convinced the elites of Westminster that they would have to find a way to accommodate Scots politicians while reducing their ability to vandalise government. Earlier regimes could not have seen these ways forward because they had tried to avoid their legislatures meeting. Hoping to rule more directly in Scotland and Ireland, they had abolished the other assemblies (as under Cromwell); they had tried to rule without calling the parliament (the usual pattern in Ireland – where the legislature did not meet at all between 1667 and 1689); or they had ruled through the Lords of the Articles (in Scotland), rather than facing the full and more independent estates.

If legislatures was essential to construct the system of undertakers, it also has to be acknowledged that it took William and his European vision to ensure these bodies met and thrived. We have already seen that the new king's continental background led to a renaissance at Westminster. The same happened in Dublin and Edinburgh. As David Hayton has shown, the years after 1688 saw a general 'rise of parliaments' throughout the Stuart realms.[16] William called *all* his legislatures because he wanted war revenue from them. Even if Ireland and Scotland were too poor to contribute much to the battlefields, they could at least ensure that they were not a financial burden on English taxpayers, whose money was then freed for Flanders. William also surrendered prerogatives to his legislatures in the north and west for the same reason he compromised with MPs in Westminster. He had to avoid crises which could distract him from the defeat of Louis. The king thus agreed to abolish the Lords of the Articles in Scotland; and accepted that the Irish Commons could revise his treaty of Limerick – in both cases losing face and prerogatives to keep funds flowing. All this meant that the Dublin and Edinburgh parliaments were regular and important bodies. Under William each met at least every two years; when they assembled they enjoyed prolonged and substantive sessions; and they both proved they could block court business until they got their way. In such circumstances the need to have undertakers to manage them became compelling – and the usefulness of the men, who could act as brokers between their kingdoms and England – was revealed.

The king could also claim credit for the religious moderation in Scotland and Ireland after 1689. We have already seen that William's continental perspective pushed him towards toleration. He had grown up in a relatively liberal society in the Netherlands, and had absorbed its reluctance to persecute. He also headed an international alliance which included states of many denominations – any of these would be offended if he attacked their co-religionists in his own realm. All of these considerations meant William could not afford to be seen as intolerant, and had pushed for religious liberty in England. In Scotland and Ireland, of course, the same conditions applied. Personally, William would be as horrified by persecution in the north and west as elsewhere, and his allies would watch his policy in Dublin and Edinburgh as closely as his rule in London.

As a result, the new king was a constant source of pressure for moderation. In Scotland, his attitudes nearly caused a problem with his accession. William initially refused to swear the traditional oaths of a Scots king on taking the throne because it included a promise to suppress heresy. He feared this would bind him to an unacceptable persecution of Catholics and Protestant non-conformists, and was only persuaded to pro-ceed when it was explained the clause was an empty form of words which had never restricted royal policy.[17] Following this, the new king worked tirelessly to prevent a return to religious strife in Scotland. Signals from the court made it clear there must be no wholesale prosecution of Catholics, and William opposed the 1689 demands to impose presbyteri-anism partly because he feared it would mean religious intransigence. He hoped Scots episcopalians and presbyterians might be accommodated in a broad church if some compromise on kirk government could be found. When William lost this battle, he still tried to protect the episcopal party. His choice of Scots ministers, and his instructions to them, indicated he wanted lenient treatment, and it was partly this pressure which led to the 1693 and 1695 relief acts. In Ireland, William's attitudes were even clearer. He supported proposed toleration bills in the Irish parliament, and the terms he granted to Catholics at Limerick proved he had no concern about popery unless it led to military resistance. As we have seen, the king's policy was undermined when the Dublin Commons refused to legislate for liberty, and emasculated the 1691 treaty. Yet even so, royal influence told. The administration in Dublin Castle made no moves to enforce the laws against Protestant non-conformists, and it is probable that treatment of Catholics was softened by knowledge of the court's position. Even the die-hard Protestants in parliament recognised that most of the clauses of Limerick must be honoured if the king were not to be humiliated, and that overly harsh anti-popery would face veto from London. Thus in Ireland, as in Scotland and England, William abated religious heats. Legislation became more liberal where the king could convince parliaments to make it so: beyond that royal pressure extended a de facto toleration far beyond its de jure limits.

Of course, nothing which has just been said alters the basic pattern of William and the three kingdoms. The 1690s were a troubled time for the British problem because the new king gave too little attention to Dublin and Edinburgh, and far too high a priority to Flanders. By the end of the reign, relations between the realms were in crisis, and radical new ideas were needed to prevent breakdown. Yet, for all this, William's true role in the Britian and Ireland can be better appreciated once we realise that it operated at two levels. On the surface, his continental obsessions led to difficulties in the three parliaments, to anger in the north and west at England's dominance, and to concrete talk of independence in both Irish and Scots press. Beneath these surface squalls, however – among the deeper currents of political culture – conditions for resolution were developing. Even as the kingdoms railed, William's European perspective was encouraging a parliamentary renaissance and a religious tolerance which would be the twin planks of eighteenth-century stability. In both Scotland and Ireland, political classes were being born who felt their interests were considered even though they were dominated by London, and whose broad satisfaction in matters of faith ensured they felt no need to interfere in their neighbours' business.

Notes

The late twentieth century saw an an explosion of writing on the British problem in the Stuart era. Glenn Burgess, *The New British History* (I.B. Tauris, 1999) provides a useful guide, while David L. Smith, *A History of the Modern British Isles, 1603–1707* (Blackwell, 1998) provides a clear account of seventeenth-century Britain and Ireland from a 'three kingdoms' perspective. The best analytical survey of interrelations between the kingdoms in the 1690s is David Hayton, 'Constitutional experiments and political expediency', in Steven G. Ellis and Sarah Barber (eds), *Conquest and Union: Fashioning a British State* (Longman, 1995); while the clearest concise narrative (ironic given the work's title) is Rose, *England in the 1690s*, ch. 7. The revolutionary settlements and disturbances are well covered in the chapters by Ian Cowan and David Hayton in Jonathan Israel (ed.), *The Anglo-Dutch Moment* (CUP, 1991). P.W.J. Riley, *King William and the Scottish Politicians* (J. Donald, 1979) is a detailed guide to Scots politics; while John Robertson (ed.), *A Union for Empire* (CUP, 1995) covers constitutional debate and commercial ideology in Scotland. Sean Connolly, *Religion, Law and Power: The Making of Protestant Ireland* (Clarendon Press, 1992) suggests Ireland was less extraordinary than has often been argued, and so suggests stability could be more easily achieved.

1 Quoted Beddard, *Kingdom without a King*, p. 45.

2 Tim Harris, 'The British dimension, religion and the shaping of political identities in the reign of Charles II', in Claydon and McBride (eds), *Protestantism and National Identity*, pp. 131–56.

3 *Acts of the Parliaments of Scotland* (1822), **9**, 9–10.

4 *An Account of the Convention of Scotland* (1689).

5 J.G. Simms, *Jacobite Ireland, 1685–91* (Routledge, 1969), pp. 50–1.

6 See James McGuire, 'The Irish parliament of 1692', in Thomas Bartlett and David Hayton (eds), *Penal Era and Golden Age* (Ulster Historical Association, 1979), pp. 1–32 – I am grateful to David Hayton for these last two references.

7 William Molyneux, *The Case of Ireland's being Bound by Acts of Parliament in England Stated* (Dublin, 1698).

8 Such an analysis is central to Riley, *King William*.

9 For the idea's early incarnation, see William Leslie Melville (ed.), *Leven and Melville Papers* (Edinburgh, 1843), pp. 383–5.

10 Riley, *King William*, p. 99.

11 *Memorial Given in to the Senate of the City of Hamburgh* (Hamburg, 1697), *CSPD, 1699–1700*, p. 347.

12 Robertson, *Union for Empire*; James Kelly, 'The origins of the Act of Union', *Irish Historical Studies* **25** (1987), 236–63.

13 Riley, *King William*, pp. 160–2.

14 Hayton, 'Constitutional experiments'.

15 See Connolly, *Religion, Law and Power*, pp. 149–70.

16 For this phrase, and most of the analysis following, see Hayton, 'Constitutional experiments', pp. 280–4.

17 Burnet, *History*, **2**, 24.

Conclusion:
William's Place in History

The British never really took to William III. In his lifetime he was unpopular for his lack of sociabililty, for his preference for old friends from the Netherlands over Britons, and for the endless drain of resources to maintain his wars. His subjects recognised that he defended their interests better than any alternative ruler, so were relieved when he escaped dangers unharmed, but there was never the warm affection which has sometimes built between people and monarch. After William's death, his subjects seemed keen to forget him as quickly as possible. The monuments planned for public places during his funeral arrangements were never built, and the annual commemoration for the Glorious Revolution, which was instituted on 5 November, soon disappeared in the older ceremonies marking victory over Guy Fawkes. By the end of the second millennium, few Britons knew much about William. Irish Protestants had turned him into a symbol of comfort in recognition of his salvation of them at the Boyne, but these friends did the king's image more harm than good. Ulster loyalism had come to mean intolerant tribalism in many sections of mainland opinion. William's association with the movement made many wary of promoting his memory. His image in Orange parades has discouraged closer investigation of either his own (very liberal) religious attitudes, or the complexities in unionist use of their icon.

It is not easy to understand why William has fallen into such obscurity. His sort of achievements – fighting continental domination, promoting parliamentary government, upholding the Protestant religion – have usually led to the British pantheon. Why should he not be as visible as Elizabeth I; Nelson and Wellington; or Britain's twentieth-century war leaders? Probably the first speech made by his sister-in-law to her parliament contains the key. When Queen Anne cast aspersions on the preceding reign by declaring her heart was entirely English, she expressed a discomfort with William's foreign origins and priorities which has dogged his reputation since. The British were happy to be rescued from French popery and arbitrary power, but were embarrassed to have received the deliverance from a Dutchman. Quite rapidly they wrote William out of the story. They transformed 1688 into a victory for Briton's own moderation and love of liberty; they retold his war as an apprenticeship for Marlborough – an appropriately British hero.

This submergence for a foreign origin is doubly unfair. First, it hides William's real contribution. In this king's reign, the British realms turned a corner. Constitutional ailments were cured, warring parties were persuaded to pursue peaceful politics, the foundations of a world-beating state were laid, and at least some progress was made towards truce between the quarrelling nations of the islands. As this book has argued, William's own actions deserve much of the credit. His rule warrants celebration, not neglect. Beneath this first injustice lies a second, deeper, one. William was forgotten because of his un-British character. Yet this was the very fountain of his achievements. In field after field, the king succeeded for the very reason he has been ignored: he was an Orange more than a Stuart. After a hundred years of crisis and failure under English rulers, Britain and Ireland needed a man from beyond their shores to cut through the Gordian knot of their politics. Only someone with a distance from entrenched disputes, with fresh thinking, and with priorities beyond his immediate subjects, could escape the old habits of power which had condemned the kingdoms to their century of troubles.

Bibliography

Manuscript sources

BL Add Ms 19253.
BL Sloane Ms 1908.

Printed primary sources

An Account of the Convention of Scotland (1689).
Acts of the Parliaments of Scotland (1822).
[Atterbury, Francis], *Letter to a Convocation Man* (1696).
Blencowe, R.W. (ed.), *Diary of the Times of Charles the Second by the Honourable Henry Sidney* (1843).
[Bohun, Edmund], *The History of the Desertion* (1689).
Bray, Gerald (ed.), *The Anglican Canons, 1529–1947* (Boydell, 1998).
Browning, Andrew (ed.), *English Historical Documents, 1660–1714* (Clarendon Press, 1953).
Bryant, Arthur (ed.), *The Letters, Speeches and Declarations of King Charles II* (1935).
By the King and Queen a Proclamation for a General Fast ... 24 March 1691–92 (1692).
[Burnet, Gilbert], *An Enquiry into the Present State of Affairs* (1688).
Burnet, Gilbert, *The History of My Own Times* (1723–34).
Burnet, Gilbert, *A Pastoral Letter ... Concerning the Oaths* (1689).
Burnet, Gilbert, *A Sermon Preached at the Coronation of William III* (1689).
Burnet, Gilbert, *A Sermon Preached Before the House of Peers ... 5th November* (1689).
Burnet, Gilbert, *A Sermon Preached in the Chappel of St James' ... 23rd of December 1688* (1689).
[Burnet, Gilbert], *Three Letters Concerning the Current State of Italy* (1688).
Calendar of State Papers Domestic.
Carr, William, *An Accurate Description of the United Netherlands* (1691).
Cobbett, William, (ed.), *The Parliamentary History of England* (1806–20).
A Collection of the Debates and Proceedings in Parliament (1695).
Commons Journals.

A Copy of the Association Signed at Exeter (1688).

Coxe, William (ed.), *Private and Original Correspondence of Charles Talbot, Duke of Shrewsbury* (1821).

Dalrymple, John, *Memoirs of Great Britain and Ireland* (1790).

[Davenant, Charles], *Tom Double Return'd out of the Country* (1702).

[Davenant, Charles], *The True Picture of a Modern Whig* (1701).

The Debate at large between the Lords and Commons (2nd edn, 1710).

The Declaration of his Highness, William Henry, Prince of Orange, of the Reasons Inducing Him to Appear in Arms in the Kingdom of England (The Hague, 1688).

The Declaration of the Lords Spiritual and Temporal, and Commons Assembled ... with His Majesties Most Gracious Answer (1689).

The Duke of Norfolk's speech at Lynn ... 12 December 1688 (1688).

The Dutch Design Anatomized (1688).

The Expedition of the Prince of Orange for England (1689).

A Faithful Account of the Renewed Persecution of the Churches of Lower Aquitaine (1691).

A Form of Prayer to be Used the Fifth day of June (1689).

A Form of Prayers Used by His Late Majesty K. William III when He Received the Holy Sacrament (1704).

A Form of Prayer with Thanksgiving ... 5th November (1689).

Foxcroft, H.C., *The Life and Letters of Sir George Savile* (1898).

The French King's Decree against Protestants ... to which is Added a Brief and True Account of the Cruel Persecutions (1689).

Great News from Salisbury (1688).

Grey, Anchitel, *Debates of the House of Commons* (1769).

HMC, *House of Lords, 1690–1* (1892).

HMC, *Report on the Manuscripts of His Grace the Duke of Portland* (1894).

The History of the Persecution of the Protestants by the French King (1689).

Horwitz, Henry (ed.), *The Parliamentary Diary of Narcissus Luttrell* (Clarendon Press, 1972).

The Humble Address of the Lieutenantry of London ... December 17 1688 (1688).

The Intrigues of the French King at Constantinople (1689).

James II, *By the King, a Declaration ... given 6 November 1688* (1688).

Japikse, N. (ed.), *Correspondentie van Willem III en van Hans Willem Bentinck* (Rijks Geschiedkundige Publicatie, 1927).

Jurieu, Pierre, *Seasonable Advice to All the Protestants in Europe* (1689).

Kerr, Russell J. and Ida Coffin Duncan (eds), *The Routledge papers* (private publication, 1928).

Lloyd, William, *A Discourse of God's Way of Disposing of Kingdoms* (1691).

London Gazette.

Lords Journals.

Luttrell, Narcissus, *A Brief Relation of Affairs of State* (Oxford, 1857).

The Means to Free Europe from French Usurpation (1689).

Melville, William Leslie (ed.), *Leven and Melville Papers* (Edinburgh, 1843).

A Memorial Drawn up at King William's Special Direction, Intended to be Given in at the Treaty of Ryswick (1707).

Memorial given to the Senate of the City of Hamburgh (Hamburg, 1697).

Molyneux, William, *The Case of Ireland's being Bound by Acts of Parliament in England Stated* (Dublin, 1698).

The Most Christian Turk (1690).

The Muses Farewell to Popery and Slavery ... a Collection of Poems, Satyrs, Songs (1689).

Nero Gallicanus (1690).

An Order of the Lords ... for a Publick Thanksgiving (1688).

A Paper Delivered to His Highness the Prince of Orange by the Commissioners (1688).

Patrick, Simon, *The Autobiography* (Oxford, 1839).

Pensionary Fagel's Letter (The Hague, 1687).

Plain English: or an Enquiry into the Causes which have Frustrated our Expectations of the Late Happy Revolution (1691).

A Praier for the Present Expedition (The Hague, 1688).

A Proclamation about the Dissolving of the Parliament, 2 March 1629 (1629).

Singer, S.W. (ed.), *The Correspondence of Henry Hyde* (1828).

Some Short Considerations Concerning the State of the Nation (1692).

[Somers, John], *A Letter Ballancing the Necessity of Keeping a Land-force* (1697).

Steele, Richard, *Memoirs of ... Thomas .. Marquess of Wharton* (1715).

[Stillingfleet, Edward], *A Discourse Concerning the Unreasonableness of a New Separation* (1689).

Temple, William, *Observations upon the United Provinces of the Netherlands* (5th edn, 1690).

Tenison, Thomas, *A Sermon against Self-love ... 5 June 1689 being the Fast Day* (1689).

Tillotson, John, *A Sermon Preach'd at St Mary le Bow ... Wed 18th June ... a Day Appointed for a Solemn Monthly Fast* (1690).

To the Commanders of Ships and all Seamen who are now Imployed in the English Fleet (1688).

[Trenchard, John and Walter Moyle], *An Argument Shewing that a Standing Army is Inconsistent with a Free Government* (1697).

True and Exact Relation of the Prince of Orange his Entrance into Exeter (Exeter, 1688).

A View of the True Interest of the Several States of Europe (1689).

[Whittel, John], *An Exact Diary of the Late Expedition* (1689).

Secondary sources

Baxter, Stephen, *William III* (Longman, 1966).

Baxter, Stephen, 'William III as Hercules', in Lois G. Schwoerer (ed.), *The Revolution of 1688–1689* (CUP, 1992).

Beddard, Robert, *Kingdom without a King* (Phaidon, 1988).

Braddick, M.J., *The Nerves of State* (MUP, 1996).

Brewer, John, *The Pleasures of the Imagination* (Harvard UP, 1998).

Brewer, John, *The Sinews of Power: War, Money and the English State, 1688–1783* (Unwin, 1989).

Burgess, Glenn, *Absolute Monarchy and the Stuart Constitution* (Yale UP, 1995).

Burgess, Glenn, *The New British History* (I.B.Tauris, 1999).

Carswell, John, *The Descent on England* (Cresset, 1969).

Carter, Jennifer, 'The revolution and the constitution', in Geoffrey Holmes (ed.), *Britain after the Glorious Revolution* (1979).

Childs, John, *The British Army of William III, 1689–1702* (MUP, 1987).

Claydon, Tony, *William III and the Godly Revolution* (CUP, 1996).

Collinson, Patrick, 'The monarchical republic of Queen Elizabeth I', *Bulletin of the John Rylands Library* **69** (1986).

Connolly, Sean, *Religion, Law and Power: the Making of Protestant Ireland* (Clarendon Press, 1992).

Coward, Barry, *The Stuart Age* (Longman, 2nd edn, 1994).

Dickinson, H.T., *Liberty and Property* (Weidenfeld & Nicolson, 1977).

Dickson, P.G.M., *The financial Revolution in England* (Macmillan, 1967).

Downie, J.A., 'The Commission of Public Accounts and the formation of the country party', *English Historical Review* **91** (1976).

Downie, J.A. *Robert Harley and the Press* (CUP, 1979).

Ellis, E.L., 'William III and the politicians', in Geoffrey Holmes (ed.), *Britain after the Glorious Revolution* (Macmillan, 1969).

Fletcher, Anthony, *Reform in the Provinces* (Yale UP, 1986).

Frankle, Robert J., 'The formulation of the declaration of rights', *Historical Journal* **17** (1974).

Goldie, Mark, 'The political thought of the Anglican revolution', in Robert Beddard (ed.), *The Revolutions of 1688* (Clarendon Press, 1991).

Goldie, Mark, 'The revolution of 1689 and the structure of political argument', *Bulletin of Research in the Humanities* **83** (1980).

Haley, K.H.D., *William of Orange and the English Opposition, 1672–1674* (Clarendon Press, 1953).

Harris, Tim, 'The British dimension, religion and the shaping of political identities in the reign of Charles II', in Tony Claydon and Ian McBride (eds), *Protestantism and National Identity* (CUP, 1998).

Harris, Tim, *London Crowds in the Reign of Charles II* (CUP, 1987).

Hayton, David, 'Constitutional experiments and political expediency', in Steven G. Ellis and Sarah Barber (eds), *Conquest and Union: Fashioning a British State* (Longman, 1995).

Herman, John, *The Navy in the War of William III, 1689–1697* (CUP, 1953).

Hill, Brian, *The Growth of Parliamentary Parties, 1689–1742* (Allen & Unwin, 1976).

Hill, Christopher, 'A bourgeois revolution?', in J.G.A. Pocock (ed.), *Three British Revolutions* (Princeton UP, 1980).

Holmes, Geoffrey, 'The achievement of stability', in John Cannon (ed.), *The Whig Ascendancy* (Arnold, 1981).

Horwitz, Henry, *Parliament, Policy and Politics in the Reign of William III* (MUP, 1977).

Horwitz, Henry, *Revolution Politicks: the Career of Daniel Finch, Second Earl of Nottingham* (CUP, 1968).

Israel, Jonathan, *The Dutch Republic* (OUP, 1995).

Israel, Jonathan, 'The Dutch role in the Glorious Revolution', in Jonathan Israel (ed.), *The Anglo-Dutch Moment* (CUP, 1991).

Israel, Jonathan, 'William III and toleration', in Ole Grell *et al.* (eds), *From Persecution to Toleration* (Clarendon Press, 1980).

Jones, David L., *A Parliamentary History of the Glorious Revolution* (HMSO, 1988).

Jones, D.W., *War and Economy in the Age of William and Marlborough* (OUP, 1988).

Jones, J.R., *The Anglo-Dutch Wars of the Seventeenth Century* (Longman, 1996).

Jones, J.R., *The Revolution of 1688 in England* (Weidenfeld & Nicolson, 1984).

Kelly, James, 'The Origins of the Act of Union', *Irish Historical Studies*, **25** (1987).

Kenyon, J.P., *Revolution Principles: the Politics of Party 1689–1720* (CUP, 1977).

The King's Apartments: Hampton Court Palace, special edition of *Apollo* Magazine (1994).

Knights, Mark, *Politics and Opinion in Crisis* (CUP, 1994).

Lake, Peter, 'Anti-popery: the structure of a prejudice', in Richard Cust and Anne Hughes (eds), *Conflict in Early Stuart England* (Longman, 1989).

Lamont, William, *Godly Rule: Politics and Religion, 1603–1659* (Macmillan, 1969).

McGuire, James, 'The Irish parliament of 1692', in Thomas Bartlett and David Hayton (eds), *Penal Era and Golden Age* (Ulster Historical Association, 1979).

McJimsey, Robert, 'A country divided? English politics and the Nine Years War', *Albion* 23 (1991).

McJimsey, Robert, 'Crisis management and political stability, 1692–1719', *Albion* 32 (2000).

Pincus, Stephen, 'The English nationalist revolution of 1688', in Tony Claydon and Ian McBride (eds), *Protestantism and National Identity, 1650–1850* (CUP, 1998).

Pincus, Stephen, *Protestantism and Patriotism: Ideologies and the Making of English Foreign Policy, 1650–1668* (CUP, 1996).

Price, J.L., *Holland and the Dutch Republic in the Seventeenth Century* (Clarendon Press, 1994).

Riley, P.W.J., *King William and the Scottish Politicians* (J. Donald, 1979).

Robertson, John (ed.), *A Union for Empire* (CUP, 1995).

Roorda, D.J., 'The peace of Nijmegen', in J.A.H. Bots (ed.), *The Peace of Nijmegen, 1676–9* (APA, 1980).

Rose, Craig, *England in the 1690s* (Blackwell, 1999).

Rose, Craig, 'Providence, Protestant union and godly reformation in the 1690s', *Transactions of the Royal Historical Society* (1993).

Roseveare, Henry, *The Financial Revolution, 1660–1760* (Longman, 1991).

Rowen, Herbert H., *John de Witt* (Princeton UP, 1978).

Rowen, Herbert H., *The Princes of Orange* (CUP, 1988).

Schama, Simon, *The Embarrassment of Riches* (Collins, 1987).

Schwoerer, Lois G.,'The coronation of William and Mary', in Lois G. Schwoerer (ed.), *The Revolutions of 1688/9* (CUP, 1991).

Schwoerer, Lois G., 'Propaganda in the revolution of 1688–9', *American Historical Review* 82 (1977).

Scott, Jonathan, *England's Troubles* (CUP, 2000).

Simms, J.G., *Jacobite Ireland, 1685–91* (Routledge, 1969).

Smith, David L., *A History of the Modern British Isles, 1603–1707* (Blackwell, 1998).

Sommerville, C.J.,*The Secularization of Early Modern England* (OUP, 1992).

Sommerville, J.P., *Royalists and Patriots: Politics and Ideology in England 1603–1640* (Longman, 1999).

Speck, W.A., *Reluctant Revolutionaries* (Clarendon Press, 1988).

Speck, W.A., 'William – and Mary?', in Lois G. Schwoerer (ed.), *The Revolutions of 1688/9* (CUP, 1991).

Spurr, John, *The Restoration Church of England* (Yale UP, 1991).

t'Hart, Marjolein, *The making of a bourgeois state* (MUP, 1993).

Western, J.R., *Monarchy and Revolution: the English State in the 1680s* (Blandford Press, 1972).

Index